CONTENTS

Preface   vii

SECTION 1   Going Places in Travel and Tourism   1

The World Is Out There Waiting   2
Defining Travel and Tourism   3
    What Is Travel? 3   What Is Tourism? 4   How Travel and
    Tourism Helps Our Economy 5   Developing and Encouraging
    Tourism 5   Tourism Development: Ready . . . Set . . . Wait a
    Minute! 5   We Love Them, We Love Them Not 6   All This
    Work and Nobody's Here?! 8
Understanding the Travel Industry   12
    What Is It? 12
Who's Who and What's What   13
    Industry Terms 13   Travel Jargon 13   Automation and the
    Travel Industry 14   Around the World with Automation 16
    Industry Associations 16   Government Agencies 17
    The Importance of Staying Current 18   Trade Publications 18
    Guidebooks 19   Brochures 19   Travel Videos 20
    Etc. . . . 20   "Being There": An Exciting Way to Stay Current! 20
The Travel Industry and You   21
    A Garden of Opportunities 21   Qualities to Cultivate 22

SECTION 2   The Travelers   25

Travelers on a Flight from Here to There   26
Travelers Today   29
    Getting to Know You . . . Getting to Know All About You . . . 31
    The Gray 90s 33   UP CLOSE: Business Travel 33
International Travelers and Things They Need to Know   35
    Passeport . . . Passa Porto . . . Passe: Don't Leave Home Without It! 36
    Proof of Citizenship and Proof of Identity 37   Be Advised 37
    Visas Aren't Credit Cards 37   Customs: Getting In, Getting Out, and
    Getting Back 38   Save the Whales—But Don't Bring Them Back in
    Your Luggage 38   Whose Picture Is on a 500,000 Lire Bill?—
    Understanding Foreign Currency 39   Leaping Over the Language
    Barrier 40   Electrical Shock 41   Take Two Ginseng Tablets and
    Call Me in the Morning 41   Don't Drink the Water—Drink
    the Beer! 41

SECTION 3   The Industry Triangle   43

Who Connects the Points?   44
    Supplier/Agent Relationship 44   These People Need Professional
    Help! 48   Traveler? Client? Who's Who? 49   Travel
    Agencies—Yesterday 52   Travel Agencies—Moving into the
    Modern World 53   Travel Agencies Today 54   Defining

Agencies Today   *54*   *UP CLOSE: American Express Travel: A Mega*
Agency   *57*   *So, You Want to Be a Travel Agent!*   *57*   *Industry*
Texts and References   *61*   *Continuing Education*   *62*
Opening Your Own Agency   63
   Options in Owning Your Business   *65*
   Travel Agencies—Tomorrow   *66*

SECTION 4   **Meet the Carriers**   69

Those Magnificent Men and Their Amazing Flying Machines   70
   Oh, What a Lovely War!   *70*
The Domestic Carriers   72
   Government Regulation and Deregulation   *73*   *Oh, Beautiful for*
   Open Skies!   *73*   *How Things Have Changed!*   *74*   *Old and*
   New, Buying and Selling, Success and Failure   *75*   *U.S. Carriers*
   Today   *75*   *UP CLOSE: The Major U.S. Carriers*   *76*
The International Carriers   77
   Who Goes Where . . . And Why . . . And How . . .   *78*
The Freedoms of the Air   80
   "Cruising" at 35,000 Feet!   *82*
What Might Tomorrow Bring?   83
Breaking the Codes   83
   Airline Codes   *84*   *Will the Real UA Please Raise Its*
   Wing Flap?   *84*   *City and Airport Codes*   *85*
Airline Routes—Not Always as the Crow Flies!   87
   Linear Routing—As the Crow Flies   *89*   *The Hub and Spoke*
   System   *89*   *Artificial Hubs—Good Idea? Or, Not Such a*
   Good Idea?   *90*   *Why Did They Name It . . . ?*   *91*
Airports   93
   Keeping the Bad Guys Out   *94*
Domestic versus International Airports   94
   UP CLOSE: Frankfurt Main International Airport   *95*
Air Fares: It's Not How Far You Fly!   97
   The Class System   *97*   *It's Just Not Fare!*   *99*   *Our "Fare"*
   Weather Friends!   *100*
Charters and Consolidators   101
   The Future of Air Charters   *102*   *Jax Fax*   *102*
   Consolidators   *102*
Employment Opportunities in the Airline Industry   103
   UP CLOSE: The Flight Attendant   *104*   *History*   *105*
   Flight Attendants Today   *105*

SECTION 5   **Aweigh We Go!**   109

Bon Voyage, Dahling!   111
   From Slow Boat to Love Boat   *113*   *Love at First Sail!*   *114*
   UP CLOSE: Carnival: A Major Cruise Line   *114*

The Modern Cruise Ship   116
    A Look Under the Hood, Behind the Doors, and in the Closets   116
    A Walk Around the Decks 116   A Room of One's Own on
    the High Seas 117   At Your Service! 121   Love Boat or Gravy
    Boat? 122   All Ashore Who's Going Ashore! 123
Up a Lazy River   123
The Dollars and Sense of Cruising   124
    Ready to Go? 126
Safety at Sea   126
The Cruise Lines International Association (CLIA)   127
Cruise Forever! Employment Opportunities in the Cruise
    Industry   128
    UP CLOSE: Cruise Director 129

SECTION 6   **A Room of One's Own**   **133**

Gimme Shelter   134
    The Basics 134
Who Owns This Place?   135
What Kind of Place Is This?   137
    Motels, Motor Hotels, and Motor Inns 137   Hotels 137
    Resorts 138   Gaming Hotels 140   Bed and Breakfast
    Inns (B & Bs) 141   Condominiums, Apartments, and Homes 142
    UP CLOSE: Club Med—An All-Inclusive Resort Chain 143
How Could We Possibly Know?   144
    Check the Ratings! 145   The AH & MA 146   What About
    Everybody Else? 146
How Much Is That Double with a Window?   148
    A Warm Bed and a Full Plate 149   How Taxing! 149   A Word
    of Warning 150
Making the Reservation   150
    Reps and Res Centers 151   More Alphabet Soup! 151
Employment Opportunities in the Hotel Industry   152
    Is This the Job for You? 152   Where Do I Begin? 152
    UP CLOSE: The Hotel Concierge 153

SECTION 7   **Behind the Wheel**   **157**

How They All Got Rolling   158
Who Wants to Drive?   158
    Who's Renting What 160   Do You Want an FCAR, or Will an
    ECAR Do? 162   We Said RENT, Not BUY! 162
Foreign Cars   164
Employment Opportunities in the Car Rental Industry   165

SECTION 8   **All Aboard!**   **169**

Getting a Leg Up on the Iron Horse   170
    UP CLOSE: Maglev: Futuristic Rail Travel 170

Rail Travel in the United States   172
    I Think I Can, I Think I Can . . .   *172*   *What Kind of Train Will It*
    Be? *173*
Making the Reservation   174
Foreign Rails   175
Rail Travel in Canada   177
Rail Travel in Europe   177
    The Eurailpass *177*   *UP CLOSE: The Chunnel* *178*
Reserving Your Seat in Europe   179
Rail Travel in Japan   179
Romantic Rides: The Great Trains of the World   181
Workin' on the Railroad: Employment Opportunities in the Railroad
    Industry   182

SECTION 9   **Tours Are Terrific!**   **183**

Tour Beginnings   184
Packages? Tours? What's the Difference?   184
    The Independent Tour *185*   *Hosted Tours* *186*
    Escorted Tours *187*   *Custom Tours* *188*   *F-Stops, Short Stops,*
    Meal Stops—Tours for Every Interest! *188*
The Dollars and Sense of Taking Tours   189
    UP CLOSE: Fall Foliage: A Tour Itinerary *191*
Selecting and Booking Tours   192
    The Cost of the Tour *193*   *Book Em'!* *193*   *Tour*
    Documents *194*   *No More Tours—Let's Have a FIT Instead!* *194*
Got You Covered!   195
Employment Opportunities in the Tour Industry   196
    UP CLOSE: The Tour Manager *197*

**Abbreviations Commonly Used in the
Travel Industry**   **201**

Glossary   **205**

Index   **225**

Travel and tourism is one of the most interesting topics and career fields in the world. But, interesting doesn't say it all! It is also exciting, stimulating, dynamic, stressful, challenging, frustrating, and FUN!

Unfortunately, many papers, books, articles and speeches about travel and tourism are, at best, dry. Their introductions should carry the warning: "Consume with a Large Glass of Water!" It's hard to figure why this is so. Granted, travel and tourism is a serious business, representing millions of jobs and billions of dollars. But, it also helps people get to business engagements and make more money, take vacations, see the wonders of the world, honeymoon, study abroad, visit relatives, cruise the seven seas, enjoy theater and ballet, visit health centers and spas, or even gamble their money away if they so choose!

Providing transportation, housing, food, and entertainment for masses of people certainly requires lots of planning, hard work, and capital. When you consider that each member of the mass tends to see himself or herself as a sole adventurer, a Marco Polo of the modern world, a soldier of fortune, a business negotiator of immense importance, or a diplomat deserving of VIP status, you can easily see that providing travel products and serving the customer can be a pretty tough assignment!

Many people who choose to write about or report on travel and tourism attempt to reduce it to a science. They provide us with numerous charts and graphs of changing trends and buying patterns and give us lots of facts about how much money it takes to build an airport, how many people travel each year between New York and Los Angeles, and what businesses expect to spend on travel each year. This can be useful information to have—especially if you are a travel analyst.

But, look around you! These travelers are having fun! Too many times, the essence of travel is missing from the texts and speeches of those who wish to teach it! Peek into the restaurants, hotel lobbies, museums, national parks, and amusement centers of the world—these people are enjoying themselves! Take a look into the meeting facilities of the major hotels of the world—the people in them are doing interesting things. Look at the passengers seated on a 747 headed for Amsterdam: arts patrons anxious to visit the great museums of Europe; Hassidic Jews on their way to Tel Aviv; jewelers headed for the diamond centers of Holland; businesspeople arriving to talk about oil, finance, or consumer products; students tasting their first real bit of freedom in the world—the list goes on and on. The inside of a 747 is a cross-section of life, not a series of charts and graphs!

We firmly believe that a book about travel and tourism should be interesting, fun, and, of course, informative. We have tried to portray what the travel industry is all about. Unless you have been hired to figure out traffic flow in and around Disney World (in which case books on city planning, road building, and migraine headache cures will serve you better), what you really need to know about travel to get started in it is how the system works, how to understand travelers, and how to help your future customers manage the many elements that make up a trip.

If you could find a "travel planning kit" it would be like a set of mental building blocks that fits together in many different ways. There are many types of travelers and many different ways to travel, but, in building a trip, one missing block can change the whole structure from an enchanted castle to a house of horrors! Consider this book a cornerstone in building an understanding of travel and tourism.

Organization. This book is organized into nine sections, with the first offering an overview of the industry and the second an introduction to the travelers themselves. The remaining sections deal specifically with the industry suppliers. At the end, you will find a comprehensive glossary of travel industry terms and abbreviations.

Objectives and industry terms and jargon are listed at the beginning of the sections. These terms appear in boldface in the text and their definitions are printed in the margins. Learning terms and industry jargon will help you better understand the material as you go along, and you won't be constantly interrupting yourself to look up unfamiliar words and phrases.

Explorations and *Enrichments* exercises appear throughout each section. Explorations are designed to "get you thinking and acting" like a travel professional by using your personal experiences and the knowledge you have gained through your reading and studies. Even if you have never traveled, you probably know a great deal more about travel than you think! Travel is a "people" business, and every experience you have had dealing with people can be "translated" into the service business of travel.

Enrichments are just that—exercises designed to enhance and enrich your knowledge of travel and the travel industry. There are many excellent resources in learning about travel, and we encourage you to seek out as many as you can! Travel and tourism is a fascinating subject that just keeps on giving us more and more to learn and enjoy. No matter how good, interesting, entertaining, or beautiful it may be, no single travel book, video, or publication can say it all!

Becoming a travel professional is as much a state of mind as it is getting good grades and memorizing facts. We hope our book will help you enjoy learning about travel, encourage you to learn more, and motivate you to use and create your own resources for personal and professional development in this exciting field.

Instructor's Guidelines. Instructor guidelines are available. They offer suggestions on lectures and pacing, supplementary exercises, and classroom discussion topics. Suggested resources, transparency masters, and section tests are also included.

Acknowledgements. Special thanks to Dave Landry who carried an extra work load during the writing of this text. We also greatly appreciate the support and patience of our coworkers: Crystal Carroll, Randall Dubois, Sue Ann Harrison, Cynthia Tellup, and Susan Van Reen.

The World Is Out There Waiting

We would also like to recognize Wilfred Spoon for his cartoon illustrations; they entertained us and we hope they entertain you!

The authors also gratefully acknowledge the time and efforts of Donna Amditis Morn, Art Institute of Florida; Martha J. Hundley, CTC, Sullivan College; and Kathy Miller, Academy Pacific Business and Travel College, who reviewed the text and offered valuable suggestions.

Going Places in Travel and Tourism

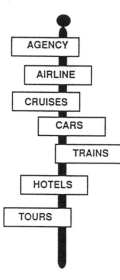

Where Are We Going?

When you have completed this section, you will:

1. Be able to define *travel* and *tourism*.
2. Understand the role of government in controlling and regulating travel and tourism.
3. Understand the regional and worldwide importance of travel and tourism and the positive and negative effects it may have on a community.
4. Understand who makes up the travel industry.
5. Know the qualities travel industry employers look for when hiring.

Industry Terms and Jargon

Agent	Computer Reserva-tion System (CRS)	Supplier
Automation		
Brochure	Familiarization (fam) Trips	

The World Is Out There Waiting

The world is out there waiting for everyone! Your decision to learn more about travel and tourism may be the most exciting one you will ever make! It will truly change the way you view the world. A career in travel is ideal for those just beginning their lives in the work place, for those who are seeking a career change, or for those who have waited until later in life to enter the job market. Travel presents exciting opportunities to all ages.

- *Where can you go in travel?* Anywhere you choose!
- *What education do you need?* A high school diploma, certainly. A college degree can be helpful, but is not necessary. Specialized career training or vocational education courses in travel and tourism can also help prepare you for the industry and, in many cases, open doors to employment possibilities.
- *What skills do you need?* Computer skills, clerical skills, and sales skills are helpful. But, if you don't have them, you can learn them!

The most important skills in this industry are people skills. Travel companies are *service* businesses. The ability to relate well to those you serve—whether you call them customers, clients, guests, or passengers—is critical to success. Travel industry professionals must deal with the public. Travelers today are sophisticated consumers. They expect superb service from well-trained and knowledgeable travel professionals. If you are personally committed to excellence in service and in your profession, you will find your place in the travel industry!

Add to your people skills a willingness to get the necessary training, to start at the beginning, to work hard, to keep an open mind, to be flexible, to learn something new about the world every day, and you will fit the description of a travel professional headed for success.

No other industry satisfies so many needs, both personal and professional. Working in the travel industry gives us the opportunity to:

- Serve and help others.
- Learn more about the world and its people.
- Become more sophisticated, cultured, and interesting.
- Experience personal growth.
- Work with interesting and exciting people.
- Meet new challenges.
- Become more independent.
- Be proud of ourselves and the job we do.
- Enjoy life and have fun!

What lies ahead in the travel industry? Dynamic gowth and many opportunities. *Cocooning,* the term coined in the 1990s to describe a desire to stay home and ignore the world, is a condition that applies to only a few. Most people want to travel. It must be affordable and relatively convenient, but the dreams of seeing new places, getting away from it all, and learning something new are alive and well!

When we look beyond the immediate uncertainties that life often presents, what is out there? Some of the most exciting developments in travel the world has ever seen! The Berlin Wall is down and many countries of Eastern Europe are welcoming tourists for the first time in many, many years. Major companies are building hotels, expanding travel services, and opening new air routes to places they have never been before! Advanced communication technology makes it easier, faster, and more economical to plan trips.

Increased government cooperation has made it far simpler to travel between the countries of Western Europe. World peace appears more attainable and, while there will always be headline news of disturbances and conflicts between people and nations, travel is truly safer than ever before!

If you pay close attention to newspapers, magazines, and television news reports, you will hear travel mentioned over and over again. You hear a lot about travel in good times and bad, because travel fascinates. Doctors, lawyers, college professors, and business executives stop their conversations when they hear you are "in travel." Once travel is mentioned, the attention centers on you, conversations become more lively, and people share their interesting experiences of the world.

EVERYONE is interested in travel, and the world is out there waiting — for you!

Defining Travel and Tourism

What Is Travel?

Webster's defines *travel* as follows: "To go from place to place or make a journey, as by airplane or car; to go from one location to another; to proceed or advance in any way; the act of traveling or journeying to different countries."* *Webster's* also tells us that *travel* is a derivative of the word *travail* which means "extremely difficult, strenuous work; toil; physical or mental hardship, pain and suffering."*

What Is Tourism?

Webster's defines *tourism* as: "The custom or practice of traveling for pleasure; the promotion by establishments or countries to attract tourists; the business or occupation of providing various services for tourists."*

Certainly, traveling in ages past was travail, and the idea of tourism—travel for pleasure and enjoyment—was virtually nonexistent. In today's world, travel does not conjure up images of hardship and pain. People travel great distances in speed and comfort. Journeys that took months by horse and carriage, weeks by ship, and days by car or train now take only hours by air. Vacations that once cost a fortune in time and money are now easily purchased by working people of more modest means. Salespeople travel to get more business, young couples save for vacations, families visit relatives and friends, and retired people travel the world for enjoyment and relaxation. Everyone, no matter what he does or where she lives, is touched by travel and tourism.

Today, the terms *travel* and *tourism* are often used together to describe the businesses associated with travel. Some travel professionals and travel educators state that travelers and tourists are synonymous; however, most people, in happy agreement with Noah Webster, consider that only those who travel for fun and leisure are "tourists."

But don't let the "fun and leisure" label mislead you! Tourism is a serious business and powerful economic force. In fact, travel and tourism is the fastest growing component of world trade and is the largest business in the world today. In the United States, travel and tourism is the largest retail business and, at the end of the 1980s, accounted for approximately 13 percent of the work force! More specifically, that means that one out of every thirteen people employed today works in some facet of the travel industry.

In the United States, the growth of service businesses is outpacing the growth of manufacturing. Many of tomorrow's workers will be employed in filling customers' service needs rather than producing or manufacturing retail goods. Travel and tourism is definitely a service business—one that encompasses the world and reaches out to all people. It is also exciting, vibrant, and full of opportunities to learn and develop, whether it is your chosen field of work or your favorite pastime!

Tourism is also a means—and a pleasurable and educational one at that—of redistributing wealth. In most cases, travel is *from* the industrialized and richer nations of the world *to* those that are less developed. In the United States alone, citizens spend more money on travel than on any other activity except eating! More and more jobs will be created to help feed this ever growing hunger for travel!

*The Living Webster Encyclopedic Dictionary of the English Language. Chicago: English Language Institute of America, 1974.

- Travel and tourism is the leading export of the United States.
- International visitors spend over $60 billion a year in the United States.
- The travel and tourism industry employs over 6 million U.S. citizens directly and many more millions in related fields, that is, fields that would not be as large without a concentration on travel and tourism, such as publishing, map making, souvenir shops, restaurants, entertainment, and so forth.
- Travel and tourism is the third largest retail industry in business gross receipts.
- Worldwide, travel and tourism is responsible for the creation of one new job every ten seconds.

Governments, citizens, and corporations throughout the world are concerned with the growth and development of tourism. Throughout the world, from the smallest villages to the largest cities and countries, there are discussion groups, task forces, councils, committees, elected officials, and private citizens who are deeply concerned with tourism. These people often work closely with industry suppliers to develop and promote tourism programs. Cooperation among the many factions of travel and tourism is critical to its success.

Although many **suppliers**—and even governments—are in direct competition with each other for the traveler's dollar, they often work together to create an attractive travel product. Even though the field is crowded and complex, the needs are fairly simple: to support and promote tourism, there must be a well-developed network of suppliers. Each of the players—airlines, hotels, tour operators, and even governments—is dependent on the others to help supply the needs of the tourist.

Supplier An airline, tour operator, hotel, car rental firm, or other business that provides or supplies the travel product.

As travel becomes more affordable and as people reach income and education levels where travel becomes important to them, the countries and businesspeople of the world look to find ways to attract travelers to their destinations, hotels, activities, events, and so on. Growth in tourism can bring money, investments, jobs, higher living standards, and worldwide recognition. And it can also bring problems.

Government control, or lack thereof, can have a far reaching effect on the impact of tourism on economies, citizens and environments. Travel and tourism is an industry that has a very close connection with the governments of the world. Governments will determine whether airports are built, whether investors feel welcome or threatened, whether tourists feel safe, and whether or not citizens welcome or reject the prospect of growth in the tourist trade.

To attract tourists, destinations must be prepared for them. All travelers (except the most adventurous explorers who usually don't bring money anyway) expect to find at least the very basic conveniences and comforts: transportation, shelter, clean water, edible food, and electricity. And, of course, most travelers expect far more than the basics. They want a choice of hotels and restaurants, shops and "things to do," such as golf, tennis, swimming, nightclubs, and sightseeing tours.

Governments wishing to attract tourists must plan carefully. For the less developed countries, creating an environment for tourism requires tremendous financial resources. Since most developing countries don't have national banks lining their few paved streets, they must look outside their borders for investors. Since investing can be a tricky business at best, businesspeople willing to spend their money will want certain concessions or guarantees to help reduce the risks they are taking, such as:

- The right to buy or control land.
- Special tax rates for the businesses they build.
- The right to bring in their own employees.
- The right to take their profits home with them.
- The right to keep competitors out.
- The right to "get involved" in governing tourism.

Without proper planning and proper understanding of the effects of tourism and investment and business growth, governments can make mistakes that could easily lead to serious problems in the future. It is not unheard of for uncontrolled tourism to create deep resentment among the citizens who now see their lives in dramatic contrast to those who have come to their homeland to make money and use its natural resources and its people.

We Love Them, We Love Them Not

Tourists often have very little regard for where they are. They sometimes see the world as their playground or amusement park and, as if they actually were in an amusement park, they expect others to both cater to them and pick up after them. Tourists are not always loved. They have been accused of polluting beaches, lakes, and rivers; ruining the countryside; defacing ruins; trashing historical landmarks; and contaminating the values of the natives.

It is not just the underdeveloped countries that suffer from the invasions of thoughtless tourists. The national parks in the United States are so popular that the sheer number of people flocking to enjoy their beauty actually destroys it. "On a summer day, the floor of the Yosemite Valley sometimes has a greater population density than Manhattan."*

Because of the economic, political, social, and environmental importance of tourism, there is a real need for organization, policies, and regulations. Although regulation is essential, it is also controversial! In principle, government intervention and regulation should be regarded as positive because the government's role is to protect resources, its citizens, and its visitors. However, lack of cooperation and coordination can seriously hamper progress, and promotion of special- (or self-) interest groups can result in decision making that helps a few but potentially harms the whole!

Some countries have developed very strict regulations while others have been more moderate, or, in unfortunate cases, very slack in policy making. Haphazard policy making leads to haphazard growth and upredictable decline. In the United States, many local, state, and federal organizations are involved in both the development and regulation of the travel industry. Listed here are some of the general areas of legislation and regulation in this industry:

Hospitality Industry: Hotels, Resorts, Restaurants

Classifications and ratings

Fire and safety codes, regulations

Health and safety codes, regulations, and ratings

Building and zoning codes

Laws and regulations governing services for the handicapped

Liquor licenses

Liability for personal property of guests, customers, and employees

Truth in advertising and promotion

Labor laws

Fair pricing and antitrust legislation

Common Carriers: Airlines, Railways, Motorcoaches, Ships, Taxis, Limousines, and so on.

Pricing controls

Licensing of businesses, services

Licensing of employees (i.e., pilots, drivers, engineers)

Safety regulations: carrier operation and equipment maintenance

Limitations of weights and capacities

Regulations regarding use of roads, rails, airspace, waterways, and public facilities

Legislation regarding free trade, fair competition, antitrust

Subsidization of routes, facilities, development, and so on

Truth in advertising and promotion

Labor laws

Taxation

*"Travel and Tourism: The Pleasure Principle," *The Economist,* March 23, 1991.

Tour Operators and Travel Agencies

Business licensing

Employee licensing: licensed guides, escorts, and operators

Definitions of responsibilities and liabilities

Truth in advertising and promotion

Labor laws

Taxation

Other areas of the industry, such as amusement parks, public and private recreation facilities, car and equipment rentals, and special events operators, have their own specific laws, codes, and regulations, as well as many of those just listed.

Although the amount of legislation enacted and proposed is astounding and, in some cases, counterproductive, people would not fly on a plane, board a ship, or ride in a motorcoach if they felt that the carrier was unsafe. Only the most courageous and adventurous (if not foolhardy) individual would want to stay in a hotel if he or she thought its elevators would malfunction, its guest room doors wouldn't lock, or that it could burst into flames at any moment. Who would enjoy dining in a restaurant that was unclean, had watered-down wine, or served liquor to children?

All This Work and Nobody's Here?!

Uh, oh. Lots of money was spent, the tables are set, the beds are turned down, the taxis and limos are waiting at the airport, and everybody's obeying the laws—but no guests! What happened?

Although travel is an important and constant force in world economics, it is a volatile field and travelers can be very fickle! There are hundreds of destinations and companies competing for travelers' attentions and their money. Many, many things can affect the popularity and acceptability of destinations to the world's travelers.

For businesspeople, travel is influenced by:

- Prospects for increasing business.
- The cost of doing business.
- Government regulations.
- Attitude of the local citizens.

Doing business within one's own country is relatively simple. The businessperson knows—or can easily find out—what the local regulations are and if his or her potential customers speak the same language, have similar customs and values, and deal in the same currency.

International business is far more complicated. Languages, customs, values, and currencies are different. The laws of a businessperson's country and the laws of the country he or she wishes to work in will be different. The languages may pose huge obstacles. The culture and people are different and a failure to understand local customs and business etiquette can be devastating. U.S. businesspeople understand each other, but they may not understand the Japanese or the Mexican or the German.

Foreigners aren't *wrong*, but they sure can be *different!* While differences may be "what makes the world go 'round," unexpected and surprising differences may make the inexperienced traveler feel that the world is spinning out of control!

In Italy, a hug—even between men—is as common as a handshake. The Japanese bow from the waist when greeting others; they are uncomfortable with even a formal handshake, and they consider direct eye contact to be disrespectful. Americans reserve hugs for close friends and family; they consider bows the sole province of performers and servants; and they believe direct eye contact is a sign of honesty and forthrightness.

Filipinos are very proud of their families and respond enthusiastically to questions about their children, spouses, and homes. An Arab, on the other hand, considers any mention of his wife (wives) highly improper. In the Northern European countries, punctuality is a must. In Latin America, it is customary to be at least fifteen minutes late and delays of up to two hours won't ruin an evening or, for that matter, a friendship or business deal. In Arab countries, unsuspecting Americans will certainly be confused, and possibly offended, by the common practice of conducting more than one meeting at a time!

If you survive the initial greetings and polite conversation, your next hurdle may well be dining with your international hosts. Many an international traveler, when faced with strange foods and stranger habits, has longed to crawl *under* the table rather than accept the seat of honored (and closely observed) guest. In Argentina, it is considered rude to eat everything on your plate. In China, it is considered rude not to eat everything, but, if you do, your dish will be immediately refilled, thereby creating a true "no-win" situation for the guest who wishes to please. In Switzerland, the highest compliment you can pay is to *request* a second helping, and, in Zambia, you must ask to be fed since it is considered impolite for a host to mention food!

Once you finally get to the table, consider consuming the following "delicacies" without flinching (or worse!):

- A sheep's eyeball in Saudi Arabia
- Roast gorilla fist in Africa
- Live fish sliced right at your table (for eating raw) in Japan
- A tiny bird (to be eaten bones and all!) in France

Refusing a specially prepared dish is tantamount to rejecting your host, his hospitality, his taste, and his country! Getting along in social, political, and business situations around the world takes understanding, patience, flexibility, and a good sense of humor! It also helps to have an iron stomach, an open mind, a blind eye, and a ready smile—the one expression that is universally understood and always welcome!

Whatever the complexities of conducting international business may be, there is one essential question the decision maker must answer: "Will this venture be profitable?" If the answer is "yes," then business moves ahead—strange customs, diets and all! If the answer is "no," then it really doesn't matter what the local government and corporate leaders have done to attract investors, or what embarrassing social gaffes were committed. Business decision makers will move on to consider other, more promising, locations and opportunities.

For tourists, the "profit" in choosing certain destinations is not monetary, but emotional. Tourists choose destinations that fill their personal needs:

- Culture
- Education
- Entertainment
- Health
- Relaxation
- Being with others
- Religion, spiritual enrichment

Once a tourist has identified the purpose of the trip, he or she wants to know that the chosen destination will fill that need and, with the possible exception of the adventurist, wants to know that the destination will be safe and comfortable. If a destination has had recent political unrest, has a reputation for "making people sick," has had severe natural problems (such as storms, fires, earthquakes), is known to be unfriendly or unsafe, or if travel magazines, guidebooks, newspapers, television, and friends report bad conditions, tourists will stay away in droves.

Although most tourists and travelers are concerned about the political stability of the destination they are considering, political unrest in other parts of the world can influence the decision to travel. Reports of terrorism, airline highjackings, threats of armed conflict involving other countries, and concerns about airline safety create feelings of insecurity in the traveling public. If potential travelers feel too insecure, they will stay home or close to home.

Good or bad weather conditions can influence tourists. A bout of extremely cold weather often has people flocking to travel agencies and airlines to plan trips to "somewhere warm." Beautiful weather, on the other hand, may keep people home, enjoying their own back yards and nearby attractions.

A surge in national pride or patriotism may also keep people closer to home. During the Persian Gulf War of early 1991, Americans who traveled, traveled close to home, mostly out of a concern for safety. After the Persian Gulf War, Americans still traveled close to home mostly out of a feeling of increased patriotism and pride in their country. For the French, national pride has long been an influence on their travel plans. It would be easy enough for French tourists to visit other European countries; however, they spend almost the same number of vacation days in their own country as they do abroad.

And, finally, but very importantly, economic conditions around the world greatly affect travel. Growth in travel and tourism is closely tied to growth in business and personal income. As people's incomes increase, the greater the likelihood they will be packing their bags for a vacation far from home. If personal income does not increase, if there is a threat that it will decrease, or if it does, in fact, decrease, potential tourists become armchair travelers at best! So, investors and destination developers may have been poised for tourism or business growth only to find that those whom they most want to attract are staying home because they simply don't have the money to go anywhere!

Explorations

We have defined—with Webster's help—both travel and tourism and have provided answers to the questions, "What is travel?" and "What is tourism?" Now, consider the following:

> You are a citizen of a small, island country. Your country has beautiful, unspoiled beaches, great fishing, and a dramatic, if somewhat stark, landscape. You raise sugar cane and bananas, but, since the country is very small, there really isn't much money to be made in agriculture. There are a few tourists who have chosen the island because it is "undiscovered," quiet, friendly, and crime free. However, unemployment is high and many citizens live in near poverty. Young people are discouraged because there is no future and they want to leave the island. Some leaders want to encourage outside investment in developing tourism while others fear the influence of foreign powers.

What position would you take?

Enrichments

Find news or magazine articles that describe:

1. Conditions that would encourage or discourage business development in a certain area.
2. Conditions that would encourage or discourage tourists to visit a certain area.

Understanding the Travel Industry

What Is It? The travel industry is difficult to understand and its size is impossible to pinpoint because there is no clear or accepted definition of the *travel industry*. If you take a simple approach and accept the statement that the travel industry gets people to a destination and back and provides them with shelter when they are there, then you are, of course, ignoring those who provide food, entertainment, local transportation, and shopping for travelers. If you include restaurants, shops, taxis, mass transit, and entertainment, your numbers will include sales to locals and will be too high. If you do not include these businesses, your numbers will be too low.

Understanding, then, that travel and tourism is a complex industry involving many, many businesses, we can say with confidence that it is huge, and nod, at least in general agreement, with the experts who say that it is one of the largest employers in the world and one of the most rapidly growing segments of world trade. But, what is it, really?

First, industry, by definition, is trade or manufacturing in general. Specifically, an industry is concerned with a particular business, such as the automobile industry or the steel industry. The travel industry is the business or trade associated with providing travel services.

Travel and tourism is more of a system than a single industry. This system is a network of industries, services, and businesses involved in selling and providing services to those who travel the world. However, those employed in travel and tourism refer to the "travel industry," not the "travel system" and, as a future travel professional, so should you!

The travel industry, unlike other major industries, is made up of many industries that are quite large in their own right:

- The airline industry
- The car rental industry
- The cruise line industry
- The hotel (or hospitality) industry
- The motorcoach industry
- The rail industry

All of these interlock and interrelate. Some companies have taken these products and combined them or added services to them to create still other companies in the travel industry:

- Guide services
- Local transportation services: limousines, buses, taxis
- Sightseeing companies
- Tour companies
- Travel agencies
- Travel writing and publishing: guidebooks, brochures, magazines, texts
- Visa and travel documentation services

All of these industries and companies are called suppliers. They supply travel products and services to the consumer, and, like all businesses, they must find a way to match their products—airline seats, tours, hotel rooms, cruise cabins, services, and so on—to the prospective buyer, the traveler.

With all these choices and all these suppliers competing for business, how does the traveler decide where to go, how to get there, where to stay, and what to do when he or she gets there? Today, over 60 percent of the traveling public uses the services of a travel agency in the planning and purchase of travel arrangements.

Travel **agents** sort through and interpret the myriad of information and choices offered by suppliers. They guide and assist their clients—the travelers—in the purchase of airline seats, cruise cabins, hotel rooms, tours, and rental cars. As you study travel and tourism, you will learn much about the components of the industry and how agents and suppliers work together to serve and sell to the traveler.

Agent (AGT) One authorized *to sell a supplier's products.*

Who's Who and What's What

Industries have their own special terms or jargon—a language that has meaning only within the context of their work. The jargon of the travel industry is extensive because it is fed by the component subindustries. For example, many terms come by way of the hotel business, others via car rental operations, and still others from shipping and cruise lines. The preponderance of terms, however, comes from the airlines and their computer systems.

Industry Terms

This text has a glossary of the most commonly used terms in the industry and also a list of abbreviations and their meanings. When you encounter a term you don't know, look it up! Knowing terms and jargon will enhance your understanding, so take the time to learn them as you go along!

You may find these terms popping up on quizzes and tests, and you will certainly hear them in lectures and discussions. The glossary is intended as an industry reference that you can use throughout your education and in your job. Not all terms in the glossary will be found in this book, but you will hear them and see them as you move through your studies in travel and tourism.

Learning travel industry jargon is necessary and fun. It is important to know the terms so you can understand your coworkers and communicate quickly and effectively with them. There simply isn't enough time in the day to say or spell out everything, but you must know when to use industry jargon and when not to. Never assume that the people you serve understand travel industry jargon. The words you are using may carry a totally different meaning for those who do not work in the industry, and the codes and abbreviations may give the impression that your typewriter ran amuck! (*Hint:* Italicized words and abbreviations can be found in your glossary.)

Travel Jargon

What do you think the following statements mean?

1. The hotel says it will give you *run of the house*.
2. The airline will not allow *open jaw* travel at this fare.
3. I need to change one of his *legs*.
4. This flight is heavily *booked* and you might get *bumped*.
5. The tour operator will give you five hundred *shells*.
6. Hotels do not like to *walk* their guests.

Now, try to decipher these coded messages:

1. CC GTY FOR CK-IN AFTER 6P
2. BKD F WL Y
3. RQTD FLT NOOP BKD OAL
4. PLZ BK LCAR W/PH RQST WKLY RTE

You can easily confuse and alienate your clients, customers, guests, or passengers (not to mention your friends and family members!) by using terms and abbreviations they do not understand. Use the terms, jargon, and codes with your coworkers and travel industry partners. Speak standard English to the public!

Automation and the Travel Industry

Getting information about travel products and services to the consumer, whether it is direct to the consumer or through an agency, is of utmost importance to the supplier. How can suppliers sell anything if the consumers don't know what they have to offer?

Many publications advertise, promote, and explain the many travel products and services available today, and they certainly serve the industry well. However, one thing you will learn about travel and travel products is that they change constantly, and the demand for up-to-date information is a daily, if not hourly, concern of most travel suppliers.

So, how does the industry keep up with this demand for information and the need to sell its products quickly and efficiently? It will come as no surprise (certainly not to those of you born within the last twenty-five years) that computers have been the solution to this problem.

To handle the challenges of working in a deregulated environment and to accommodate the rapid growth and stiff competition of the late 1970s and 1980s, the airlines began making major improvements to their reservations processes through computerization. Advances in communication technology made fantastic things possible, and the major airlines quickly realized that, by placing their reservations systems in the offices of their distributors, they could expedite bookings, speed up communication, and *make more money!*

Airlines leased their reservation systems to travel agencies, and they also began charging each other to display schedules, fares, and seat availability. Agency **automation** became "Big Business" for the airlines, and the development and advancement of these reservation systems became a high priority.

Automation   The computerized reservation and accounting systems used by travel vendors, most commonly travel agencies.

Not only did agencies find great value in having computerized access to airline seats, but other vendors quickly saw the advantage of "being in an airline system." The systems quickly expanded to include hotels, car rentals, vacation packages, cruises, and rail travel. They also began offering comprehensive information on such varied subjects as weather, local transportation, Broadway shows, train reservations, and documentation requirements for travel to foreign countries.

Hotels, car rental companies, cruise lines, tour operators, and travel information services found that the airline systems provided them with immediate and widespread access to the traveling public. Airlines welcomed the interest of other suppliers because they could charge them to be in their systems, and the more suppliers represented in a system, the more valuable the system became to the agencies who leased them from the airlines.

Automation changed the jobs of reservationists, ticketing agents, and travel counselors by eliminating the time-consuming routine tasks of:

- Searching for schedules and fares in huge, fine-print reference books.
- Handwriting tickets and typing itineraries, invoices, and statements.
- Making multiple calls to suppliers to book airline seats, hotels, car rentals, and so on.

In the United States, the vast majority of all airline reservations and over 90 percent of all airline tickets are handled through computers. Today, there are four major automated reservations systems in the United States:

Apollo: Covia Corporation, a partnership that includes United Airlines, USAir, and others. Apollo was once solely owned by United and many industry professionals still refer to Apollo as "United's system."

Computer Reservation System (CRS) The automated reservation systems developed and marketed by the airlines and used by most travel agencies to book airline seats, hotels, and rental cars. The major systems are Apollo, Sabre, System One, and Worldspan.

Sabre: American Airlines. American was the great innovator in airline automation systems and today still commands a large share of the **Computer Reservation System (CRS)** market. Automation has been very important to all carriers, but none more so than American. Its Sabre system is believed to be the most profitable division of the holding company that controls the airline, the reservations system, and other interests.

System One: Also known as SODA, which stands for System One Direct Access. System One was originally developed and owned by Eastern Airlines and later purchased and operated as a subsidiary of Texas Air Corporation. Problems at Eastern and later problems at Texas Air affected the expansion of this system as many users were concerned about the stability of the company. In 1990, Electronic Data Systems Corporation purchased 50 percent of System One, making this system one of the few to have nontravel industry partners.

Worldspan: A recent (1990) merger of Delta Airlines' system (DATAS II) and TWA's system (PARS). Northwest Airlines is also a partner in this group. The joining of these two systems made Worldspan a formidable competitor with Sabre and Apollo/Covia, the two largest in the nation.

Around the World with Automation

At the same time as they have been changing, growing, and merging in the United States, automation vendors have also been pushing their technological wares in other parts of the world, primarily in Europe and Canada. Covia Corporation purchased one-third of Canada's Gemini Group Automated Distributors (known more simply as Gemini), and Sabre has been busily increasing its installations there as well!

Unlike Canada, which has only two competing systems, Europe has more competitors. In addition to the U.S. systems entering the market, there are also two European vendors: Galileo and Amadeus. Amadeus and Galileo claim more agency locations, but, unlike their U.S. counterparts, they are systems that have not yet achieved full functionality. The U.S. vendors are intent on worldwide growth, and we can safely predict that there will continue to be changes, mergers, partnerships, buyouts, and exciting developments driven by stiff competition in global automation.

Industry Associations

Large industries foster the formation of associations and institutions. These organizations exist to set policies and standards, improve business conditions, or offer education and the exchange of ideas. Memberships in such organizations can be an indication of industry commitment and high professional standards.

Trade associations are organized to serve their members, but the major trade associations often provide indirect benefits to agents who are not members. In your glossary, you will find descriptions of the following major trade associations:

American Hotel and Motel
  Association (AH & MA)
1201 New York Avenue, N.W.,
  6th Floor
Washington, DC 20005

Airlines Reporting Corporation
  (ARC)
1709 New York Avenue, N.W.
Washington, DC 20006–5288

Air Transport Association
  (ATA)
1709 New York Avenue, N.W.
Washington, DC 20006–5288

American Society of Travel
  Agents (ASTA)
1101 King Street
Alexandria, VA 22314

Amtrak, the National Railroad
  Passenger Corporation
400 N. Capitol Street
Washington, DC 20001

Association of Retail Travel
  Agents (ARTA)
25 South Riverside
Croton-on-Hudson, NY
  10525

Cruise Lines International
  Association (CLIA)
500 Fifth Avenue, Suite 1407
New York, NY 10111

Institute of Certified Travel
  Agents (ICTA)
148 Linden Street, P.O. Box
  82–56
Wellesley, MA 02181

International Air Transport
  Association (IATA)
26 Chemin de Joinville
P.O. Box 160, 1216 Cointrin
Geneva, Switzerland

International Airlines Travel
  Agent Network (IATAN)
300 Garden City Plaza
Garden City, NY 11530

Meeting Planners International
  (MPI)
1950 Stemmons Freeway
Dallas, TX 75207

National Business Traveler
  Association
1650 King Street, Suite 301
Alexandria, VA 22314

National Tour Association, Inc.
  (NTA) and National Tour
  Foundation
North American Headquarters
P.O. Box 3071
Lexington, KY 40596

United States Tour Operators
  Association (USTOA)
211 East 51st Street, Suite 12B
New York, NY 10022

Government Agencies

Travel would not be possible without the supporting services and facilities of the communities and countries of the world. Airports, harbors, roads, bridges, and public utilities must be able to handle the ever-increasing numbers of travelers. Governments are responsible for seeing that these needs are met today and in the future.

Governments know that promoting tourism can provide jobs to thousands. They also know that uncontrolled and unplanned growth in tourism can create major problems for their citizens. All governments have agencies that support and regulate travel. Some of the most important United States federal agencies and offices are:

- Department of Commerce
    U.S. Travel and Tourism Administration

- Department of State
- Department of Transportation (DOT)
- Federal Aviation Administration (FAA)
- National Transportation Safety Board (NTSB)
- U.S. Customs Service

Government tourist offices, commonly known as national tourist offices (NTOs) throughout the world, offer assistance and information to travelers and travel agencies. They work to promote travel and tourism to their countries. They provide sales assistance and marketing support to travel vendors and maintain extensive supplies of printed information.

Governments also maintain embassies and consulates in foreign countries. These offices perform many functions and exist primarily as local political and cultural liaisons for their governments. While their primary focus may not be tourism or tourists, they do provide assistance to their citizens who are traveling or living abroad.

The Importance of Staying Current

The hallmark of the travel industry is change and growth. Some change is due to the technological advances in automation, but a great deal is due to political and economic factors. When war breaks out or revolution erupts, travel suppliers around the world feel the effects as surely as politicians in Washington, D.C.

Similarly, the travel planning decisions of industry suppliers and their customers are influenced by the bankruptcy (or threatened bankruptcy) of other suppliers and the mergers and acquisitions of travel industry companies. The constant upheaval in the airline industry over the last decade has created news items of great interest to the general public and of critical importance to those who make their livings in the travel industry. When there is a major storm, earthquake, or fire, your customers' plans and your business could be affected—sometimes dramatically.

You must be aware of these events as they happen and stay abreast of the public's response to them. The easiest way to stay up to date is to become a regular reader of newspapers and news magazines. If you are already a news "junkie," that's great; but if you haven't acquired the habit, get hooked now! You can begin by browsing through various papers and magazines and clipping articles for research or discussion. Some excellent sources of travel news are:

- Any major city newspaper
- *The Wall Street Journal*
- *USA Today*

Trade Publications

Since every sector of the industry has its own publications, the amount of material available to industry professionals is considerable, if not overwhelming! The major trade organizations publish magazines, newspapers, and guides. There are also trade newspapers that contain

business articles as well as destination and supplier information. Some popular travel publications are:

- *ASTA Agency Management*
- *Business Travel News*
- *Tour and Travel News*
- *Travel Age*
- *Travel Agent*
- *Travel Weekly*

Guidebooks

Guidebooks offer excellent, detailed information on destinations, hotels, restaurants, and shops. When using guidebooks, it is important to remember they are generally written from one person's point of view and reflect his or her taste in hotels, restaurants, shops, and attractions. Some popular guidebook series are:

- *AAA Guides*
- *Blue*
- *Frommer*
- *Baedecker*
- *Fielding*
- *Michelin*
- *Birnbaum*
- *Fodor*
- *Mobil*

Brochures

Travel **brochures** are distributed by suppliers for the purpose of selling their products and always present them in the best possible light. Responsible suppliers will take care not to misrepresent their products. They will also include helpful information about local customs, documentation, currency, electrical current, health advisories, and so forth.

Brochures may be one-page flyers or sophisticated, multicolored "magazines" of tour offerings and destinations. Airlines, hotels, tour operators, cruise lines, and governments spend millions of dollars every year in creating and distributing these sales pieces. While the photography may be beautiful (even eye-popping!), and the language inviting and effusive, the wise buyer will know how important it is to carefully read "the small print" and to seek out other opinions such as those of a travel agent or those found in guidebooks and travel articles.

Brochure *A printed folder that contains information about hotels, cruises, tours, and so on. It may be a simple flyer or as large as a magazine. Agencies keep brochures on file as aids in selling travel and making bookings for clients.*

Travel Videos

Travel videos were originally produced to sell travel to the consumer, but they have proved to have great educational value for the travel professional as well. Many videos are produced and distributed by suppliers and national tourist boards to promote their products and countries. Generally, these are available at little or no cost to agencies. Travel agents use them for their own training and often lend them to clients or have a special viewing area in their offices for those who are considering the destination or supplier.

Etc. . . .

Travel is often a subject in popular magazines, books, films, and television shows. Anything you read or see that builds on your knowledge of the destinations of the world will make you that much more of an expert in your chosen field.

A traveler who has recently returned from a trip can provide up-to-date information and impressions of carriers, suppliers, and destinations. Usually, travelers are pleased and complimented to be asked for their opinions.

"Being There": An Exciting Way to Stay Current!

Familiarization (Fam) Trip
A free or discounted trip for travel agents designed to familiarize them with a destination or travel service to stimulate travel sales to that area/supplier.

Travel can be a necessity and a pleasure. Leaving home, however, even on happily anticipated trips, is stressful for most people. Travel builds confidence and knowledge for industry employees and helps them make their customers more comfortable with their travel choices.

Airlines, cruise lines, tour operators, and governments sponsor **familiarization (fam) trips** to many destinations so that travel industry employees can learn about destinations and services firsthand. These trips include visits to airports, hotels, resorts, restaurants, and local attractions and may also include seminars and workshops. Fam trips can be wonderful and exciting, but the intent of the trips is educational. They are part of an employee's professional development. While fam trips are a benefit of the job, they should be taken seriously.

Personal vacations also enhance your knowledge of the world. Travel industry employees are often offered reduced-rate transportation and hotel discounts that greatly offset the cost of travel. Personal travel serves to familiarize and make the travel professional more sympathetic and understanding of his or her client's concerns and stresses while traveling. Although fam trips are an excellent way to educate and familiarize, the suppliers do take care of all the details for the participant. Often, the sponsor and host of a fam trip will go to great lengths to make the travel trouble free—a luxury the "regular" traveler rarely has!

It is not possible to visit every destination; you would never be in the office to serve the client! Destinations and suppliers change—sometimes quickly and dramatically. What was true of a place two years ago may not be the case today. Travel professionals must be able to research, discuss, and sell destinations they have not visited. The foundations of destination and supplier knowledge are the many industry references available in books, on the computer, and on video tapes. As you study travel and tourism, you will take a "familiarization tour" of the many resources available to you.

Explorations

Write a report on a destination or hotel. If you have not traveled recently, write a travel review of your own town or a special site, hotel, or restaurant located there. Remember! The traveling public is looking to *you* for good ideas on what to do!

OR

Interview a family member or friend about a trip he or she has recently taken and report on his or her findings. Once again, remember that you are responsible to the traveling public. Ask questions that will help you develop a picture of this destination:

- What did the traveler like?
- What did the traveler dislike?
- Is it a good place for families, couples, and young people or old?
- How was the service?
- How was the food?
- Would the traveler go back?

These are by no means all the questions you might ask, but they will get you started.

Enrichments

1. Check the local TV listings for travel programs and watch them.
2. Check out a travel video from your school, library, or local video store.
3. Read a travel magazine (or travel article), guidebook, or travel book.

The Travel Industry and You

A Garden of Opportunities

The travel industry offers a wide variety of employment opportunities, requiring skill levels from very basic to highly technical and offering compensation from minimum wage to highly paid executive levels. There are jobs in the travel industry that require college degrees or professional training and there are those that offer on-the-job training.

This industry offers everyone unlimited opportunities to grow—whether that growth direction is to manage or own a travel agency, manage a corporate travel department, market or run a hotel, be an airline sales representative or a professional tour manager, become a meeting planner, or become a travel educator and trainer.

The travel industry strongly supports the philosophy that the best way to learn is from the bottom up. Ask a hotel general manager where she began her career, and she will very likely tell you "front desk" or reservations; ask an airline sales representative where he began, and he will tell you reservations, baggage handling, or as a gate agent; ask a travel agency manager where she began, and she will tell you delivering tickets, filing brochures, or answering phones.

The travel industry can also take pride in the fact that it is "friendly" to women and minorities. There are many women in the travel business—in fact, the industry is 84 percent female! If you compare the travel industry to others, you will find that, traditionally, it has been more open-minded about hiring and promoting women and minorities.

What opportunities are out there? Where could you begin and where will you go? As you learn about travel and tourism, you will be introduced to the opportunities the companies that make up this industry may offer. At the end of this section you will find a listing of entry-level and career opportunities. As you consider them, it is important to keep an open mind, explore all possibilities, and remember that experience in any travel field will lead to opportunities in others.

Qualities to Cultivate

Travel is a service business. While efficiency is valued, accuracy is critical, and knowledge is power, the ability to work with others (whether they are customers or colleagues) is of utmost importance! If you are entering the travel field from a career in another industry, you have probably already learned much about business etiquette and the pleasures and pitfalls of working with others. If you are new to the business world, it is important to know what qualities employers look for and reward in employees. Following is a partial list:

- Sympathy, patience, and even temper under stress.
- A willingness to solve problems rather than complain about them.
- Punctuality, neatness, organization, and accuracy.
- Attention to detail.
- Flexibility and versatility.
- Knowledge of the industry and an eagerness to learn more.
- Willingness to learn a new way to do an old job.

- Interest in the long-term growth of the business.
- Congeniality and cooperation with coworkers.
- Respect and deference (but not servility) in dealing with customers.
- Politeness, poise, professional attire, and good grooming.

Your education and training in this field may get you to an employer's front door, but it is the impression you make that will determine whether or not you get the job. Travel is a service business and the customer must always come first! Employers will look at you through their customers' eyes; if they do not believe that those who do business with them will like you, they will not hire you.

Travel Career Growth

Entry Level	Career
Travel Agency	
Travel Agent—Domestic	Travel Agent—International
Accounting Assistant	Agent Supervisor
Outside Sales Representative	Officer Manager
Receptionist	Controller
Marketing Assistant	Accounting Supervisor
Secretary	Marketing Director
	General Manager
	Outside Sales Representative
	Special Projects Supervisor
	International Supervisor
	Domestic Supervisor
	Commercial Supervisor
	Tour and Group Sales Manager
	Owner
Air Carriers	
Reservationist	Marketing Director
Ticket Agent	District Sales Representative
Flight Attendant	Regional Sales Manager
Customer Service	Director, Agency Relations
Dispatcher	Director of Automation
Clerical	Director, Group and Charter Sales
Operations	Traffic Manager
Accounting	Director, Tour & Convention Services
Tour Company	
Receptionist	Tour Director
Secretary	Account Supervisor
Tour Guide	Marketing Director
Sales Representative	Sales Director
	Ground Services Director

Travel Career Growth (continued)

Entry Level	Career

Cruise Company

Entry Level	Career
Reservationist	Sales Representative
Secretary	Marketing Director
Clerical/Accounting	Group, Charter & Incentive Director
Public Relations	Scheduling Director
	Passenger Service Representative

Travel Trade Organizations

Entry Level	Career
Secretary	Marketing Director
Receptionist	Executive Director
Membership Representative	Research & Analysis Director

Hotels

Entry Level	Career
Reservationist	Catering Director
Receptionist	Housekeeping Director
Front Desk Clerk	Sales Director
Secretary	Group & Incentive Sales Director
Clerical/Accounting	General Manager

Other components of the travel industry that offer employment opportunities include car rental companies, corporate travel departments, Amtrak, travel publications, city convention and visitors bureaus, foreign country and state tourist offices, Chambers of Commerce, and so forth.

The Travelers

Where Are We Going?

When you have completed this section, you will:

1. Understand what motivates people to travel.
2. Be able to identify the three basic categories of travelers.
3. Understand demographic and psychographic market research.
4. Know the important differences and basic requirements of international travel.

Industry Terms and Jargon

Boarding Pass	Documents	Meet and Assist
Coach Class Fare	Duty	Nonstop Flight
Connecting Flight	Frequent Flyer	Visa
Customs	International	

Travelers on a Flight from Here to There

People travel for many reasons and their attitudes toward travel vary greatly. By understanding the travelers themselves, you will be well on your way to understanding travel industry suppliers and the keys to success with them.

Scene: A flight from Chicago's O'Hare Airport to the West Coast
Time: A Thursday afternoon

Coach Class (1) The sections of an air carrier where lower cost seats are located. (2) The actual class of service paid for.

1. A *business woman* who will return home tomorrow evening has paid the full **coach class** fare of $700 for her round-trip ticket. The trip was booked at 8:00 this morning, and her travel agent had to send a special courier on RUSH delivery to get it to her. The business emergency and the last-minute arrangements put everyone in her office in a panic, and she is on edge about the trip. To add to her discomfort, she could only get a middle seat; she prefers an aisle. She tried to use her **frequent flyer** status to upgrade to first class, but, like the rest of the flight, first class was sold out.

Frequent Flyer Program Airline program in which members accrue miles (points) for flights taken. The miles/points are usually redeemable for free travel arrangements.

2. A *family of five (mother, father, and three children)* are traveling to see their cousins. All low-cost seats were sold out on the **non-stop flight** when they called to make their arrangements. The airlines reservation agent booked them on a **connecting flight** through Chicago and they were able to get the special fares. The youngest child is only six months old, and, since her mother will hold her on the trip, she travels for free. One of the children has spilled orange juice, another is complaining loudly about not having a window seat, and the other child is crying. The father is nervous because the passenger next to him seems aggravated by all the commotion. The mother is wishing they were on the nonstop flight, but she does take some consolation in knowing that the special-fare tickets were half the price of regular coach fare.

Nonstop Flight A flight that does not stop between point of departure and destination.

Connecting Flight Air transportation arrangement that requires a passenger to change planes en route to his or her chosen destination.

3. An *elderly gentleman,* whose final destination is Denver, had to make a connection in Chicago. He planned his trip several weeks ago and, because he is staying over a Saturday night, he was able to get the lowest fare. He broke his hip earlier this year and was very concerned about making the connection— sometimes the gates can be very far apart at O'Hare. His travel agent requested that the airline's agents meet him on arrival with a wheelchair and also told him to mention it to the gate agents at his first flight so they could double-check on the wheelchair request. His agent also suggested he tell the flight attendants about his condition so that, if anything went wrong with the arrangements, they would be prepared to help him. Everything went smoothly, but he really appreciated his travel agent's concern and good advice!

4. A *rabbi* is traveling to speak at a theological conference in Vancouver. He accepted the engagement at the last minute when

the original speaker canceled. The university sponsoring the conference paid over $1,000 for his ticket. He will make flight connections on the West Coast. He is concerned that his request for kosher meals might not have been received by all the airlines he will travel on today.

5. A *brother and sister* are going home for a college break. One has a nonrefundable fare of $258. They both are staying over Saturday night and made their reservations more than two weeks in advance, but the brother kept changing his return and delayed in purchasing his ticket. By the time he decided to stick with his original plans, the lowest fare was no longer available. His fare is $400, and he is thinking how annoyed his mother is going to be that he fooled around and didn't get the lowest fare. He wishes he could have a cigarette, but smoking isn't allowed on flights in the United States.

6. A *professional musician* is seated near the brother and sister. His tuba is extremely valuable, and he will not allow it to be placed in the baggage compartment. Since it will not fit under his seat or in the compartment overhead, he had to purchase a ticket for it. It is strapped in the seat beside him. He booked a discount fare, but the total cost for him and his tuba was still nearly $800.

7. A *nicely dressed couple* is having champagne cocktails to toast the beginning of vacation. They are traveling free to Hawaii—first class! The husband has enough frequent flyer points for two tickets to Honolulu. He will also receive a free rental car and a 50 percent discount at their hotel on Waikiki Beach.

8. A *child, eight years old and traveling alone,* has the lowest fare to Portland, Oregon, but his parents had to pay an additional charge for **Meet and Assist** service. This extra charge is required by this airline for unaccompanied minors making connections. The child is seated in the bulkhead section of the coach compartment so the flight attendants can keep a careful watch over him. They are responsible for seeing that he gets safely off the plane and is met by an airline representative who will take him to his next flight.

Meet and Assist An airline term meaning a client needs to be met by a customer service representative when his or her flight arrives and assisted with making a connecting flight. This request is most often made for elderly, disabled, young, or first-time flyers.

9. A *travel agent whose ticket cost $158* received an agent's discount of 75 percent off full coach fare. She is returning home from visiting hotels for a meeting her agency will be handling. She asked for a first-class upgrade when she checked in. The gate agent said the flight was showing full in first class, but he offered to hold her ticket until the last minute to see if a first-class passenger "no-showed." No such luck this time, and she's stuck near the crying baby!

10. A *lawyer* who hoped to be going home today received an emergency call from his office at his hotel late last night. His partner asked him to rearrange his schedule to fly to the West Coast before coming home. He hates to mess with exchanging tickets and decided to purchase a new ticket in Chicago and

have his old ticket refunded by the travel agency. He called his agency's toll-free number first thing this morning and was relieved to get his favorite agent on the phone. She booked his flight (even though she couldn't issue the ticket!) and took care of the hotel and car rental reservations. He prefers to call the agency because they have his profile in their system, and everything can be handled with just one phone call.

11. Another *travel agent* on this flight paid nothing for his ticket. His agency paid for a familiarization trip that will take him to Hong Kong, Singapore, and Thailand for ten days. He is eager to see these fabulous places, although he will have a very full itinerary and a tiring layover on the West Coast. He knows he will be wined and dined by the hotels and the tour company that organized his "fam," and he is looking forward to the exciting days ahead. He will take detailed notes on his trip so he can file a written trip report with his agency when he returns.

12. A *retired couple* is returning home after taking a deluxe cruise in Scandinavia to see the fjords. They had a wonderful time and can't wait to tell their travel agent all about it. She really made a great recommendation and even had a bottle of wine delivered to their table on their first night! They had the ship's photographer take a picture of them toasting each other with the first glass of wine, and they brought her a copy. The only problem they encountered on their entire trip was on this flight when they found another couple in their assigned seats. After checking the **boarding passes,** the flight attendant discovered that the other couple belonged two rows back.

Boarding Pass   A permit for the traveler to board a ship, plane, train, or other form of transportation. Part of the check-in process. Travel agencies now provide advance boarding passes to air travelers—a very popular service that saves travelers time and frustration and lessens their chances of being bumped by the airlines.

These travelers are all very different people, but they do have one need in common: transportation. In this case, that need is very specific—a seat on an airplane. Their reasons for wanting a seat on this plane are as different as their ages, backgrounds, and personalities. Some are traveling on business; some for pleasure. Some travelers have a choice in the matter; others do not. Some travelers are alone; others are not.

Explorations

1. Most travelers pay for their transportation. What does this scene reveal about air fares?

2. Travelers also have secondary needs in travel that are met in a variety of ways by different people. What are some of the needs these travelers have?

3. What does the airplane scene reveal about:
   a. Airline services?
   b. Travel agency services?

4. If you were planning a trip, would you call a travel agency? Give your reasons why or why not.

Enrichments

Interview a traveler you know:

1. What does he or she like about traveling?
2. What does he or she dislike about traveling?
3. What was one of this traveler's favorite travel experiences?
4. What was one of this traveler's worst travel experiences?

Travelers Today

We've all heard funny and distressing tales of the "ugly _(fill in the nationality of your choice)_ tourist". Unfortunately, there are those who travel who believe that, just because customs or life styles are different from their own, they are wrong or inferior. These travelers make no effort to adapt to their new surroundings and apply the standards of where they live to the neighborhoods, cities, and countries of others. They are the worst type of traveler, and they have been roaming the globe for centuries. When the Greek philosopher Socrates was told that a narrow-minded acquaintance had gained nothing from traveling abroad, he replied, "I very much believe it, for he took himself with him."

However, the good news is that travelers are, for the most part, "gentle invaders." They bring their cultures, businesses, friendships, and money to others and take their new-found awarenesses of others home. Travel broadens a traveler's perspective of the world and the perspectives of those who come into contact with him in the host destination. If a traveler sees better things while traveling, perhaps she will bring these new ideas home. If, on the other hand, a traveler sees conditions worse than those in his own country, perhaps he will better appreciate what he has.

There are as many types of travelers as there are destinations, hotels, and means of transportation to serve them. Where one traveler may find great satisfaction in spending hours in an art museum, another may fill up on culture very quickly and be happiest with a quick visit to the masterpieces of the world and a leisurely afternoon at a sidewalk cafe.

Enthusiastic travelers flock to Miami every week to board luxury cruise ships for three-, four-, seven-, and fourteen-day voyages where constant entertainment, sightseeing, shopping, and dining are all promised and delivered! Others find the idea of vacationing on a gently rolling ship in open waters unappealing—if not nauseating!

Millions of families have traveled great distances to enjoy amusement parks of every variety, while other mothers and fathers would rather vacation in a pit of vipers than take yet another roll of film of their youngsters holding hands with six-foot cartoon characters in 95 degree heat.

Some business travelers stay in deluxe hotels and conduct business meetings in spacious suites or over an expensive meal. Others may be much more concerned with expenses and will seek out moderately priced hotels and dine alone. Some businesspeople travel frequently between major cities while others may have more complicated itineraries to visit remote oil fields, military bases, or manufacturing plants.

Those who have the freedom to decide where they are going, when they are going, and, most importantly, *if* they are going, are *discretionary* travelers. Those who have very little choice about whether they travel or not are *nondiscretionary* travelers. Travel industry suppliers more often refer to these travelers as:

- Vacation or leisure travelers (discretionary)
- Business or corporate travelers (nondiscretionary)

These distinctions are broad and ignore those who travel for reasons other than vacation or business, such as those attending to personal or family emergencies or students returning to school. These are relatively small groups, and, since they are not business travelers, they are usually lumped in with the vacation or discretionary group. People who are traveling to a meeting they are not required to attend but which will further enhance their professional knowledge or add to their personal development are not vacation travelers; nor are they business travelers.

Those who are traveling together on group tours are classified as vacationers, but the planning and handling of these trips is different from planning travel for individuals. Travel suppliers that handle groups traveling or meeting together consider them a separate category altogether. Thus, we have:

- Vacation (or leisure) travelers
- Business (or corporate) travelers
- Group and meeting travelers

Within each category, there are many different types of travelers, each with their own needs and expectations.

Vacation Travelers	Business Travelers	Groups and Meetings
Families	Salesmen	Sales
Singles	Executives	Corporate
Young singles	Professionals	Professional
Divorced singles	Doctors	Medical
Widows/widowers	Lawyers	Legal
Couples	Accountants	Associations
Honeymooners	Consultants	Clubs
Working couples	Education	Education
Gay couples	Government	Trade Fairs
Retired couples	Clergy	Conventions
Handicapped	Technicians	Vacation

While certain preferences, interests, and needs can be assigned to each category, there are further distinctions within the categories themselves. Some travelers will have lots of money to spend while others will be on more restricted budgets. Some travelers will be very independent in their planning and others will need guidance and very specific recommendations. Some travelers will want every detail covered while others will be more free-spirited and loosely organized.

Some travel suppliers specialize in handling travel for one of the three main groups, or even for a specific subgroup such as a travel supplier specializing in ski vacations. Others, such as the airlines, wish to attract the business of all groups and individuals and create departments within their companies to work with specific types of travelers. They also create many different types of advertising promotions with messages designed to appeal to a certain type of traveler.

ABC Corporation Customer Questionnaire

You recently purchased one of our newest products, and we do hope you are pleased with it! Would you now take a moment to complete the following questionnaire and return it to us in the postpaid envelope? Your answers will help us serve you better in the future!

A. Age group (check one):

( ) 18–24   ( ) 25–34   ( ) 35–45   ( ) Over 45

B. Family Income (check one):

( ) $15,000–$19,000   ( ) $20,000–$29,000   ( ) $30,000–$39,000

( ) $40,000–$50,000   ( ) Over $50,000

C. Education (check one):

( ) High School Graduate   ( ) 1–2 Years Postsecondary/College

( ) College Graduate   ( ) College+

Getting to Know You . . . Getting to Know All About You . . .

And, the questions go on and on. . . .

Have you ever received one of these forms or been contacted by telephone to "answer a few questions" for a local business, pollster, or marketing research firm? Probably so, because finding out about you and others like you will help businesses determine how you spend your money, how much money you have to spend, and how to get you to spend it with them!

Travel suppliers, like other businesses, spend time and money to find out about you, the potential traveler. They want to know who they should sell to, how they should sell to them, and how they can best reach them. Market research has shown that travelers with similar backgrounds have similar purchasing habits. Analyzing answers to questions such as those on the ABC Corporation questionnaire may result in statements such as "75 percent of our customers are 25–34 years old and have some college education." This type of research and analysis is demographic—or, more simply put, research based on facts and figures.

Demographic information describes groups according to age, sex, marital status, income, family size, education, occupation, religion, and so forth. Demographics compiled by market researchers from the travel industry have provided the following information about vacation travelers:

- They are more urban than rural.
- They are likely to have college degrees.
- They prefer group travel if they are blue-collar workers.
- They prefer individualized travel if they are professionals.
- Their propensity to travel is based on age:

  65% of ages 16–24 travel

  40% of ages 50–64 travel

  17% of age 65+ travel

- Those with higher income and education travel by air and stay in hotels.
- Those with lower income and education travel by car or bus and stay with friends or relatives.
- Most people who travel to foreign countries do so more than once.

If ABC Corporation wishes to attract older or wealthier buyers, it needs to find out what this group wants. To get this type of information, it will need to ask more "life-style" questions such as:

- Do you dine out once a week or more?
- Do you prefer going to movie theaters or renting videos?
- Do you plan on taking a vacation next year?
- Do you shop frequently by mail?
- Have you read one or more books in the last three months?

These questions are psychographic. Psychographic information reveals more subjective information. Researchers ask travelers to describe their activities, interests, needs, and attitudes. Analysts then come to certain conclusions about a group's motivations and preferences, such as young people are more likely to travel for excitement and are therefore willing to endure some hardships; older people are more likely to travel for pleasure and prefer luxurious accommodations and being pampered.

Psychographic information can also be used to predict future buying trends—something of great interest to travel suppliers. Such information will help suppliers decide which destinations will be popular, which types of trips will be preferred, and which population segments will be most likely to spend their money on travel.

The Gray 90s

One population group that receives almost constant research attention is the "baby boomers." As this much watched and frequently questioned group moves into middle age in the 1990s, everyone from local travel agencies to major airlines wants to know: "Where do you want to go?" Psychographic research has uncovered answers to this question and many more about their likes and dislikes. You can be sure that sales and marketing experts are busy designing travel products to appeal to this group. What have these graying "baby boomers" told them?

YES   to travel outside the United States.
NO   to family-oriented attractions.
YES   to more luxurious accommodations
NO   to longer vacations
YES   to more weekend trips
YES   to more active, adventurous vacations
YES   to expecting higher levels of service
NO   to highly organized tours
YES   to independent tours and cruises

UP CLOSE

Business Travel

Type: Nondiscretionary.
Purchasing: ■ Company pays, not the individual.
                     ■ Frequent use of credit cards.
Planning/Booking: ■ Often last minute (highest fares).
                     ■ Frequent changes, cancellations, rebooks.
                     ■ Often handled by secretary or assistant rather than the traveler.

	▪ Reservations made by phone, fax, or computer link-up.
Trip Components:	Primarily air and hotel, frequent car rentals.
Length of Stay:	▪ Domestic trips: 1–3 days.
	▪ International trips: 4–7 days.
Frequency:	Tend to be high frequency travelers—as often as once a week.
Travel Days/Times:	Most commonly Monday–Thursday; early morning/late afternoon.
Travel Seasons:	No travel over holidays; light travel in late summer; otherwise, no high/low seasons.
Special Services:	Specialized accounting and purchase/booking reports, special discounts, commission sharing, on-site reservations equipment or personnel, ticket delivery, travel policy monitoring, toll-free numbers, twenty-four-hour emergency assistance, flight insurance, and so forth.
Company Concerns:	Price and cost control: travel policy monitoring, expense account reconciliation, negotiated rates with vendors, frequency/necessity of trips, and so on.
Traveler Concerns:	▪ Efficient booking process, accuracy, on-time delivery, no delays, and personalized service from the travel agency.
	▪ On-time performance, comfort, frequent flyer programs, seat assignments/location and good service from the airlines.
	▪ Ease in check-in/check-out, room service, airport shuttle service, and frequent guest programs from hotels.
	▪ Ease in pick-up/drop-off, express check-in/check-out, and equipment dependability from car rental firms.

Explorations

The hotel you work for needs to increase its "corporate" business and you, as a sales assistant, have been asked to look at new markets. You have just read about the growing numbers of women traveling alone on business.

1. What do you think a single woman's major concerns are when traveling?
2. What special needs might a businesswoman have?
3. How would you advertise to this market?

Enrichments

1. Take another look at the list of travelers on page 3. Are there others you would add?
2. Read a travel article on a specific destination or examine a travel vendor's brochure. To which of the traveler types do you think this destination or travel product will appeal?

International Travelers and Things They Need To Know

Don't forget to declare your genius! When asked by U.S. customs officials in New York if he had anything to declare, the great poet Oscar Wilde quipped, "I have nothing to declare but my genius." Wilde got away with it; you probably won't!

International travel is truly fascinating! It involves the manipulations of governments at the highest level and results in the free flow of passengers among countries that once vowed mutual destruction. International air travel has literally caused the entire planet to shrink! However, easy though international travel may be, there are preparations travelers should make and requirements they must meet or run the risk of encountering difficulties, discomfort, and delays.

Whenever travelers leave the United States, enter foreign countries, and return to the U.S. they will probably need to obtain permission from at least one government. This permission may be in the form of a passport or other proof of citizenship, it may require a visa or tourist card, or it may be accompanied by a health certificate or other official

International   Between countries.

Documents *(1) All the confirmations, tickets, itineraries, and so on, a passenger receives for a fully prepaid trip. (2) The forms/papers required by a foreign government to enter its country: passport, visa, tourist card, and others.*

documents certifying that the traveler has met the requirements for entry into the country.

The airlines are particularly keen on the subject of documents since they are held responsible if they bring a passenger into a country with improper documentation. The carrier is subject to a fine and must provide return transportation for the rejected traveler. Airlines are not eager to be put in this position and protect themselves by refusing to allow passengers to board international flights unless their "papers" are in order. This makes the international carriers a generally reliable source of information concerning documentation required by the countries to which they fly.

Passeport . . . Passa Porto . . . Passe: Don't Leave Home Without It!

A *passport* is a document issued by a country for its own citizens. It establishes the travelers' identity and nationality, enables them to enter foreign countries and return to their own, and requests protection for them while on foreign soil. Most countries require passports for visitors from other lands, but some do not. This depends upon the good relations the countries enjoy, and like goodwill in any aspect of human endeavor, it could turn to ill will at a moment's notice.

U.S. passports are issued for each individual in the family and they cost from $40 to $65 each, plus the cost of two photos. These photos also must be of a special size and format—not just any old snapshot will do. Adults must renew their passports every ten years; children every five. Applications for U.S. passports are available from most post offices and state and federal court buildings. Well-supplied travel agencies keep copies of both the initial applications and the forms for renewal by mail and may also offer passport photo services.

The traveler-to-be must submit the completed form, photos, fee, and proof of citizenship to any passport office, federal or state court clerk's office, or designated post office. The processing time varies, so travelers should allow two to four weeks minimum. In an emergency, a traveler can appear in person at one of the many passport offices and try to "walk it through." Sometimes your local congressman or senator will expedite the issuance of a passport, especially if the applicant made a substantial contribution to his or her political campaign.

A passport may be renewed by mail if it was issued within the past twelve years. A lost passport may be reissued by a U.S. *embassy* (the official residence of the ambassador to the country) or *consulate* (the office of the consul, an official appointed to represent the commercial and private interests of U.S. citizens abroad). There is a U.S. embassy in most of the world's major capitals and there are consulates located in major cities other than capitals.

If the United States does not have diplomatic relations with the country, it does not maintain an embassy or consulate; but, since most U.S. citizens aren't likely to visit those countries, they probably won't be losing passports there! There is a brisk trade in stolen passports worldwide so travelers should keep passports in a safe place at all times! Travelers should *never* pack a passport in a suitcase. They must be presented to the authorities before luggage is collected.

You won't be surprised to learn that Washington, D.C., is home to the embassies of most foreign countries, and there are plenty of consulates located in our other major cities.

Proof of Citizenship and Proof of Identity

Countries that do not require passports from U.S. citizens, such as Mexico, Canada, and many of the island nations in the Caribbean, will generally settle for proof of citizenship. This can be a certified copy of a birth certificate (with a raised seal to distinguish it from a photocopy) or a voter's registration card.

Some of our neighboring countries may require only proof of identity. Proof of identity may be a driver's license or other document that has been issued by an official source and that bears a picture of the owner. *Please note:* It is a common misconception that a U.S. social security card or a military registration card is proof of citizenship. They are not.

Given the fundamental instability of foreign relations, it is a good idea to take a valid passport when leaving the continental U.S. It is the one document that provides indisputable proof that you are who you say you are.

Be Advised

Countries that do not have diplomatic relations do not honor each other's passports. The U.S. State Department issues *travel advisories* whenever conditions occur that make travel difficult or unsafe. These advisories might include information about natural disasters such as earthquakes or hurricanes or manmade ones such as strikes, riots, war, terrorism, disease, or even a shortage of hotels rooms. The State Department may, in some dire cases, ban travel to a particular place altogether. That doesn't mean you can't go—this is, after all a free country—but, if you do, you go at your own risk and without the nation's official participation in your adventure.

Visas Aren't Credit Cards!

The government issues your passport, but another country's government issues you a **visa** for travel in that country. Sometimes it is a separate document, but most often it is a stamp placed in your passport indicating how long you may stay. In certain circumstances a *transit visa* will suffice, allowing you to pass through the country to get to another one.

Visa An endorsement in a passport by a foreign government official that indicates the passport has been examined and the holder may travel to that country. Not all countries require visas. Since the officials in the country in question have the final say, on rare occasions a visitor may be denied entry even though he or she has a valid visa.

Most visitors qualify for regular tourist visas, but students who wish to study abroad for a full year will probably require a special student visa and businesspeople who are actively engaged in commerce (really buying and selling or manufacturing—not just attending meetings or looking around) may need a special business visa.

It is not a good idea to wait until you are met at the border by an armed guard with an oversized dog to get your visa, though it can sometimes be done. Since you will probably have to send your passport to an embassy or consulate, you won't want to wait to get started. If you need visas for several countries and wait until a week before departure, even a visa service charging top dollar may not be able to bail you out. Express mail services may be fast and reliable, but they can't work miracles. Also, foreign citizens living in the United States may have to produce special documentation to *leave* this country.

A *visa does not assure a traveler of entry into a country.* The government of that country always has the last word, and just because one of their bureaucrats in Washington slipped up and issued a visa doesn't mean the guard at the border with the big, mean dog won't turn a hapless traveler away at gunpoint. But, be of good cheer, this seldom happens: most countries admit most of the travelers to whom they grant visas. It never hurts, however, to be on your best behavior when traveling in someone else's country—just in case. . . .

Customs: Getting In, Getting Out, and Getting Back

Customs A government agency charged with collecting taxes on imported items and preventing the entry of prohibited items. International travelers may not enter a country until they have been "cleared" by a customs agent.

Duty The import tax charged on certain goods brought into a country.

One of the reasons U.S. citizens are welcome in so many countries the world over is our willingness to go into hock buying everything that isn't red hot or nailed down. To this nation of shoppers, the world often appears to be a giant mall. International travelers need to be well advised about foreign currencies (affectionately known as "play money") and about **customs** (and we don't mean eating with the left hand or standing up every time the jukebox plays "God Save the Queen").

Virtually every country in the world places restrictions upon the value and kinds of items that travelers can bring in. They do not want international visitors corrupting their youth by bringing in subversive literature (communist countries have frequently designated Bibles as such) or tight blue jeans (except for your own use, of course); and they may suspect a traveler of competing with local merchants if he or she declares 15 wristwatches or 27 cameras or 100 cartons of cigarettes.

At best, a **duty** (tax) will be charged on these items; in the worst case, the goods will be confiscated. But unless you are a known smuggler, you will probably follow the line marked "nothing to declare" and breeze right through. Coming home to the United States with all your loot may not be so easy.

All travelers arriving in the U.S. (foreigners and returning U.S. citizens) must go through customs and immigration. This is always done at the first city of arrival into the United States. These cities are known as *international gateway* cities.

Save the Whales—But Don't Bring Them Back in Your Luggage

Those valiant public servants who guard our nation's coffers never sleep. They are particularly eager to see that travelers do not sneak back home with a suitcase full of great bargains upon which they have absolutely no intention of paying U.S. tax. U.S. citizens do have the right to bring in $400 worth of items purchased abroad duty-free ($600 from the Caribbean). The ante is upped to $1,200 if the goodies were bought in The U.S. Virgin Islands, American Samoa, or Guam.

This does not include (great bargains though they are in some countries) such items as narcotics, guns, switchblades, endangered species, or any plants or animals likely to bring U.S. agribusiness to its knees. Confine your toxic substances to the specified quantities of alcohol, cigarettes, and cigars allowed and you should clear customs without a hitch.

You cannot take the local merchant's word that the items he or she is selling you are OK to take home. A more reliable source of information is the U.S. Customs Service pamphlet, *Know Before You Go*. It is available free of charge from the USCS, Publications Reproduction Branch, 6 World Trade Center, New York, NY 10048.

If a customs agent is the suspicious type, he or she might question travelers about their own possessions. International travelers should carry only the amount of prescription drugs they will need for the trip, and these should be clearly labeled and, if possible, accompanied by a prescription form or a doctor's statement of their necessity.

Maybe you really do need 1,000 ten-milligram tablets of Valium to get you around the Pacific Rim, but if a customs agent finds them in an unmarked bottle in one of your socks, the best thing that can happen is that he will question you at some length, then invite two or three of his colleagues to ask you the same questions over again a few more times just to make absolutely sure that they didn't miss a key part of your explanation.

Other items that may slow you down are cameras, furs, and jewelry for which you carry no proof that you bought them in Peoria rather than Hong Kong (from which you have just returned and where they are dirt cheap). Proof of purchase could be the receipt for the item, but the best way to protect yourself is to register personal items that may be in question prior to your trip. Any U.S. customs officer should be able to answer your questions or send you to the official who can.

And, don't think you can slip your items in by mailing them back! All packages mailed to the United States must carry customs declarations and are inspected on arrival. You are allowed to mail a certain amount of gifts home duty-free, but, regardless of whether it's your birthday, anniversary or graduation, the gifts can't be for you without counting in your total allowance!

Whose Picture Is on a 500,000 Lire Bill?— Understanding Foreign Currency

One of the items most likely to be regulated by a government is currency. Some governments want one country's currency but not another's; some will let you bring yours in but not take theirs out, while others will let you take theirs out by the wheelbarrow load as long as you leave yours behind. Still other countries won't even let you have their money—they insist you spend your own currency in designated tourist shops, restaurants, hotels, and so on.

Using foreign currency can be rather confusing, especially since the money of many countries is so colorful. The U.S. dollar is among the most boring looking in the world. The thing to know about money is that our form is not accepted by every shopkeeper, hotelier, and restauranteur on the planet: most of them prefer their own; after all, it bears the image of their favorite queens, poets, or dictators and is printed in their favorite ink, and, furthermore, it costs them money to have our currency converted to theirs.

Travelers will need to have enough foreign currency to get them through the first day or so. They can probably get it at the airport bank upon arrival, assuming they arrive during business hours, but they will probably be too tired or excited to give the transaction the attention it deserves. Getting some travelers checks (only suicidal fools or people who can afford bodyguards carry large sums of cash these days) before leaving home is a wise idea, and a small packet of foreign bills and coins for transfers, tips, and a meal or two can make arrival in a foreign country a little less stressful.

The main thing to remember about changing, or "exchanging," money is that you lose and the bank usually gains every time. You are buying the money, and the bank is not in the business of coming out on the short end. During the trip, as you pass from country to country, you should not exchange any more money than needed for a few days. It will not be a wonderful homecoming to find that you lost money yet again by having the odds and ends of foreign bills (banks won't even bother with small change) converted back into U.S. dollars and cents. Travelers will probably get a better rate of exchange from banks and American Express offices than they will in most hotels and shops.

Travelers can also expect that, in many of the world's most popular spots, they can use credit cards and go deeply into debt just like they can back home. The big difference is that their purchases will be in marks, francs, yen, yuan, and so forth, and that the price they pay the credit card company is based on the rate of exchange at the time the charge is posted. This could be quite different from the rate in effect on the day the purchase was made. Widely accepted though plastic money may be, you can't use credit cards to bargain with street vendors and the average Third World taxi driver probably doesn't keep a validator in his glove box.

Leaping Over the Language Barrier

Even though one may *know* that the "French speak French," it is, nonetheless, impossible to imagine the real effects of not being able to communicate with others. It can make people who are normally quite self-sufficient feel helpless, afraid, and angry. Phrase books can be helpful, but most travelers quickly realize that if you ask a question in a foreign language, you will be answered in that language!

Most people are not going to learn a language simply because they want to vacation in a foreign country. And, not knowing a language should not prevent people from traveling to distant lands. It is important to realize, however, that many travelers have misgivings about language barriers and need to be reassured and advised on how to deal with this very real problem.

To ease the language barrier, travelers should:

- Consider making their first destination one where English is the official or second language.
- Take a hosted or escorted tour where they will have the security of having someone to turn to if communication becomes too stressful or difficult for them.

- Stay in hotels (usually the larger or chain properties) where English is spoken.

Electrical Shock

Electricity in many foreign countries is different from our own. Electrical current in the U.S. is 110 volts. In other countries, such as those of Europe, the current is 220 volts. What this means is that travelers *cannot* use their hair dryers or other small appliances without a voltage converter unless the appliance is specifically designed to run on either current. To attempt to use a U.S. appliance in a 220 outlet would destroy the appliance and risk serious electrical shock.

To further complicate matters, the current is not the only difference. The outlets themselves are also different. Sometimes there are several different designs in one country alone! (Britain is notorious for this!) The prongs may be round, flat, odd sizes, or positioned differently. It is terribly confusing and, in some countries, no one can predict just what type of outlet a given hotel room will have. In some cases, there won't even be an obvious or available outlet. Electricity in most countries is *extremely* expensive and since hoteliers do not want to encourage its use, outlets may be hidden or inaccessible.

Take Two Ginseng Tablets and Call Me in the Morning

Travelers have many fears and one of the most common has to do with being sick or injured while abroad. The world is a much healthier place than it once was thanks to medical science, and you can now travel to many places without fear of contracting the diseases that used to decimate entire populations. Smallpox, for example, has been virtually eradicated and vaccination for it is no longer required. Other diseases such as cholera and yellow fever are present in a few locales, but vaccination is not required unless you are coming from an infected area. Malaria still exists and cannot be prevented by vaccination, but travelers can take preventive drugs in pill form.

The Centers for Disease Control publishes a bulletin entitled, *Biweekly Summary of Health Information for International Travel*. A company can get on the mailing list by getting in touch with the Quarantine Division, Centers for Disease Control, Atlanta, GA 30333. But, remember! No matter how many of these bulletins you've read, unless you are licensed to practice medicine, you should always advise others who seek your advice to consult a physician before journeying anywhere in the world where serious communicable diseases are still endemic in the population.

Don't Drink the Water—Drink the Beer!

A change of food and water always seems to have some effect upon travelers, but to keep adverse effects to a minimum, it's a good idea to practice caution. Water treated with chlorine, as it is in most major cities in the developed countries, is generally safe to drink. In less developed countries, you are taking a chance unless you drink bottled or boiled water. Don't make the mistake of pouring your Perrier over locally produced ice cubes, however. The bacteria that are killed by boiling aren't necessarily killed in the deep freeze.

If you are seriously worried about the water, then you should be worried about glasses and utensils washed in water that may have been tepid and soapless. It may well be safer to drink from a bottle or can (wiped clean) than a recently washed glass. When traveling in Third World countries, some travelers take their own cups and utensils, and Western-style hotels often provide carafes of boiled water in the room for brushing teeth, taking medicine, and so on. There are also tablets you can get to treat water, or you can take along a pot or heating element and boil your own (but don't forget about electrical current differences).

If you wouldn't drink it, don't swim in it either! The last word on water and disease is available from the Centers for Disease Control in Atlanta. If the country's hygiene and sanitation are poor, you don't want to drink their milk or eat their milk products unless you are sure these have been pasteurized. Raw fruits and vegetables, unless peeled, can also be risky.

Explorations

You are going to India, and there's lots of work to do!

1. Obtain a passport application and complete it. (For the purposes of this exercise, you are NOT required to actually go through the expense. Whether you get a passport or not is up to you, but going through the application process will help you better understand documentation requirements. Remember! Having a passport is indisputable proof of your identity and nationality—not a bad thing to have on hand in any case!)

2. Contact an embassy, consulate, visa service, or airline to determine what type of documents (visa, tourist card, etc.) are required for U.S. citizens to travel to India.

3. Call your public health department to see what shots are recommended or required for travel to India.

Enrichments

Check to see how your bank handles foreign currency information and exchanges:

1. Can it give you current exchange rates?
2. Does it exchange money?
3. Does it sell travelers checks in foreign currency?
4. If it cannot help you with these transactions, who in your area does the bank recommend?

The Industry Triangle

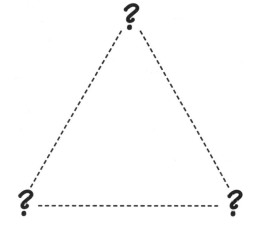

Where Are We Going?

When you have completed this section, you will:

1. Understand the supplier/agent relationship.
2. Understand the agent/client relationship.
3. Know how a travel agency makes its money.
4. Be able to describe the travel agencies of today.
5. Understand the many aspects of a travel agent's job.
6. Be familiar with the basics of owning your own travel agency.

Industry Terms and Jargon

Airlines Reporting Corporation (ARC)	Commission	Override
	Distribution	Preferred Supplier
Base Fare	Net Rate	Profile

Who Connects the Points?

This industry is so complex, it is often difficult to see how it all fits together. Although there are many parts and ways these parts relate to one another, the travel agent stands out as the one central, independent means of "bringing it all together." You will learn much about the travel industry as you look through the eyes of the travel agent. Suppliers and clients both rely on the travel agent for help in the complicated world of travel!

To distribute their products economically and efficiently, industry suppliers turn to independent companies to sell on their behalf. In most industries, these independents are known as agents, distributors, or independent sales representatives ("reps"). In the travel industry, the travel agency fills this role. Although many industry suppliers have their own reservations and sales facilities, it would be impossible for them to have offices everywhere. The cost would be prohibitive and suppliers simply could not afford such an arrangement.

Airlines Reporting Corporation (ARC) *Corporation jointly owned by most of the major U.S. airlines. It collects payments for tickets sold by travel agents, distributes the monies to the airlines, and supervises the appointment of travel agencies to sell airline tickets.*

Travel suppliers authorize or appoint travel agencies to sell their products. These appointments may be very formal such as the ones through the **Airlines Reporting Corporation (ARC)** and the International Air Transport Association (IATA/IATAN). Others are quite informal—perhaps just an oral agreement. To sell airline tickets, an agency must be "ARC Approved." The approval process is detailed and a prospective agency must show proof of financial backing and stability. It would be very risky for the airlines to appoint "just anyone" to have blank airline tickets to issue and sell to travelers. A validated airline ticket is as good as cash and, if the agency doesn't pay, the airline is out a lot of money!

Suppliers need agencies to sell their products, and reputable travel suppliers want to deal only with reputable travel agencies. However, some suppliers, such as cruise lines, do not need to be as careful and may not have such stringent requirements as the airlines. Since cruise companies issue their own tickets, they can better control the payment process; that is, they can and do demand deposits and payments up front. If the agent doesn't pay, the client doesn't cruise.

Hotels may also work with independent reps or salespeople who are not ARC approved. Since virtually all guests pay by credit card on checkout or with cash or check prepayment, hotels do not need to be as concerned with the financial stability of the person booking the reservations. If the guests cannot offer proof that they can pay for the room when they check in, the hotel can simply refuse to accommodate them.

Supplier/Agent Relationship

Suppliers and agents depend on each other and, for the most part, have professionally friendly and cooperative relationships. Many suppliers have special sales or agency relations employees who work solely with travel agencies. Airlines have sales representatives, special numbers, and "help" desks just for travel agents. Cruise lines also have special reservation numbers, sales representatives, and sales managers devoted solely to travel agents. However, despite everyone's best intentions, it is

See How They Sell

Supplier	Sells Through

Airlines	Travel agencies
	Direct: Reservation centers (800 numbers)
	        City ticket offices, airline counters
	        Reservation equipment on customer's
	          locations, including personal
	          computer shopping
	        Cruise lines
	        Tour operators

Cruise Lines	Travel agencies Cruise-only agencies Tour operators *Direct:* Reservation centers (800 numbers); some reservation offices
Car Rentals	Travel agencies *Direct:* Reservation centers (800 numbers) Offices at airports, hotels, and so on Package tour arrangers

Trains	Travel agencies
	Direct: Reservation centers (800 numbers)
	        Local (city) offices
	        Train stations
	Tour operators, packagers

Hotels	Travel agencies *Direct:* Reservation centers (800 numbers) Direct to hotel Airline reservation centers Hotel representatives Tour operators and packagers
Tour Operators	Travel agencies *Direct:* Reservation centers, offices (very few) Airlines

not always easy for an airline employee or a hotel manager to see the business world from an agent's point of view. And, of course, it is also not always possible for an agent to see things from "the other side."

Supplier/agency relations are improved through industry associations where suppliers and agents meet and also through visits to the "front line." Hyatt Hotels began a program in the early 1990s to familiarize agents not only with the hotel, but with its operations as well. Agents were treated to a view behind the scenes—from reservations to housekeeping to food services—to see how things really work. About the same time Hyatt introduced its program, United Airlines sent 500 of its employees out to spend a day in a travel agency. United employees from accounting, sales, customer service, and even the executive levels set out to learn what agents do and what they want from their suppliers. Programs such as these clearly enhance understanding and cooperation in the business world—something that ultimately benefits both the travel professional and the traveler!

As you can see from the chart, travel agencies are a primary source of distribution. Travel agencies are virtually everywhere: in small and large cities, airports, shopping centers, malls, and corporate office parks. They provide travel suppliers with a direct link to markets and consumers. It would be an enormous task for a supplier to maintain offices in every major city—not to mention the smaller ones!

Agency distribution makes sense because it is the most economical way for a supplier to get information about its products into the hands of potential travelers. If paying commission was not the best and least costly method of distribution, suppliers would not support agencies. It is a financial, not a friendship, arrangement.

Commission The percentage paid to a travel agency by suppliers for selling travel arrangements.

To compensate agencies for the sales their agents make, suppliers pay them a portion of their selling price, known as **commission.** The price to clients is the same whether they buy from an agency or direct from the supplier. Some suppliers sell primarily through agencies; others sell both ways. For example, many tour operators sell only through agencies, while airlines sell both through agencies and direct to the traveler.

Net Rate (1) The airfare, tour price, hotel rate, or cruise price less commission. (2) A price quoted to a sales agent without standard commission built in. Group hotel rates, chartered aircraft rates, chartered motorcoach rates, and group tour rates are often quoted net, noncommissionable by a supplier. The agency handling the trip must then add on its charges to cover handling and profit.

How much is an agency paid? Surprisingly little! A 10 percent commission is the rule of thumb, although, in a few cases, it is actually less, and in other cases, it is more. There are also times when an agency receives no commission or is quoted a "net" rate. It is then up to the agency to add service fees or profit margins. **Net rates** are commonly quoted by hotels for group bookings and may actually be lower than the full rate, less commission.

It is important to know not just what the commission rate may be, but also how it is calculated. On airline tickets, the commission is paid on the **base fare**—that is, the fare *before* any taxes are added. The sale of a ticket that has a total fare (base and tax) of $544.00 does not put $54.00 commission in the agency's bank account.

Base Fare The air fare set and charged by the airline before taxes are added. The tax is federal tax on transportation.

Commission for a hotel stay is paid on the room rate only. If an agent thought he or she would be paid commission on the entire bill, he or she would be counting chickens that did not even exist! Exceptions to this would be hotels and resorts that may offer a "package" that

See How They Pay

Supplier	Standard	Exceptions
Airlines	10%—Domestic 8%+—International	**Overrides** based on volume Additional commission on designated flights, special promotions, groups
Cruise Lines	10%	Overrides on **preferred supplier** programs Additional commissions offered on special sailings, promotions, groups
Car Rentals	10%	Some preferred supplier overrides Additional payments sometimes offered on special packages, programs Lower commissions (5%+) paid on corporate, special discount rates
Trains		Basic 10%
Hotels	10%—US 8%—International	Additional commissions on promotions packages Some preferred supplier programs Groups commonly quoted net rates
Tour Operators	10%	**Preferred supplier** overrides Group overrides

Override Additional commission paid to agents by a supplier as a bonus for overall volume, increased sales, or as an incentive to book particular arrangements.

Preferred Supplier The suppliers an agency chooses to sell over others. The choice of preferred supplier is usually made based on commission rate paid, service, and quality. Some agencies have "preferred supplier lists" and sell those suppliers exclusively.

includes the room and other features. In most cases, the full "package price" is commissionable.

Ticket Breakdown: Base Fare * Tax * Agency Commission

Greensboro/Atlanta
Full Coach Fare: $544.00

Airline Base Fare = $494.55

U.S. Tax
$49.45

Agency
$49.45

Commission for cruises and tours is paid on the full rate for the cabin or tour package. If air fare is included, commission is also paid on that amount. As with air tickets and hotel room rates, commission is not paid on any included taxes or service charges.

These People Need Professional Help!

Since many suppliers are very large and have their own reservation agents who are easily reached by phone, why does a traveler use an agent, a "middle man"? The choices a traveler faces today are mind-boggling. Airlines are constantly changing their fares, hundreds of hotels and resorts compete fiercely for travelers' attentions, the number of cruise ships sailing the world's waters has multiplied dramatically in the last ten years, and car rental companies offer hundreds of options and incentives to drive their cars! Increasingly, the confused traveler turns

The World Is Out There Waiting

to the professional who can translate the jargon, figure the fares, check the regulations, issue the tickets, describe the options, make informed recommendations, and deliver it all in a cohesive, understandable form.

Travel, especially to faraway places, is very expensive. It is unlikely that a consumer who is about to commit large sums of money and time to a purchase would make a decision without investigating the choices and comparing prices. Since agencies represent the vast majority of travel suppliers, the traveler can call on an agent for all his or her travel needs: air tickets, car rental, hotel reservations, tour packages, cruises, passport pictures, and even traveler's checks! Calling each supplier, checking out competing companies, and then putting together an itinerary would take the individual traveler lots of time. By calling an agent, the traveler reduces his or her work to one call and, at the same time, reduces the chances of making the wrong choices. A bad travel experience cannot be fixed or replaced with a better one!

Furthermore, travel agents not only sell to the client, but they inform and serve them as well. This "extra" help usually does not cost the traveler any more than making the reservations direct with the supplier. In fact, it often costs the traveler less because the agent is knowledgeable about and free to recommend the products and services of numerous, competing suppliers.

Suppliers would find it difficult to spend the amount of time travel agents spend with their clients. Over 85 percent of all discretionary travelers who use a travel agency not only ask for assistance in making reservations, but also for guidance and recommendations in choosing where to go! Suppliers want to hear from the agent when the client is ready to buy. Suppliers are in business to sell seats on a plane or rooms in a hotel, and they are happy to leave the time-consuming task of counseling to the agent!

Why then is an agent willing to invest so much time in helping a traveler when a particular trip won't earn that much in commission income? Because, to the agent, the traveler represents more than one sale. This year the client may book a two-hour flight to visit her sister; next year, she may take a European tour. Also, satisfied clients will tell others about the good service they received. "Word of mouth" is powerful advertising!

Who is the professional both suppliers and travelers need? The professional is the travel agent!

Traveler? Client? Who's Who?

All of an agency's clients are travelers, but not all travelers are an agency's clients.

The airplane scene in Section 2 gives a brief profile of some specific travelers and illustrates the point that travelers are different. We can identify their needs and see their reasons for being on the plane. To flight attendants, the travelers are passengers whom they will assist for approximately an hour and a half and then will probably never see again. They are important to the flight attendant, but he or she does not know them or have the time to get to know them.

Traveler Data Sheet

Completing the following information will save you time in booking reservations and help us address your travel needs. Traveler data is automatically transferred onto each reservation. All traveler data is kept confidential. After completing an original sheet, you need only advise us of changes.

Name:_____ Title:_____

Company:_____ Charge Code:_____

Mailing Address:_____ Department:_____

_____ Delivery Address:_____

Home Address: _____ _____

_____ Business Phone:_____

FAX #:_____ Home Phone: _____

If your secretary/assistant makes travel arrangements for you, please provide:

Name:_____ Extension #:_____

How should your <u>business</u> travel be charged?   ( ) Invoice   ( ) Credit Card

    Type of Card:_____ Card Number: _____
    Name of Card:_____ Expiration Date:_____

How should your <u>personal</u> travel be charged?   ( ) Invoice   (Credit Card)

    Type of Card:_____ Card Number: _____
    Name of Card:_____ Expiration Date:_____

If you use more than one credit card for business or personal travel, please attach a list, as outlined above, indicating business or personal use.

I hereby authorize Travel Solutions upon my approval to use the listed credit cards as payment and/or guarantee for travel arrangements. This authorization remains in effect until cancelled in writing.

_____   _____
       Date   Signature

Airline Information:

Seat Preference: ( ) Non-Smoking   ( ) Smoking   ( ) Aisle   ( ) Window
                    ( ) Special Instructions:_____

Frequent Flyer Information:

Airline	Member #	Name (exactly as appears on membership)
( ) American	#_____	_____
( ) Continental	#_____	_____
( ) Delta	#_____	_____
( ) United	#_____	_____
( ) US Air	#_____	_____
( ) Other	#_____	_____

If your spouse or children have frequent flyer or guest numbers, please attach a list of the airlines, member numbers and names.

Please add any additional information we need to expedite your travel arrangements; special meal requests, First Class only, handicapped requirements, senior citizen, preferred airline, military, etc. _____

_____

An agent knows his or her travelers. They are his or her clients. They have a business relationship.

The agent traveling to Chicago on that flight knew none of the passengers around her. If asked, she could not say why any of those people were on the plane. However, if one had been a client of hers, she would have known much more than what that brief scene revealed.

We guarantee hotel reservations for late arrival. A guarantee obligates you to pay for at least 1 night unless you cancel according to the hotel cancellation policy. For hotel reservation guarantees, please indicate:

( ) Guarantee to credit card listed on previous page.
( ) Guarantee to credit card # _____ Name _____ Exp. Date _____
( ) Never guarantee my hotel reservations.

International Travel

Passport # _____ Date Issued : _____ Expiration Date: _____

Place of Issue: _____ Birthplace: _____ Birthdate: _____

Name On Passport: _____ Citizenship: _____

Car Rental Information:

Preferred Car Company And Your Personal ID#:

Alamo - ID # _____
Avis - ID # _____
Budget - ID # _____
Dollar - ID # _____
Hertz - ID # _____
National - ID # _____

Preferred Car Size:

( ) Economy
( ) Compact
( ) Mid-size
( ) Full-size
( ) Luxury

Hotel Reservations:

Preferred Hotel Chain and Frequent Guest #:   ( ) Smoking   ( ) Non-Smoking

Courtyard # _____   Ramada # _____
Hilton # _____   Radisson # _____
Holiday Inn # _____   Sheraton # _____
Hyatt # _____   Stouffers # _____
Marriott # _____   Westin # _____
Omni/Dunfey # _____   Other # _____

Who, in your company, plans corporate meetings and seminars? _____

Do you belong to any associations, clubs, groups who plan travel? _____ If so, what is the organization name and who is the travel contact?

When people choose an agency and agent to work with, they will share information about themselves so there will be an understanding of their needs and expectations. Since the agent clearly wants to fulfill these needs and expectations, he or she will solicit information that will make this goal easier to achieve.

This information gathering could begin with polite questioning or by requesting that the client complete a "Traveler Data Sheet." From the information gathered, the agent creates a computer file—known as a **profile**—of the client that can be referred to, updated, and shared with others in the agency who may also have occasion to work with him or her.

As you can see from the Traveler Data Sheet, the agent knows a great deal about his or her clients. Some agencies go even further in their questionnaires to uncover not only the facts about how their clients travel but also what types of travel their clients like or hope to do in the future.

Profile   Detailed computer file that contains information on a traveler or company and contains such information as charge card numbers, frequent flyer numbers, addresses, phone numbers, travel preferences, and so on. Agencies use these profiles to insure speed and accuracy in making reservations for their regular clientele.

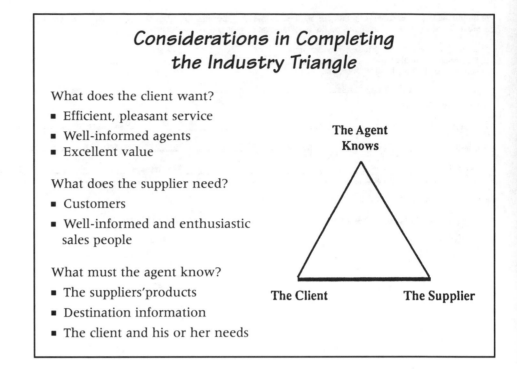

Considerations in Completing the Industry Triangle

What does the client want?
- Efficient, pleasant service
- Well-informed agents
- Excellent value

What does the supplier need?
- Customers
- Well-informed and enthusiastic sales people

What must the agent know?
- The suppliers' products
- Destination information
- The client and his or her needs

The Agent Knows

The Client   The Supplier

Travel Agencies— Yesterday

Thomas Cook is most often credited as being the father of travel planning as a business. Over 150 years ago, on July 5, 1841, he chartered a train to take 570 participants to a temperance convention. It was a day's excursion—twenty-two miles between Leicester and Loughborough, England.

Cook's first thoughts were directed to advocating temperance and exposing the evils of alcohol, and he was interested in involving more and more people in events such as the one in Loughborough. However, by 1845, he had changed from a volunteer travel planner to a travel entrepreneur by opening a commercial excursion agency. His first excursions were within England, but he quickly expanded to include tours to the Continent. He and his son (Thomas Cook & Son) dominated the early travel industry. In fact, "taking the Cook's Tour" became a common expression for tours of any type and is still heard today!

In the United States, the concept of travel for pleasure was slower to develop. Businessmen traveling by train and staying in big city hotels was pretty much all there was to the traveling public. Hotel porters would often be called upon to make train reservations for the businessmen staying in their hotels and can certainly be considered one of the early relatives of today's travel agents. The porter received a small commission from the railway for handling these arrangements and he would also add a charge for picking up and delivering the tickets.

Agents for shipping lines were also forerunners of today's travel agents. Steamship companies opened ticketing offices to arrange passage from Europe to the United States, and their representatives rode on horseback to outlying areas to collect money from those who wished to bring their families to America.

By the end of the nineteenth century, the idea of organized travel assistance, such as Thomas Cook & Son offered, had spread to the United States, and numerous agencies were in operation. At this time, agencies catered mostly to the wealthy, selling steamship tickets and making arrangements for grand tours of Europe.

After World War I, when commercial aviation was just beginning, the airlines realized that the railways were their biggest competitors. They turned to the hotel porters to help sell and deliver tickets. In those early days, suppliers considered the steamship agent and the hotel porter as distributors of tickets for business that already existed. Very little expertise was required; there weren't that many routes or fares, and competition was minimal.

Travel Agencies— Moving into the Modern World

After World War II, the developing interest in personal or leisure travel, the greater demand for international travel, and the increased public acceptance of air transportation propelled the entire travel industry into rapid growth. The flight of the first transatlantic passenger jet in 1958 introduced a whole new era of personal and business travel for millions of people. In only twenty years—1960 to 1980—the number of passengers on U.S. scheduled flights increased 378 percent to almost 300 million! The growth in air travel has been matched by growth in every other sector of the travel industry, including travel agencies. While there were only about 1,000 agencies in existence in the early 1940's, there are over 35,000 in business today, and the Bureau of Labor Statistics predicts a shortage of 150,000 trained travel agents by the turn of the century!

Before 1958, a travel agency was, in most cases, a part-time business, had a staff of only one or two agents, and was often located in the back office of the bus depot, in a local restaurant, or in a small office in a local hotel. There were no computerized reservation systems giving agents immediate access to worlds of information. Long distance and international calling was terribly expensive and often difficult, if not impossible, to complete. There were no fax machines to provide immediate written confirmations. Making arrangements for travel and accommodations in faraway places was done by letter and planning a tour could take months!

Agents wrote tickets by hand and either wrote or typed out travelers' itineraries. Each individual air carrier, tour operator, or steamship line approved them. To even be in the business of selling airline tickets, agencies had to have the sponsorship of one airline and the approval of two-thirds of the carriers whose tickets the agency would sell. Airlines could actually control whether or not an agency existed. If a person wished to open a ticketing office where the airline felt there was "no need" (that is, the carrier had or was planning to have its own ticket office), the agency could be denied sponsorship or approval by the two-thirds majority.

In 1959, the Civil Aeronautics Bureau, which governed just about everything to do with air travel, abolished the control an individual airline could exert, and opening an agency became a question of an individual meeting operating and financial qualifications rather than qualifying on competitive (or, more accurately, noncompetitive) grounds.

Travel Agencies Today

The travel agency today is vastly different from the early agency operating out of a bus station or café. Agencies offer many, many services that no one even dreamed of forty years ago! And, although the vast majority of agencies are still small businesses, small is just not what it used to be!

The small agency of today is computerized and has immediate access to worldwide travel information. It can issue a ticket and printed itinerary in less than ten seconds. It can fax a hotel on the other side of the world and have a confirmed reservation for a client in a matter of hours, if not minutes!

The early travel agency was primarily concerned with leisure travel. Today's agencies, both large and small, are primarily concerned with business travel. Automation has provided agencies with the means to handle the many changes a business traveler makes, not to mention the last-minute nature of his or her travel planning. When reservations were made by telephone or letter and when tickets and itineraries were written by hand, the business traveler was more trouble than he or she was worth! Today, that is no longer true, and agencies are constantly seeking new corporate travel business.

Defining Agencies Today

The early travel agencies were easy to define. They all did about the same thing and were all about the same size. Changes in travel—primarily its availability and affordability—have caused changes in agencies. Today, many types of agencies exist, literally side by side! Some industry experts prefer to define agencies by size (how much business they do) while others believe agencies are more accurately defined by concentration (the type of business they do). Let's take a look at both!

Bigger than a Bread Box? What is small, what is large, and who determines it? For years, the industry defined large and small by analyzing air ticket sales, or ARC revenue. Today, while air ticket sales are indeed important to an agency, other sales are becoming more and more important. In the 1980s, analysts estimated that anywhere from 65 to 85 percent of an agency's business was air travel. Today that figure has dropped to less than 60 percent. Agents are booking more hotels, car rentals, cruises, and tours than they were fifteen years ago, and those commissions really count!

In today's world, all the business an agency transacts counts in determining its size, and size is quoted in gross sales, not commission revenues:

Small $2 million or less
Midsized $3 million–$24 million
Large $25 million–$49 million
Very Large $50 million and over

"Very large" agencies that have offices in many cities, at airports, and perhaps even in foreign countries are more commonly known in the industry as *mega agencies*. The mega agencies, such as the American Automobile Association, American Express, The Carlson Group, Thomas Cook Travel USA, IVI Travel, and Rosenbluth Travel are most concerned with major corporate travel accounts such as those of IBM, DuPont Industries, General Electric, AT&T, Coca-Cola, and the like.

Because these mega agencies control such enormous amounts of travel purchasing, they have become like the giant discount houses of the retail trade. Through volume overrides and bulk purchasing, they can offer large corporations savings and even rebate a portion of the commissions they earn. They also offer many sophisticated services, such as expense account monitoring, account reconciliation, and management reports.

"Large agencies" and "very large agencies" that concentrate on developing business in a more restricted area, such as the West Coast or Southeast are most commonly referred to as *regionals*. Regional agencies command a smaller travel volume, but they are certainly large enough to be stiff competition for the "megas." Regional agencies often compete with the mega agencies by promoting the fact that they are locally owned and managed and offer more "personal" service.

Although the amount of business handled by mega agencies and regional agencies is staggering and represents the largest proportion of travel agency sales today, most agencies in existence are not megas or regionals. They have single offices, are privately owned, have three to six employees, and average under $3 million in sales per year. In fact, only 9 percent of the travel agencies in the United States handle $5 million+.*

What kind of bread box? As we have seen, travelers have many different needs and there are as many types of travelers as there are people in your hometown! Different types of agencies have emerged to

Source: Travel Weekly, August 13, 1992.

serve different markets. In this categorization, volume of business is not the distinguishing factor—market focus is.

Full-Service Agency. Most agencies fit into this category. They handle all types of travelers—corporate, leisure, group, and so on—and they also handle all types of reservations—air, car, hotel, cruise, tour, and so forth. An experienced full-service agent is comfortable in planning travel for school groups and executives, backpackers and jet setters, adventurists and cruisers. Larger full-service agencies usually departmentalize, and their individual agents may be more specialized in what they do, such as arranging travel only for corporate, leisure, group, international, or domestic travelers.

Commercial/Corporate Agency. These agencies specialize in business travel planning. Most truly corporate agencies are very large (regional or mega). Agents in these companies are primarily reservationists, highly skilled on the computer, and do very little travel counseling. Commercial agencies usually have locations that are removed from the general public and very often have special arrangements with their clients for handling their travel:

In-house/On-site: The agency has employees working at the client's location to make reservations, and issue and deliver tickets.

Satellite Printer: The agency has a ticket printer at the client's location for immediate delivery of tickets and itineraries.

CRS on Site: The agency arranges for the client to have computers at its location so that employees can access reservation information and send reservation requests via computer to the agency's local office.

Vacation/Leisure Agencies. This is pretty self-explanatory! These agencies promote their vacation-planning expertise and work with both groups and individuals. Predominantly vacation/leisure agencies tend, for the most part, to be smaller than full-service or commercial agencies. In larger metropolitan areas, some vacation/leisure agencies specialize in one type of travel (i.e., adventure travel, senior citizen, religious) or in a specific destination (i.e, the Orient, Europe, Hawaii).

Cruise Only. Cruises are relatively easy to sell, customer satisfaction is high, and compensation for the agent is good. A number of travel professsionals have decided that cruises represent greater business potential than any other travel product. These agents have decided to specialize in "cruise only" and have moved away from offering full service. In fact, many "cruise only" agents have even moved away from computer systems because they are not really critical to the sale. This type of leisure travel business has grown and, in 1985, formed its own trade association, the National Association of Cruise Only Agencies.

American Express Travel: A Mega Agency

Although its beginnings were not in travel planning for groups or individuals, American Express is most often credited with being the first travel company in the United States. American Express was founded in 1850 as a subsidiary of the Wells Fargo stage coach line to handle express cargo shipments of goods, valuable papers, and money. The travel division really began after James Fargo, the son of the original president, took over the company.

James Fargo ran American Express for thirty-three years. In 1882, he introduced the American Express money order, and, in 1891, he introduced the American Express Traveler's Cheque. In 1895, he opened the company's first European office in Paris. With offices in Europe, American Express became a focal point for travelers and, by 1912, the company was issuing rail and steamship tickets and was organizing and selling sightseeing tours.

Today, the American Express Company is well known in the fields of investments, banking, insurance, and travel-related services. Although American Express was not the first charge card company (Diner's Club was), it has certainly been the most recognized around the world. From the original "green card," American Express has expanded its individual card services to include the Gold Card and the Optima card and has added a "business card" system for companies to offer to their employees who travel.

American Express operates retail travel agency offices throughout the United States and around the world and is the largest travel agency in the United States. American Express also operates over 1,500 tours a year which are sold both in American Express travel offices and independent travel agencies. American Express Travel is both a competitor of and a supplier to travel agencies.

So, You Want to Be a Travel Agent!

Being a travel agent can be fun and rewarding, but it isn't easy! Most agencies today that are looking for entry-level employees first look at graduates of reputable travel schools. A few agencies will train "from the ground up," but most want you to have some exposure to the industry, a clear understanding of the work involved in being a travel agent, and, at the very least, basic training on one of the reservation systems.

Most agencies, both large and small, start an entry-level employee out answering the phones, putting tickets together, delivering tickets, and stamping and filing brochures. In smaller agencies, your progression to "agent" will, in most cases, be quicker, because a smaller agency

A Morning in the Life of a Travel Agent

(Hint: If you want to really know what is going on, look up all the boldface words and abbreviations in the glossary.)

8:15 A.M.   The work day begins by signing into my **CRT** and reading the daily briefing. There's a health warning for Peru and enhancements to international faring.

8:20 A.M.   I check my messages and **queues** for changes to any of my clients' **PNRs.** Looks like I've got several time changes, four seat assignments to make, a **WL** that has cleared and—OOPS!—a flight I thought was confirmed for Mr. Jones has come back as a **NO OP!** I also have seven **tix** to issue today! First things first—got to fix Mr. Jones' trip! I begin checking for him and, luckily, there is another flight leaving an **hr** later. I grab a seat for him and call his secretary to advise of the change.

8:30 A.M.   Phones are now officially on, and the clients waste no time getting to us! My first call is from Sue at Wallace Corp., who is the president's secretary. The **flts** I booked for her boss yesterday will have to be changed for a Wednesay departure, not Thursday, and she wants the tickets delivered this pm. While talking to Sue, Pat, my coworker, leaves me a message to call Mrs. Williams **ASAP.**

8:45 A.M.   Before I could get to Mrs. W., Mr. Tomms called to book himself to NYC next **wk.** He always knows exactly what he wants, so that didn't take too long!

9:00 A.M.   Quick run for coffee, then back to call Mrs. Williams. But, no! There's a client at my desk. She wants to pick up **tix** that Julie (another coworker who's on a fam to Hawaii) **bkd** for her. No problem! Julie issued them before she left, so all I have to do is get them from the **pup** box, go over the **itin** with her, take her **pmt** and write her a receipt.

9:10 A.M.   Now back to my desk to call Mrs. Williams, and there's another note for me from Dr. Burns who wants to know if his cruise tickets have arrived. I call Mrs. Williams first. She wants to talk about going to Paris. Her husband says they are going for their anniversary in two months. We discuss fares, where to stay, package deals, etc. She also wants to know about getting a passport. Her husband has one, but she doesn't. I tell her what to do, and she wants to come in this afternoon to talk more and get her passport photo done with us. (Hope I can remember how to operate that camera!)

9:30 A.M.   I call Dr. Burns. The cruise **documents** aren't here yet, but it is four **wks** before he leaves. I tell him not to expect anything until 2-3 **wks** prior. Of course, I told him

Continued

	that when he brought in his final **pmt,** but it seems like everyone gets anxious before a trip—even doctors!
9:40 A.M.	My coffee's cold. Back for more! Carol in processing stops me with a question about a tkt that should be delivered today. We get that fixed, and I'm back to my desk to find another msg!
9:50 A.M.	Another business client who needs to make reservations for later this wk. I call him back and get that taken care of—except for the **htl.** He wants me to find the one closest to his customer's place of business. I found two in the *Travel Planner,* but he couldn't decide which one he wanted. He said he'd call back later.
10:00 A.M.	A quiet moment! I issue two of the tix, make a couple of seat assignments, and call one of the clients who had a time chg. Nothing else new on my queues except for the tkt for Sue's boss. I issue that one right away since it must be delivered today. My phone's ringing again!
10:30 A.M.	That call was from Mrs. Blackmon who has decided to **xl** her trip to San Diego. She's decided it's too expensive plus she doesn't think her daughter really wants her to come out there to see her. She tells me all about their conversation last night—poor lady! It really didn't sound all that serious (probably just trip jitters for her too!), so I told her to wait a day or two because she won't get this good fare again if things work out for her to go after all.
11:00 A.M.	Well, that took some time! But then, Mrs. Blackmon usually does. At least she didn't decide to come in to tell me all about it! Now I have a couple more messages for call backs. I decide to take a few minutes to clear out the work on my queues before getting tied up in other phone conversations.
11:15 A.M.	Finished the queues. Pat asks me about hotels in Cancun since I was just there last month. I make some suggestions for her client and take just a couple more minutes to tell her a story about one of the people on that fam.
11:30 A.M.	I make my call backs. One xl and two more bookings. If we stay this busy for a while I'll probably make my bonus for this month! I get another call—this one from a new client who wants **info** on a Caribbean cruise.
12:00 P.M.	What a morning! Time for lunch—although I wonder if I should go. So much is happening here!

doesn't have the luxury of having a full-time receptionist. Everyone has to "do everything" and new agents must be productive right away.

Agents laugh about this, but it is true: an agency usually hires only when it is "desperate" for help and needed someone "yesterday." Also, agencies often hire one person when what they really need is one and a half to two more employees! Why such close planning? Employees are an agency's greatest expense, and wise managers and owners want to be absolutely sure the "busy-ness" they are experiencing isn't temporary. Also, it can take up to one year for an employee with no training to be a productive agent, so new people represent a major expense to the business. Luckily, good travel training programs in quality schools have proven that this "introductory" time can be dramatically reduced for the agency and new agent as well!

How productive must an employee be? A travel agency employee making $15,000 a year must handle at least $600,000 a year in travel sales to simply cover his or her existence in the office! If this person is "support" for trained agents, then the agency manager should be able to say that this support will enable the other agents to produce an additional $600,000. In other words, a new agent is a major cost to an agency until he or she can prove his or her worth in real dollars and cents!

The best employees in any service business are those who have high ability, great willingness to work, and who do best when left alone to do the job! Except for working in the largest corporate agencies where agents function more as reservationists, the travel agent has varied duties and multiple responsibilities. A travel professional wears many important hats:

- *Receptionist:* How an agent greets a client by phone or in person creates a lasting impression of both the agent and the agency. Except in very large agencies where calls may be routed either electronically or by a full-time operator, agents are expected to be responsive to all incoming calls. Over 90 percent of an agency's business is handled by phone! In most companies, all agents are "front office," which means they are immediately accessible to clients entering their doors. They must be attentive to receiving these guests and making them feel welcome.
- *Secretary:* Even in today's highly automated world, a great deal of clerical work goes along with being an agent. An agent must keep accurate records of activity on a client's trip, file, keep track

of payments, send out confirmations, send thank you notes and welcome home notes, and stamp, file, mail, and request new brochures, and so on.

- *Computer Operator:* This is an automated business! Your productivity, efficiency, and overall success in this job will depend to a great degree on how proficient you are in working on a computerized reservation system. Although this is a service and people business, technical proficiency is very important.

- *Service Rep:* An agent is the person who works with the client, provides the service, listens to the complaints, and solves the problems. Often, the only experience a client has with an agency is with the individual agent, and clients frequently expect that agent to single-handedly conquer the world of travel for them!

- *Counselor/Consultant:* The agent is the travel expert. Travelers look to agents for professional advice. However, unlike other counselors and consultants, agents do not get paid for the professional advice they give. They get paid for booking and selling trips.

- *Salesperson:* Last on our list, but by all means, most important! Excellence in all other aspects of the job will not make up for failure to make sales. After all, as we have pointed out, that's how the money comes into the agency and, of course, into the agent's pocket as well!

For those who are just starting out in the business, the most commonly voiced concern is, "How can I do it all?" It takes practice, experience, confidence, and skill. Some new agents are most concerned about the computer, others worry they will make mistakes, others fear the selling process. By far and large, however, the most common fear is "product knowledge," or, "How can I sell something I haven't done or seen?"

All good agents do. It is not possible to experience everything and see every place. In Section 1, we talked about staying current with newspapers, magazines, guidebooks, brochures, videos, travel programs, and personal travel. For the agent, there is also the support of coworkers who have been to places they have not or who have sold packages or trips they have not. There are also many texts and reference books for agents which address specific needs.

Industry Texts and References

One indispensable text for agents is the *ARC Industry Agents' Handbook,* published by the Airlines Reporting Corporation. For the highly automated business, ARC also offers a computer disk version of the handbook. This book (whether printed or on computer disk) contains explanations of many industry terms and practices and step-by-step instructions for:

- Issuing handwritten tickets
- Completing all ARC documents
- Completing the ARC sales report

- Calculating transportation taxes
- Applying for ARC approval

Neither the novice nor the experienced agent will remember every requirement for issuing tickets and other ARC documents. Today, most ticketing is automated, that is, generated by computer. The *ARC Industry Agents' Handbook* serves to refresh an agent's memory when handwritten tickets or other documents are required.

Other important industry references that you will find described in the glossary are:

- CLIA (Cruise Line International Association) Manual
- Cook's Timetable
- Hotel and Travel Index
- Official Airline Guide (OAG)
- Official Hotel Guide (OHG)
- STAR Service
- Travel Industry Personnel Directory
- Travel Planners: Business (North American), European, and Pacific Editions

There are also a multitude of destination reference materials available: promotional material from the destination visitor's board, geography books, and books written specifically for the travel agent on destination geography and selling "unknown" destinations.

Continuing Education

One of the great benefits of being in the travel business is that it is so much fun to continue to learn about the world! Industry associations, travel schools, and independent consultants offer many opportunities for continuing your professional development. Courses in sales, management, geography, international faring, marketing, group and meeting planning, and so on are readily available to the interested agent and are usually very inexpensive! Education for the travel agent is often combined with the opportunity to travel—which is, of course, one of the most thrilling and sought after experiences in the world!

Licensing of travel agents is often discussed, but very little has been done in that direction. The Institute for Certified Travel Agents (ICTA) in Wellesley, Massachusetts, works as a center for continuing education and professional development for travel agents. A number of agents in the United States have pursued the Certified Travel Counselor (CTC) designation offered by ICTA. This program of individual and group study is open to experienced agents only (generally five years) and is primarily geared to owners and managers. ICTA also offers the Destination Specialist (DS) designation for agents of all levels of experience. This is primarily a self-study program involving in-depth reading and practical exercises on specific destinations around the world.

Becoming a DS or a CTC takes time and commitment and is an important achievement for those who undertake the study programs. The

DS and CTC designations are not requirements in the profession and, while they are generally recognized in the travel industry, they are not designations that most clients understand or look for in choosing an agency or agent.

Being a Travel Agent: Pros and Cons

The Pluses

- Independent work
- Always learning about the world
- Opportunities for personal growth
- Entrepreneurial field
- Rarely ever boring
- Travel benefits

The Minuses

- Low entry-level pay
- Narrow profit margins
- Highly competitive
- Stressful
- Constant changes

Opening Your Own Agency

You've weighed the pluses and minuses and decided that travel agency life is for you. Many have gone before you and, even though they may have been tired and frustrated at times, most never regret the lifestyle they have chosen. In fact, nearly 80 percent of all agents polled in the 1990s expect to be in the agency business at the turn of the century.

Like many people in this business, you yearn to have your own agency! The initial investment is relatively low. There's no inventory to buy, heavy equipment to lease, or large blocks of real estate to rent. The major expense you will face is personnel, followed by rent, computers, and telephones. The process can be confusing to the inexperienced and there are some very definite qualifications you must meet!

Remember that many people want to own a business because they love the work they do. Being a good travel agent does not mean you will be a good businessperson. Once you undertake owning and managing your own agency, you are no longer primarily a travel counselor. You are now manager, owner, cash flow specialist, budgeting expert, advertising whiz, public relations specialist, negotiator, and, if you are like most small business owners, also a secretary, janitor, personal problems counselor, and the person everyone runs to when the printers need new ribbons!

There are a number of books and manuals about starting your own agency, and you may want to invest in one or two. However, the most important first steps are:

1. Talk with people who know the business. If other agents are unwilling to share information with you (remember, it is a competitive business!), call a travel school near you or the department of travel and tourism at your local community college, technical institute, or university. Often they can direct you to industry experts or, if they have the expertise, consult with you themselves.

2. Contact the Airlines Reporting Corporation (ARC) to begin the process of application. To obtain an ARC appointment, you will have to meet certain criteria:

   a. Proof of financial stability: Personal financial records and work histories of all key people will be required.

   b. Letter of credit or proof of security bond filed. This amount will be no less than $20,000.

   c. Experienced people on staff. Both management and ARC ticketing experience are required.

   d. Certain qualifications about location and physical facilities will also have to be met: Signage, office layout, security for ARC documents, and so on.

3. Contact ASTA for information about their services and assistance.

4. If there are local or regional travel associations in your area, contact them as well.

Once you get the basic information, your next steps SHOULD ALWAYS BE:

1. Take a close look at yourself:
   - How hard are you willing to work?
   - How much expertise do you really have?
   - How much expertise can you depend on from others?
   - What do you really know about this business?
   - What do you really know about running a business?

2. Take a look at your own finances and income needs:
   - How much money will this really take?
   - How much money must I make?
   - How much money am I willing to lose?
3. Take a look at the marketplace:
   - How will you fit in?
   - There are lots of travel agencies. . . . How will you be different?
   - Who is your competition?
4. Develop a business and marketing plan:
   - Where are you now?
   - Where do you need/want to be one year from now?
   - How will you get to where you need to be?

Just because you have no business ownership experience does not mean that you should not undertake this very big step. It is often the inexperienced who bring new ideas and innovations to an industry. But, inexperience should be balanced with knowledge. Don't waste time learning on your own what others can easily teach you. An investment in education, advice, and experienced help can save you precious time and money!

Options in Owning Your Business

Purchasing an Existing Business. Agencies, particularly smaller ones, are not all that expensive. Before staring an agency from the "ground up," you should check what may be available for purchase. Purchasing an existing agency may be more expensive (on paper) than starting your own, but don't forget you are buying an *existing* business. If you do your homework and know what you are buying, you should walk in the door with an established income flow!

Before purchasing any business, you should have already established a good working relationship with an accountant and a lawyer. However, remember that the travel business is "different." Many accountants and lawyers do not understand the nature of this agent-client-supplier-based business. Seek out the assistance of an experienced travel industry consultant—you won't regret it!

Purchasing an Interest in an Existing Business. Becoming a partner in an existing business can be less risky than starting your own business and less expensive than buying another business outright. Many of the issues of investing in an existing business are the same as purchasing an existing business. Other considerations in a partnership would be:

- Why is this business in need of an investor/partner?
- What is the personal chemistry between me and my partner(s)?
- What do I need from this relationship?

Joining a Franchise. A number of national franchises offer assistance in setting up agencies: office design, computer leases, ARC applications, advertising, and so on. Franchisors charge an up-front fee and an on-going fee or percentage of commissions. For the inexperienced, franchises may appear the best route to take. However, in most cases, it is not the best decision. Why?

1. Initial franchise fees are very high. In some cases, they are substantially higher than reasonable projected start-up costs.

2. On-going fees can be onerous. Once you have had the assistance to get on your feet, the real work is up to you. A national franchise does not know your marketplace or your competition. Many of the services they supply are "boilerplate" and very possibly not suited to the needs of your business and your clients.

3. Many of the services—computer leases, newsletters, negotiated rates, training programs, users' meetings, and so on—are readily available elsewhere and very possibly at lower costs!

Becoming an Independent Contractor. You may decide that investing in a start-up agency or purchasing an existing business is not for you. It is possible to work as a travel consultant from your own home or existing business without going through the expense of obtaining ARC and IATAN approvals. Some experienced agents establish working relationships with local agencies to handle their air ticketing while others align with national organizations that have been established to support and promote independent operators.

Working as an independent operator can be rewarding, but you must be careful to select an agency or operator that has an established procedure for working with independent contractors. If you are interested in becoming an independent contractor, you should do a thorough background check of the agency or organization with which you plan to work. Your travel school or a travel industry consultant may also be able to asssit you in establishing an independent contractor business.

Travel Agencies—Tomorrow

What does the future hold in store for today's agent, agency manager, and owner? Many predictions are made, and some will prove to be accurate, while others will miss the mark. The one thing everyone will agree on is that there will be continuing changes in this field.

For forty years—from the mid-1940s until 1984—travel agencies had the exclusive right to sell airline tickets. No other company, independent agent, or representative—other than the airlines themselves, of course—could sell and issue airline tickets. In 1984, the Civil Aeronautics Board (CAB) abolished agent exclusivity on the grounds that it was anticompetitive.

This ruling, known as the *competitive marketing decision*, allowed new channels of **distribution** for airline ticket sales. A number of companies and entrepreneurs have taken advantage of this ruling, and more are still to come! The full effects of this ruling on the travel industry are still not clear, but some changes that have already taken place are:

Distribution *The network of branches, subsidiaries, and independent agencies through which a travel supplier sells its products.*

- *Automated Ticket Machines (ATMs).* These ticketing machines (similar to automated banking machines, have been installed in airports. Future installations may be in supermarkets, hotels, and shopping centers.

- *Personal Computers (PCs).* Computer programs now exist for individuals to access airline schedule and fare information and to request tickets via home computer.

- *Home Television Shopping.* There are now home shopping programs that offer air tickets and other travel products.

- *Business Travel Departments.* Travel departments in large companies once had to have an affiliation with an approved agency or directly with an airline to have computer access to airline information and ticketing services. Today, business travel departments may be approved to issue and sell airline tickets—essentially operating their own "travel agencies."

There are some who see these new developments as a serious challenge and threat to travel agencies and the "old" distribution system. Others see them as interesting sidelines that will have little effect on the continuing need and demand for travel agency services. Travel pricing will continue to be complicated, choices will probably increase in number, and competition will continue to be fierce. Under these conditions, it is difficult to see how machines and television shopping could take the place of professional travel counseling.

For agents, many changes—mostly automated—are in the cards for the future:

- *Laser Imaging.* It may sound futuristic, but it's just around the corner! Agents will be able to access not only written, but visual, information right at their desks! Consider taking an electronic fam with on-screen pictures and descriptions of destinations and properties!

- *Automated Quality Control.* These programs already exist and are used by both large and medium-sized agencies. Future developments will make them more widely available to agencies of all sizes. These programs allow quality control agents to handle bigger workloads and help eliminate "human error."

- *Computerized Travel Data Bases.* Agents can now subscribe to data bases that offer a virtual library of travel information. Some have agreements with the airline/agency systems and can be accessed through the agency CRT for an additional monthly fee, or sometimes, they are free to subscribers. Others are programs that are purchased individually (third-party vendors) and installed on office PCs. These data bases are often more up to date than printed reference materials and can cut research time in half!

How will the agent's job be transformed in this age of automation enhancements? Agents will have to be more and more technically proficient. Although many of these advances may cut an agent's research and booking time, there is little danger that travel counselors will become extinct. Travel is about people going places and people meeting other people—a computer can only do so much!

Explorations

1. Develop questions to add to the Traveler Data Sheet that would give your agency information about what appeals to your clients in leisure travel.

2. If you have dealt with an agency, write a brief report of your experience:

   - What was your initial impression of the business?
   - What was good about the service?
   - What was bad about the service?
   - What would you do differently if you were an agent?

or

If you have never worked with an agency, describe what you would expect an agent to do for you in helping you to plan one of the following:

a. Your honeymoon

b. Your family vacation

c. Your trip with friends to a ski resort

Enrichments

Make a list of agencies in your area (maximum of five). Indicate what you think their size (small, medium, large, mega agency) and focus is. (Ways to determine: newspaper advertisements, Yellow Pages advertisements, visits/calls to agency, personal experience.)

Meet the Carriers

Where Are We Going?

After completing this section, you will:

1. Understand the importance and continuing effects of the 1978 Airline Deregulatory Act on U.S. airlines and consumers.
2. Know the major U.S. carriers.
3. Understand who governs and controls international air travel.
4. Know about airline, airport, and city codes.
5. Have a basic understanding of how air fares are set.

Industry Terms and Jargon

Airline Code

Airport Code

Charter

City Code

Commuter Carrier

Consolidator

Deregulation

Direct Flight

Domestic Travel

Hub and Spoke System

International Air Transport Association (IATA)

International Airlines Travel Agent Network (IATAN)

Promotional Fare

Those Magnificent Men and Their Amazing Flying Machines

The desire to fly is as old as humankind—actually *doing* it is something quite new! Although modern aviation really didn't begin to get off the ground until the end of the 1800s, there were some important landmarks that helped pave our way to the stars:

c. 215 B.C.	Archimedes discovered the Principle of Flotation which was used 2,000 years later in making balloons!
c. 100 B.C.	Hero discovered the Principle of Jet Propulsion which, 2,000 years later, was key in the development of jet aircraft.
1490	Leonardo Da Vinci made drawings of a parachute, helicopter, propeller, and a flying machine with wings.
1783	Francois Pilatre Rozier sailed 300 feet above Paris in a hot air balloon, only to be killed two years later in an explosion of a balloon filled with a combination of hydrogen and hot air.

Although it took the civilized world quite some time to take to the air in great numbers, once things got going, the development and spread of air travel has been—just like the machines themselves—amazing!

The growth of air travel has been the single most important factor in the growth of the travel industry. The airline business takes the central role in the travel industry. All the other component industries—hotels, car rental firms, tour operators, cruise lines, and travel agencies—depend on its success.

Oh, What a Lovely War!

A discussion of the development of commercial aviation would not be complete without a mention of what two world wars contributed. In the early 1900s, flying machines were for daredevils and, to some minds, the ungodly. Many believed that man was not meant to fly, and all this buzzing about in machines was a frivolous pastime, if not an affront to nature! The curious flocked to fairs to watch stuntmen fly their machines and sail above the ground in balloons, but very few onlookers took the idea of air transportation for themselves seriously—if they thought of it at all!

It took a war to educate the world about flying and what could be accomplished in the air. Unfortunately, one of the first things accomplished (other than prewar entertainment) was destruction. Between 1914, when World War I began, and June 28, 1919, when the Treaty of Versailles was signed, warring nations began manufacturing war planes with metal bodies (rather than wood) and developed more powerful engines to increase speed and flying distance.

Following the war, organized air service developed rapidly in Europe. By 1921, government subsidies for developing aircraft were in

Important Dates and Developments in Air Travel

1891   First successful manned glider flights by Otto Lilienthal in Germany. Gliders were the first "heavier-than-air" aircraft and the design model for the first "engine-powered" airplanes.

1903   Wilbur and Orville Wright man the first successful engine-powered, heavier-than-air, flight at Kitty Hawk, North Carolina. The flight lasted twelve seconds and covered a distance of only 120 feet.

1908   Louis Bleriot makes a daredevil flight across the English Channel from France to Great Britain.

1910   Count Ferdinand von Zeppelin established the first commercial "lighter-than-air" airline, using dirigibles to transport passengers between German cities.

1922   Calbraith T. Rodgers makes the first U.S. transcontinental flight. Rodgers' accomplishment took forty-nine days and nineteen crash landings and covered 4,231 miles!

1918   Airplane pilots are first required to obtain licenses to fly by proclamation of President Woodrow Wilson.

1919   The first nonstop transatlantic flight is made by British fliers Captain John Alcock and Lieutenant A. W. Brown from St. John's, Newfoundland, to Clifden, Ireland, taking sixteen hours and twenty-eight minutes and covering 1,936 miles.

1923   Lieutenants J. A. Macready and Oakley G. Kelly make the first nonstop U.S. transcontinental flight, taking twenty-six hours and fifty minutes and covering 2,516 miles.

1924   The first round-the-world flight made by U.S. Army biplanes. They traveled 26,345 miles in 175 days!

1926   U.S. government offered subsidies to private airline companies to carry the mail, giving the carriers the boost they needed to get commercial aviation "off the ground."

1927   First nonstop transatlantic solo flight made by Charles Lindbergh from Roosevelt Field, New York, to Le Bourget, France. His flight of 3,610 miles took thirty-three hours and thirty minutes.

1929   The airship Graf Zeppelin flew around the world from Lakehurst, New Jersey, in twenty-one days and eight hours.

1932   Amelia Earhardt became the first woman to fly solo across the Atlantic. She flew from Canada to Ireland in fifteen hours and eighteen minutes.

1936   The DC-3, a twenty-one-person commercial airplane, was introduced to the airline industry. This twin-engined aircraft flew at a speed of 170 miles per hour and quickly won a reputation for dependability, safety, and comfort. The DC-3, like its sister of the road the Model T, became the standard for commercial air travel and is still in use today!

1937   The first maneuverable helicopter was built in Germany. The dirigible Hindenburg crashed and burned, bringing an end to passenger travel by airship.

1939   The first jet-propelled aircraft was built in Germany. Pan American World Airways (Pan Am) began regularly scheduled transatlantic service.

1947   Captain Charles Yeager of the U.S. Air Force broke the sound barrier flying over 760 miles per hour.

1949   The first nonstop, round-the-world flight was made by Captain James Gallagher and his crew aboard the *Lucky Lady*. The flight took three days and twenty-two hours and covered 23,452 miles.

1955   The first turbo-prop (early jet) aircraft was introduced into service in the United States.

1958   Pan Am's Boeing 707 jet traveled nonstop between New York and Europe in seven hours!

1960s   All major airlines added jet aircraft to their fleets.

1970   Pan Am introduces the first jumbo jet, the Boeing 747. This marvel of an airplane is as tall as a five-story building, has a range of 5,800 miles, has a capacity of up to 500 passengers, and is over 200 feet long. Orville and Wilbur Wright's entire first flight could have taken place *in this plane!*

Continued

1976	The supersonic transport aircraft (SST) was introduced through a joint development effort of Britain and France. This space-age passenger plane carries 100 to 125 passengers, travels at a speed of 1,350 miles per hour, and makes the transatlantic journey from the east coast of the United States to Britain in only four hours!	1991	The MD-11 jet, the first new, wide-body, long-range aircraft in almost a decade was introduced in the United States.
		2000	**World air traffic predicted to reach two billion passengers!**

place and most of Europe's major cities were linked by air service. The United States was a little slower to take to the skies. It wasn't until 1926, when the government subsidized private air carriers to transport the mail, that the industry really got up and flying.

In September 1939, Germany invaded Poland, and the world was back at war again. This time, airplanes played an even larger and more important role than before! Warfare accelerated research into advanced aerodynamics—fighting nations needed planes that could fly higher, faster and longer!

Fighting in the air, while fierce and deadly, was also exciting and romantic. The reports from the front were full of news about our daring pilots and their successful raids both during the day and night. Air warfare gave credibility to flying, and, odd though it may seem, helped convince the public that flying was truly safe.

The Domestic Carriers

In the United States, we refer to carriers that operate flights between and within the fifty states as our *domestic carriers*. Airlines that are based in or owned by other countries are commonly referred to as *foreign carriers*. Airlines that fly between countries are *international carriers;* many of our U.S. carriers are international as well as domestic. Of course, domestic and foreign designations are relative to where you live: in France, Air France is the domestic carrier and Delta is a foreign carrier. Both Air France and Delta are international carriers regardless of where you live!

Even though airlines in the United States are privately owned, they are regulated by the federal government. The rationale for this regulation is that the airlines use federal airways and engage in interstate commerce.

Federal regulation actually began in 1926 when the government awarded contracts for mail delivery to private carriers. However, as passenger travel grew, government involvement quickly changed from awarding mail contracts to enforcing economic and air safety regulations. The federal government considered air transportation a public utility even though the service was provided by private companies.

The Civil Aeronautics Act of 1938 was the most influential piece of legislation in federal government control and regulation of the airlines. It strengthened the government's powers and led to the creation of the Civil Aeronautics Board (CAB) and the Air Safety Board, a forerunner of the Federal Aviation Administration (FAA).

The CAB had five members that:

- Reviewed route requests and granted authorizations.
- Established a uniform system of rates and fares.
- Approved airline mergers, acquisitions, and new entrants.
- Ruled on unfair competition.

The CAB awarded "certificates of convenience and necessity" to domestic airlines and assigned carriers to specific routes. To indicate their size and scope, certified air carriers were classified along geographical lines:

Trunk lines (an old railroad term) were the large carriers that flew coast to coast, long-distance (long-haul) routes between major metropolitan areas and medium-sized cities.

Regional lines served a specific area of the country. For example, Southern Airlines served the South, and Allegheny Airlines served the Northeast. These carriers were originally referred to as "feeders" as they "fed" the trunk lines by bringing passengers and cargo from the smaller cities and rural areas to the major cities.

If an airline wanted to expand its routes or fly to a new destination, it had to request permission from the CAB. The procedure was unbelievably complicated and cumbersome. It could take months, even years, for the CAB to make a decision on a carrier's request, and, even then, it was often denied.

If an airline wanted to increase fares, it also had to file a request with the CAB and wait for approval. Air fares were the same for all carriers. The fare between Chicago and Atlanta would be the same on any airline you chose to fly. The CAB published all approved fares, and agents and airlines alike used the same source for determining the price of a ticket.

On October 30, 1978, President Jimmy Carter signed the Airline Deregulatory Act into law. This **deregulation** of the airlines instantly and dramatically changed every aspect of not only the airline industry but

Government Regulation and Deregulation

Oh, Beautiful for Open Skies!

Deregulation *The elimination (by law in 1978) of U.S. government control of airline routings, fares, and schedules.*

the rest of the travel industry as well. Airlines were given the freedom to set their own prices and apply for new routes that were once closed to them.

Although it has been over fifteen years since deregulation, the effects of such a dramatic act still reverberate throughout the industry. The debate on whether deregulation has been good or bad for the travel industry and the consumer still rages on—you will hear it mentioned again and again. There is, however, one thing no one in the industry can deny: deregulation has made life as a travel professional more interesting, exciting, and demanding than ever before!

A large part of the 1978 legislation was the phasing out of the CAB and, of course, the elimination of the power and control it once exerted over the airlines. Although many people were excited about the changes they believed deregulation would bring to U.S. airlines and consumers, others knew that an industry that had been regulated for forty years could not manage such dramatic change overnight.

It took a number of years to dismantle the CAB—it actually ceased to exist at midnight December 31, 1984. Since that time, the Department of Transportation (DOT), which was created in 1966, has watched over the U.S. airline industry from a distance. Although the powers of the DOT are more limited than those the CAB had, Congress did intend, in writing the Airline Deregulatory Act of 1978, to see that the federal government *alone* would regulate the airline industry. Federal regulations on any airline industry issue take precedence over the rights of the states or individuals to legally challenge any carrier's business practices.

The DOT regulates and monitors all transportation industries and transportation safety issues in the United States. Because the job is so big and covers so many industries, there are, of course, specialized administrations under DOT whose authority is specific to one type of transportation.

The Federal Aviation Administration (FAA) is a part of DOT and plays an extremely important role in the continued regulation of air safety. The FAA has absolute authority over anything larger than a seagull that passes through the U.S. airways. Its duties include:

- Certifying new aircraft as safe for service.
- Examining and licensing pilots, flight crews, mechanics, and technicians.
- Staffing control towers throughout the United States.
- Setting standards for new aircraft and equipment.
- Investigating air carrier accidents (along with the National Transportation Safety Board).

How Things Have Changed!

Since deregulation, the geographical distinctions of the trunk and regional classification system have become hazy. Regional carriers applied for new, longer-haul routes, purchased larger aircraft, and companies merged to form new and larger airlines.

As the regional carriers spread their wings, they found that the smaller towns and cities they once served were no longer profitable. Before the dismantling of the CAB in 1984, airlines could not terminate service to an area without the approval of the CAB, and the CAB rarely gave that approval. With the changes of deregulation, regional carriers were given approval, not to leave an area, but to farm out their least productive routes to airlines that operate much smaller aircraft—the **commuter carriers.** Ironically, the commuter now serves the regional as the regional once served the trunk.

Commuter Carrier *Carrier that operates smaller equipment and services smaller cities or population areas that cannot support major aircraft or traffic.*

Old and New, Buying and Selling, Success and Failure

The established carriers, both trunk and regional, jumped at the chance to expand their route systems. They all wanted long-haul flights between major cities where they felt they could attract the most passengers and make the most money. What was not readily apparent (since the airlines had not competed in over forty years) was that the introduction of more carriers in the large markets simply meant that no planes were full. Since pricing was now in the hands of the carriers, they did what all businesses do when supply exceeds demand: they lowered their fares. In the early 1980s, price wars were so fierce that, in some cases, an airline ticket between two cities was cheaper than bus fare!

As the established carriers added routes and struggled with pricing, others saw the opportunity to create new airlines. Some of these new lines were "no frills." They offered basic transportation with none of the amenities passengers had come to expect from the established carriers such as meal service and interline baggage handling. These "no frills" carriers charged less and added unwelcome pressure to the other carriers' economic struggles.

The 1980s saw airlines grow and shrink; merge with others, lose their old identities and create new ones; open their doors for the first time; succeed beyond anyone's imagination; and fail miserably. This intense, often frantic, competition led Robert Crandall, president of American Airlines, to remark in a *Travel Weekly* (June 11, 1992) interview: "There is no industry. There is just a group of savagely competitive individuals who agree on nothing."

U.S. Carriers Today

Today, airlines are classified by the amount of business they produce, not by where they fly. This classification system is more realistic and more accurately describes the airline industry.

Major carriers such as American, United and Delta serve the major cities of the U.S. and many foreign destinations as well. They earn at least $1 billion a year.

National carriers such as USAir and Northwest also serve many of the major U.S. cities and some foreign destinations. However, the nationals serve fewer cities and offer fewer flights and, therefore, have fewer passenger sales. They earn between $75 million and $1 billion a year.

Regional carriers may have schedules outside the United States, but generally very few. They may fly to many areas in the United States, but their concentration is generally in one area, such as America West in the West and Southwest. They earn between $10 million and $75 million a year.

Commuter carriers operate smaller aircraft and fly between smaller cities or ferry passengers from smaller airports to major airports. Commuter carriers may have agreements with or be subsidiaries of larger carriers and share their names and codes. They earn less than $10 million a year.

After deregulation, many new carriers were vying for positions in the U.S. skies. Because of fierce competition, poor management, lack of equipment and technological expertise, overexpansion and, in some cases, just rotten luck, virtually all the new carriers of the 1980s do not exist today. Furthermore, many established U.S. carriers also had their wings clipped: some went out of business (Eastern and Pan Am) and others merged with or were purchased by larger or financially stronger carriers (Western Air with Delta, Piedmont with USAir), and some just got smaller (Continental and TWA). Today, there are only three U.S. carriers with *major carrier* status, and they are often referred to as "The Big Three": American Airlines, Delta Airlines, and United Airlines.

UP CLOSE

The Major U.S. Carriers

Note: Numbers given are approximate. Changes in employment, cities and countries served, and aircraft in service are frequent.

American Airlines

Headquarters:	Fort Worth, Texas
Established:	1926
Employees:	90,000+
Aircraft:	600+
Countries Served:	30+
Cities Served:	190+
U.S. Hubs:	Dallas-Fort Worth, Chicago, Nashville, Raleigh-Durham, Miami, San Juan
Reservation System:	Sabre Travel Information Network

Delta Airlines

Headquarters:	Atlanta, Georgia
Established:	1929
Employees:	60,000+
Aircraft:	500+
Countries Served:	15+
Cities Served:	190+
U.S. Hubs:	Atlanta, Dallas-Fort Worth, Cincinnati, Salt Lake City, Los Angeles, Orlando
Reservation System:	Worldspan

United Airlines

Headquarters:	Elk Grove Township, Ill. (suburb of Chicago)
Established:	1926
Employees:	80,000+
Aircraft:	475+
Countries Served:	20+
Cities Served:	160+
U.S. Hubs:	Chicago, Denver, San Francisco, Washington-Dulles
Reservation System:	Apollo

Explorations

1. What is the closest commercial passenger airport to where you live?

2. Name the domestic airlines that serve this airport and give their size classification: major, national, regional, or commuter.

3. Do any of these airlines maintain the following in your city or at your airport?
   - Reservation center
   - Major maintenance facility
   - Sales office
   - City ticket office

Enrichments

Check your local newspaper over the next three days for articles about U.S. domestic airlines. Classify these articles as primarily concerned with:

- Fares
- Business conditions (i.e., discussions of financial stability, selling, merging, cost cutbacks, expansion, etc.)
- New services, routes
- Labor issues
- Customer service (i.e., quality rankings, on-time performance, etc.)

(*Hint:* Don't just check the front page! Remember to investigate the business and travel sections too!)

The International Carriers

When you first enter the travel business, you are not likely to be called upon to prepare a traveler's air itinerary or figure an international fare

from Washington/Dulles to Frankfurt to Budapest to Bombay to Karachi to Kathmandu to Sydney to Tokyo to Los Angeles to Atlanta. There are experienced industry professionals who specialize in the complexities of international travel, and although you may not choose to be one, no travel professional who expects to do well in the business can remain totally ignorant of it. Besides, international travel is fascinating! It involves the manipulations of governments at the highest levels and results in the free flow of passengers among countries that once vowed mutual destruction.

Who Goes Where . . . And Why . . . And How . . .

International Air Transport Association (IATA) *A voluntary membership organization of the airlines which, by setting rates and establishing conditions of service and safety standards, provides a unified system of worldwide air transportation.*

The fundamental issue is that *travel from one country to another depends upon agreements between governments.* Governments, like people, have a variety of motivations for their actions, but their most obvious motivations are money, power, and national pride. Attempting to ride herd over these mixed motives and bring a semblance of order to the airways of the world is the **International Air Transport Association (IATA).**

Founded in 1919 by a group of European airlines and reorganized after World War II, IATA has attempted to maintain order and stability among the international air carriers by providing a forum for the airlines to meet and discuss mutual concerns, recommending fares and tariffs, representing the airlines in travel agency affairs, promoting air safety, and encouraging worldwide air travel. Membership in IATA is strictly voluntary, and its agreements are subject to the approval of its members' governments. Such approval is relatively easy to obtain for those carriers that are government owned. These "flag carriers" (so called because of the implication that they promote their nations by "showing the flag") generally know in advance the fares and routings their governments will accept. In fact, because many of these flag carriers receive subsidies from their governments, they can offer lower fares even if it means they operate at a loss. The privately owned carriers, such as those we have in the United States, find such competition

The World Is Out There Waiting

unfair. Consequently, it is much less certain that our government will approve IATA agreements.

Furthermore, we involve the Departments of Justice, State, and Transportation and even the White House in these decisions. Our government has never looked favorably upon IATA's role as a price-setting cartel and has sometimes rejected agreements and pressured IATA to liberalize its system. Even though more Third World carriers have joined IATA, it is still primarily controlled by its European members.

Although air travel has brought the nations of the world closer to one another—obviously not in miles but in time it takes to travel the miles—the world is still a big and complicated place. To better manage the needs of nations and the carriers who serve them, IATA divides the world into three traffic conferences (areas) and attempts to set rates and services levels within and between them.

Remember! Membership in IATA is voluntary and most carriers and their governments have very clear ideas about how they want the business of international air travel conducted in and around their countries.

The IATA traffic conferences are:

Traffic Conference 1: North and South America and the Pacific as far west as the international date line.

Traffic Conference 2: Europe, Africa, and the Middle East.

Traffic Conference 3: Asia, Australia, and the Pacific as far east as the international date line.

For many years after 1945, IATA had a system for regulating the number of agencies that could sell international air tickets in a given geographical area. There was what was known as a "need clause" which allowed airlines to appoint agencies according to the need for them. The "need" was based on the airlines' assessments. This agency program was designed to ensure that U.S. agents were competent, reliable, and financially stable; but it also permitted IATA to set fares and commissions.

The CAB disapproved the need clause in 1960 as an antitrust measure and, in 1979, launched an investigation into the competitive marketing of international air transportation. By the end of 1984, the balance of the antitrust immunity IATA had enjoyed was withdrawn as part of the overall deregulation of the U.S. airline industry.

This left the U.S. market wide open for anyone to become an international air ticketing agent and collect commission. Professional travel agents were no longer protected from the possible dilution of clientele and revenue, and the general public faced being left without reliable, professional guidance in the purchase of air travel products.

To help counteract the possible negative effects of U.S. deregulation and its effects on international air travel, the **International Airlines Travel Agent Network (IATAN),** a private, nonprofit wholly owned subsidiary of IATA, was organized in 1985 to replace IATA as the organization that appoints U.S. travel agents to sell tickets for the international carriers that serve the United States. It is dedicated to maintaining professional standards among travel agents by endorsing them as qualified by experience, integrity, and fiscal responsibility.

International Airlines Travel Agents Network (IATAN) A wholly owned subsidiary of IATA with voluntary membership among the airlines and other travel industry suppliers. It appoints travel agencies to sell tickets for international travel on IATA member carriers.

But, back to the foreign governments. Each country in the world is a sovereign nation, and at last count, there were close to 200. That means each of these countries claims the land within its boundaries, part of the waters that border it, and all of the air above it, from the ground to infinity. No nation can do much at the present time to regulate satellites orbiting the earth, but they can create havoc with the prop planes that fly close to the earth and even with the jets cruising at 35,000 feet. The world's nations have agreed, therefore, that any time an aircraft registered in one country flies through the airspace of another, it must do so as an invited guest.

This host-guest relationship has been carefully delineated in a formula called the "Flying Freedoms" or the eight "Freedoms of the Air." The first five were formulated by a convention of UN members (except the Soviet Union) in 1944; the last three are unofficial and have been added to the list over the years. They provide countries with a foundation for international negotiations.

The Freedoms of the Air

1. The right of an airline to fly over one country to get to another.
2. The right to stop over in a foreign country for technical reasons such as fuel, maintenance, or a crew change, but not to do business.
3. The right of a carrier to drop off passengers from its country of origin in another country.
4. The right of a carrier to pick up its native passengers in another country and fly them back home again.
5. The right of a carrier to transport passengers from its home country to a second country and even to a third as long as the flight originates or terminates in the carrier's home country.
6. The right of an airline to transport passengers from one country to another via its home country.
7. The right of a carrier to operate entirely outside its home country.
8. The right of an airline to operate flights between cities in a foreign country.

Examples of the Freedoms:

First Freedom: Delta Airlines departs Atlanta and flies over Great Britain en route to Paris.

Second Freedom: Singapore Airlines departs Amsterdam and lands in Toronto on its way to Singapore. The stop in Canada is a scheduled stop for refueling, service, and crew change. However, Singapore Airlines *may not* carry passengers to or from Toronto. That is, all passengers on board the flight are traveling from Amsterdam to Singapore. No passenger gets off or boards the flight in Toronto.

Third Freedom: United Airlines departs from Chicago, Illinois, and carries passengers to London.

Fourth Freedom: United Airlines departs Hong Kong and carries passengers to Los Angeles, California.

Fifth Freedom: Delta Airlines departs Atlanta, stops in Paris (where some passengers disembark), boards additional passengers, and continues to Stuttgart, Germany.

Sixth Freedom: Northwest Airlines, carrying Norwegian passengers from Oslo bound for the Orient, may stop over in Detroit, a gateway city.

Seventh Freedom: KLM (Dutch Airlines) flies between Frankfurt, Vienna, and Milan and returns—all outside KLM's home country (the Netherlands).

Eighth Freedom: American Airlines, a U.S. airline, carries passengers between Frankfurt and Munich—all within Germany.

The first two freedoms, called *transit rights,* have been widely accepted. Hardly anyone could go anywhere if one nation's planes could not fly over another nation. As long as nations do not feel that passenger planes are being used to spy on their countries, everything generally proceeds smoothly. However, when there is suspicion of foul play, tragedy can be the result.

In August 1983, Korean Air Lines flight 007 was flying to Seoul when it wandered into U.S.S.R. air space. Suspecting a spy plane (or worse), the Soviets fired on the plane, causing it to crash and killing all 269 persons aboard. The international community was enraged that a country could shoot down a defenseless civilian aircraft. Although the Soviets certainly had the right to regulate who entered their air space, most nations believed that international custom and the First Freedom of the Air clearly dictated that a country's rights should not be exercised in such a drastic way.

The next four freedoms, called *traffic rights,* have not yet been completely accepted. The last two, as you can undoubtedly imagine, are allowed only under special circumstances since they bring carriers more directly into competition with each other.

Access to foreign markets has long been a controversial issue in aviation. Governments and carriers alike are anxious to expand air business into and within other countries. Of course, many of these same governments and carriers are also anxious to keep other countries and carriers out of their own markets. These mixed motives create confusion and fierce debate throughout the world. Some countries see "open skies" as the way to go. Others are dead set against it.

Why Be "For" Open Skies? To create new business. In the United States, many carriers believe that the potential for new business wholly within the U.S. is minimal; the market is pretty "tapped out." Flying to and within foreign countries represents new opportunities and untapped markets.

The largest increases in passenger traffic are predicted to be from the Pacific Rim where future economic growth is expected to outpace that of the rest of the world. In fact, fewer than 5 percent of the population of the countries of this area have ever been on an airplane. As economies improve and individual standards of living rise, people will begin to travel. Some industry analysts believe that 40 percent of the world's passenger traffic will be to, from, and within the Pacific Rim by the turn of the century!

Why Be "Against" Open Skies?   To prevent unwanted competition within your own country. Many government-owned and government-supported airlines have a monopoly on air travel within their countries, control the air fares into and within their borders, and have the power to restrict the entry of other carriers into their markets. Open skies would undoubtedly change all that and would make doing business far more complicated and difficult than it already is!

"Cruising" at 35,000 Feet!

You have probably noticed that the airlines have borrowed language from the maritime world: the pilot of a plane is the "captain," the copilot is the "first officer"; speed and distance are partly measured in "knots"; passengers sit in "cabins" in front of a "bulkhead," luggage is stored in the "hold," and flight attendants prepare food in the "galley" while the aircraft "cruises" at speeds in excess of 500 miles per hour. Other maritime traditions that have been passed along to these airships that ply the atmospheric oceans include the red and green running lights on the port and starboard sides (respectively) of a plane and the custom of flying the nation's flag.

For centuries, ships flew their nation's flags over the stern while in foreign ports; so do airplanes bear their nation's painted-on flag on the tail section or rear-mounted engine pod. You will see the tricolor on the Air France Concorde, the Union Jack on the British Air Concorde, the rising sun on the planes of Japan Airlines, and on the Scandinavian Airlines planes you will see the flags of Norway, Sweden, and Denmark.

What Might Tomorrow Bring?

Increased Air Passenger Traffic. Numbers are expected to reach 2 billion after the turn of the century. Almost 50 percent of that number—*or nearly one billion passengers*—will be traveling on U.S. carriers!

Open Skies. Despite difficulties nationally and internationally, the European Economic Community is expected to finish dismantling the trade barriers established after World War II. This international deregulation will create skies without borders, lower fares, and more routes.

More Buying, Selling, Merging, and Disappearing. Deregulation in the United States brought forth a rash of new airlines, most of which no longer exist. But, some have learned from the mistakes of others, and new players are once again entering the U.S. skies. New carriers, such as Midwest Express, which serves business markets from its home base in Milwaukee; North American Airlines, which operates feeder service from Miami and Los Angeles for El Al's New York-Tel Aviv service; Carnival Air, which caters to the leisure market; and MGM Grand Air, which caters to wealthy travelers, will probably continue to enter the market place—this time more profitably and successfully than before.

International deregulation will increase the buying, selling, and merging of carriers that U.S. airline deregulation began. Already, international carriers are investing in one another, signing joint operating agreements, and becoming private, rather than government-owned, operations. However, it will not be all rosy—some carriers will not survive the new competition and will shrink in size and influence, or cease to exist altogether.

New Technological Developments. These include faster, more fuel efficient, and, hopefully, for the passenger, more comfortable airplanes.

Breaking the Codes

We have already explored the rationale for industry jargon and mentioned that the travel industry has its own jargon, abbreviations, and codes, many of which come from the airlines and their computer systems. Although there are many codes and abbreviations, and although they can at first be overwhelming, there is usually a simple logic to them and learning and using them can be fun!

Because computers have become such an integral part of the travel industry and because they must transmit a lot of information quickly, their codes have come to form the basis of the industry's jargon. City, state, country, airline, and other codes permit agents to communicate rapidly and precisely. Anything that saves keystrokes saves time and money! You may think of all this as "alphabet soup," but, in the travel business, it is your "bread and butter"!

Airline Codes

Airline Code The two-character code designation of an airline.

All airlines have a two-character code that is uniquely their own. Most **airline codes** consist of two letters although a few are one letter and one number. In computer language, letter codes are referred to as alpha codes and number codes are referred to as numeric codes. When you have both a letter and a number, the code is said to be alphanumeric.

Some codes are the first letter of each of the airlines' two names:

It's Easy		Try Some!	
American Airlines	**AA**	Hawaiian Air	_____
Air France	**AF**	British Airways	_____
United Airlines	**UA**	Air Canada	_____

Other codes may be derived from the first two letters in the first name of the airline:

USAir	**US**
Iberia	**IB**

And still others may be taken from letters in the first name of the carrier:

De**l**ta Airlines	**DL**
North**w**est Airlines	**NW**

Other two-character codes will make sense when you learn more about the carrier and its country. For example, the code for Aeroflot, the Russian airline, is SU, the beginning letters of the Soviet Union. Even though the Soviet Union is now divided into many countries and independent entities, it is not likely that the two-letter code will change since it has long been established in the worldwide travel industry.

And, finally, there are codes that make no sense, such as KX for Cayman Airways, UP for Bahamasair, and WN for Southwest Airlines. If you use these codes frequently, you will soon have them committed to memory. If you rarely work with an airline, you may not recognize its code and will have to look it up. You can always find the codes in the *Official Airline Guide* (OAG) or in the computerized reservation system.

Will the Real UA Please Raise Its Wing Flap?

You board UA 1077 only to find that it isn't a United flight at all. It's a twenty-four-passenger commuter flight with a name you've never heard of before!

or

A travel agent looks up a schedule from his home city through New York to Rome and is surprised to find that TWA shows a flight from his home city since they have never had service there! He calls the airline only to find that the TWA domestic flight is actually a USAir flight.

Things are not what they seem! Surprisingly, the airline code on a ticket or in a printed or computerized schedule may not be the carrier on which the passenger will actually fly.

Q: How can this be?
A: "Code sharing."

Code sharing does not mean much to the average traveler—until, of course, he or she ends up on a strange airline whose name bears little or no resemblance to the one printed on his or her itinerary. The practice of one carrier using the code of another began in the 1960s when Allegheny Airlines (which later became USAir) used its code AL in front of the flight numbers for its connections on smaller commuter carriers.

In the 1980s, other airlines followed suit. A ticket could, for example, show Delta Airlines as the carrier from San Francisco, California, connecting in Cincinnati, Ohio, with the final destination being Greensboro, North Carolina. The flight from San Francisco to Cincinnati is indeed a Delta jet, but the flight to Greensboro is a commuter carrier operated by Comair as the "Delta Connection."

In addition to this practice, carriers may also establish joint operating agreements, lease planes from one another, and "pool" aircraft. The case with TWA is an example of this. In order to show "direct" connections and fares from a smaller domestic market through a major city to an international destination, carriers will work out "code sharing" and service agreements with other carriers.

Code sharing, although disliked by, and confusing to, consumers, was accepted by federal regulators and the practice became widespread. Today, DOT policy requires airlines in "any direct oral communication" to alert consumers as to what airline they will actually fly. Printed schedules and computer displays also have an indicator (usually a *) by the flight number to indicate a "commuter" flight.

City and Airport Codes

City and **airport codes** (and these are, more often than not, the same) are either made up of the letters of the city, such as ATL for Atlanta *and* its airport, Hartsfield International, or SFO for San Francisco *and* its airport; or else they are taken from the name of the airport, such as SDF for Standiford Field in Louisville, Kentucky. Sometimes the airport has grown and changed locations and the origin of the name is no longer readily apparent. This is the case with MSY, the code for the international airport in New Orleans.

The following cities have a generic city code in addition to the code for their airports:

City Code *Three-letter designation used by airlines to identify cities. Many city codes are identical to the three-letter airport codes.*

Airport Code *The three-letter code designation of an airport.*

City Name	City Code	Airport Names and Codes
New York, NY	NYC	LaGuardia (LGA) John F. Kennedy Int'l (JFK) Newark, NJ Int'l (EWR)
Washington, DC	WAS	Washington National (DCA) Dulles International (IAD)
Chicago, IL	CHI	O'Hare International (ORD) Midway (MDW)

Decoding Airline Codes

AA	American Airlines		LI	LIAT-Leeward Islands Air
AC	Air Canada		LM	ALM-Antillean Airlines
AF	Air France		LR	Lacsa
AI	Air India		LY	El Al Israel Airlines
AM	Aeromexico		MS	Egyptair
AN	Ansett Airlines		MX	Mexicana
AQ	Aloha Airlines		NH	All Nippon Airways
AR	Aerolineas Argentinas		NM	Mount Cook Airlines
AS	Alaska Airlines		NW	Northwest Orient
AV	Avianca		NZ	Air New Zealand
AY	Finnair		OA	Olympic Airways
AZ	Alitalia		OS	Austrian Airlines
BA	British Airways		PL	Aeroperu
BL	Air BVI, Ltd.		QF	Qantas Airways
BW	British West Indies Airlines (BWIA)		RG	Varig
CA	CAAC		RJ	Alia-Royal Jordanian
CI	China Airlines		SA	South African Airways
CO	Continental Airlines		SH	Sahsa
CP	Canadian Pacific Air		SK	SAS-Scandinavian Airlines
CX	Cathay Pacific		SN	Sabena
DL	Delta Airlines		SQ	Singapore Airlines
DO	Dominicana		SR	Swissair
EI	Aer Lingus		SU	Aeroflot
EU	Equatoriana		TG	Thai International
FI	Icelandair		TN	Australian Airlines
GF	Gulf Air		TP	Air Portugal (TAP)
HA	Hawaiian Air		TW	Trans World Airlines
IB	Iberia Airlines		UA	United Airlines
IT	Aer Inter		UP	Bahamasair
JL	Japan Airlines		US	USAir
JM	Air Jamaica		UT	UTA French Airlines
KE	Korean Air		VA	Viasa
KL	KLM Royal Dutch Airlines		VE	Avensa
KX	Cayman Airways		VP	VASP Brazilian Air
LA	LAN Chile		VS	Virgin Atlantic
LH	Lufthansa			

The World Is Out There Waiting

Encoding Airlines Codes

Aer Lingus	EI	Egyptair	MS
Aeroflot	SU	El Al Israel Airlines	LY
Aerolineas Argentinas	AR	Finnair	AY
Aeromexico	AM	Hawaiian Air	HA
Aeroperu	PL	Iberia Airlines	IB
Air Canada	AC	Icelandair	FI
Air France	AF	Interflug	IF
Air India	AI	Japan Airlines	JL
Air Jamaica	JM	Lacsa	LR
Air New Zealand	NZ	LAN Chile	LA
Air Portugal (TAP)	TP	LIAT-Leeward Islands Air	LI
Alaska Airlines	AS	Lot Polish Airlines	LO
Alitalia	AZ	Lufthansa	LH
Alia-Royal Jordanian	RJ	Mexicana	MX
All Nippon Airways	NH	Mount Cook Airlines	NM
ALM - Antillean Airlines	LM	Northwest Orient	NW
Aloha Airlines	AQ	Olympic Airways	OA
American Airlines	AA	Qantas Airways	QF
Ansett Airlines	AN	Sabena	SN
Austrian Airlines	OS	Sahsa	SH
Avensa	VE	SAS-Scandinavian Airline System	SK
Avianca	AV	Singapore Airlines	SQ
Bahamasair	UP	South African Airways	SA
British Airways	BA	Swissair	SR
British West Indies Airlines (BWIA)	BW	Australian Airlines	TN
CAAC	CA	Trans World Airlines	TW
Cathay Pacific	CX	United Airlines	UA
Cayman Airways	KX	USAir	US
China Airlines	CI	UTA French Airlines	UTA
Continental Air Lines	CO	Varig	RG
Delta Air Lines	DL	VASP Brazilian Air	VP
Dominicana	DO	Viasa	VA
Ecuatoriana	EU	Virgin Atlantic	VS

Airline Routes—Not Always as the Crow Flies!

People may have always wanted to fly like the birds, but when they take
to the air aboard a commercial carrier, they fly higher and faster—but
rarely straighter! Obviously, airplanes fly between airports because they
are the delivery and pickup points for passengers and cargo. An airline
route is the path an airplane takes in delivering its services, and making the most efficient use of an airplane is a high priority for all carriers. Routes are planned carefully using two systems: linear routing and
the hub and spoke system. When looking at airline route systems, it is
helpful to note that routing of any type is affected by air traffic, weather

Identifying City/Airport Codes

This map has numbers representing most (but not all) of the major airports in the contiguous United States. Above the map are the three-letter codes for those airports and/or cities. See how many of the codes you can break by placing them in the correct numbered blanks. *Some of the blanks should be filled in with more than one code.* The answers appear at the end of Section 4.

ALB	BIS	DCA	GTF	JAX	MCO	ORD	PWM	SEA
ABQ	BOS	DFW	GSO	JFK	MCI	OMA	PHX	STL
ATL	BUF	DTW	GEG	LAX	MKE	ORF	RNO	SFO
BDL	CHS	DSM	HOU	LGA	MEM	PVD	RDU	SDF
BOI	CLT	DEN	IAD	LIT	MSY	PIT	RAP	TPA
BWI	CLE	EWR	IAH	LAS	NYC	PHL	SAN	TUS
BNA	CVG	ELP	IND	MIA	OKC	PDX	SLC	WAS
BHM	CHI	GSP	JAN	MSP				

1. _____	10. _____	19. _____	28. _____	37. _____	46. _____	55. _____
2. _____	11. _____	20. _____	29. _____	38. _____	47. _____	56. _____
3. _____	12. _____	21. _____	30. _____	39. _____	48. _____	57. _____
4. _____	13. _____	22. _____	31. _____	40. _____	49. _____	58. _____
5. _____	14. _____	23. _____	32. _____	41. _____	50. _____	59. _____
6. _____	15. _____	24. _____	33. _____	42. _____	51. _____	60. _____
7. _____	16. _____	25. _____	34. _____	43. _____	52. _____	61. _____
8. _____	17. _____	26. _____	35. _____	44. _____	53. _____	62. _____
9. _____	18. _____	27. _____	36. _____	45. _____	54. _____	

conditions, air rights, noise control, and so on, and often deviates from what would appear to be the obvious, common-sense approach to getting from one place to another.

Linear Routing— As the Crow Flies

In a linear route, an airplane usually flies the shortest and straightest line between two points. That is, an airplane begins its journey in Los Angeles, flies directly to Seattle, then turns around and comes back. A linear route may have intermediate stops to pick up more passengers or cargo. For example, a **direct flight** from Atlanta to Las Vegas may have an intermediate stop in Dallas where the airline can pick up or leave off passengers.

Direct Flight   *A flight that does not require a passenger to change planes during intermediate stops; also known as a through flight.*

If the flight between Los Angeles and Seattle made no stops along the way, it is called, quite naturally, a nonstop flight to Seattle. If, however, the flight makes intermediate stops between L.A. and Seattle, it is called a direct flight.

Linear routing is simple, straightforward, and creates very few scheduling headaches for the airlines and easy booking for the reservationists. However, it really only works for travel into and out of larger cities. There are plenty of people who want to go to—and leave—Chicago. So, it should come as no surprise that there are flights from large and small cities direct into Chicago.

But what about those few who want to fly from Charleston, West Virginia, to Wichita, Kansas? They certainly wouldn't fill a plane, so it would be impossible to convince an airline to dedicate an expensive plane and crew to a "linear route" (nonstop or direct) between these two points. Chances are, the occasional traveler between these two cities will have to connect through the "hub" of Chicago.

The Hub and Spoke System

Picture a wagon wheel with its center, the hub, and the spokes that extend from it to the rim. Then, consider a large metropolitan city, such as Atlanta, as the hub and outlying cities such as Birmingham, Savannah, Jacksonville, Cincinnati, and New Orleans as the endpoints of the spokes and you will get the basic idea of the hub and spoke system.

An airline uses an airport as the center, or hub, to receive as many flights as possible from outlying cities at the same time. The airlines can provide more service between a greater number of cities and, through careful scheduling, can make sure that they do not lose passengers connecting to other airlines. The airlines also use their smaller planes to bring passengers from the less populated outlying cities and "feed" their own flights between major metropolitan areas. Interestingly, this hub and spoke concept allows major carriers to serve as regional carriers as well.

Using the **hub and spoke system** can mean that, to travel from New Orleans to Birmingham by air, a passenger will connect in Atlanta. Hardly a route the birds would choose, but, for the airlines, routing through large cities is a natural, and they have set up administration centers, reservation centers, and aircraft maintenance facilities in them. However, the rapid growth of airline traffic over the last ten years and the competition for new routes has saturated the natural hubs such as

Hub and Spoke System   *An airline's system of using a large city or area airport as a connecting point for its flights from smaller cities.*

Atlanta, Chicago, Denver, New York, and Dallas. During the busiest flight times of the day, there isn't enough room for a crow to land, much less an airplane!

The new era of competition has spawned creativity and, in an effort to increase their routes, keep passengers from choosing or connecting to competing airlines, and ease congestion at major airports, the airlines have created "artificial" hubs at destinations that are not yet saturated with heavy air traffic. Where the largest airports of the nation may serve many carriers as hubs, the artificial hubs are dominated by one carrier and, thus, are also called single airline hubs. USAir in Baltimore and Charlotte, American Airlines in Raleigh/Durham and Nashville, and Delta Airlines in Cincinnati and Salt Lake City are just a few examples.

Typically, in creating "artificial" hubs, an airline designates an airport as its "new" hub and invests in—or gets the local community to invest in—expanding the airport to be able to handle more flights. Artificial hubs are typically more regional than national and serve more "short-haul" flights than "long-haul" flights. USAir may have a couple of flights from Baltimore to Bermuda, but to fill them, the airline must have many flights from smaller, surrounding cities bringing in passengers.

Artificial Hubs— Good Idea? Or, Not Such a Good Idea?

The artificial hub and spoke system, at first glance, appears to be an excellent alternative to the major city hub system. That is indeed true, but there can be a down side for the passenger. In the major hubs, many

A Natural, Major City Hub

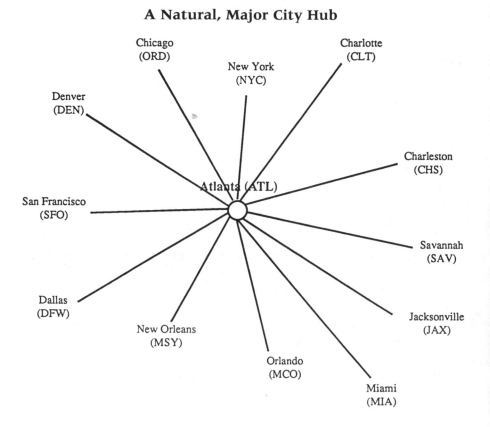

An Artificial or Single Airline Hub

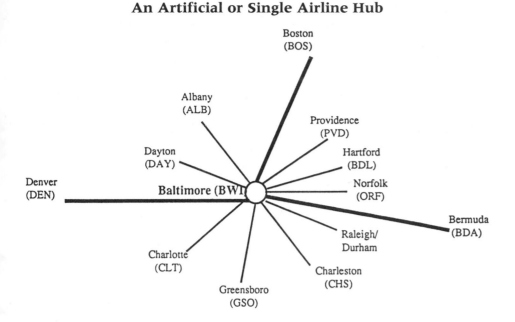

airlines interact to serve the passenger. If one carrier has a seriously delayed arrival or a mechanical problem that prevents a departure, its passengers can be rerouted to other carriers, often with a minimum of inconvenience. At the artificial hubs where one carrier is the dominant player, passengers may have no alternatives when flights are delayed or cancelled. When one spoke of this wheel breaks, the whole wagon can come to a halt.

Artificial hubs developed so quickly that airport facilities have not always kept pace and, in some cases, are inadequately sized or staffed to handle the transiting passengers comfortably. Airports are not most people's favorite places to spend hours of their time, and travelers in need of efficient service and back-up alternatives often find the major airports more to their liking.

Travelers who look to the major airports as the best places to connect are, by and large, the business travelers who pay the highest fares. In an effort to boost revenue, improve service, and meet the needs of the important business traveler, some airlines have altered their concentration on the hub and spoke system and are increasing nonstop and direct flights.

A return to more direct and nonstop flights does not signal the abandonment of artificial hubs. Both major city and artificial hubs will exist. Predictions are that demand for air travel will continue and as many as thirty more U.S. airports will reach flight saturation over the next few years. The only solution to continued crowding of the airways over the existing hubs will be to create more hubs.

The names of airports and other public facilities are often tributes to heroes or outstanding individuals who have made significant financial, social, or political contributions to their communities. Time often fades local memories and most modern-day travelers changing planes in a

Why Did They Name It . . . ?

busy metropolitan airport have little or no knowledge of local history. Life on the road is hectic, and, if asked, most harried businesspeople (who may have changed planes in Chicago hundreds of times) would tell you (if they agreed to speak to you at all) they never gave the first thought to why O'Hare is called O'Hare.

But, since you are in a "learning phase" and not yet in a harried business phase, it can be interesting to learn why an airport carries the name it does. Plus, someone should remember these great folks who pioneered aviation and, maybe one day, while circling O'Hare in a snow storm, you can entertain your seatmate with "airport trivia"!

In 1943, in Washington, D.C., President Franklin D. Roosevelt presented the Congressional Medal of Honor to Navy Lt. Edward "Butch" O'Hare, a native Chicagoan and one of the greatest combat pilots of all time. Back in Chicago, troop and cargo planes were being built at a factory known as Orchard Place. After the war, the city purchased the land for use as a municipal airport. The facility was coded ORD (for ORcharD Place) and named for the hometown hero, Butch O'Hare.

LaGuardia Airport in New York (LGA) was named after the city's last independent mayor, Fiorello H. LaGuardia—the man who single-handedly pushed New York City into the forefront of aviation. Of course, there is a story to this flamboyant politician's exploits on behalf of his city!

In 1934, LaGuardia flew home from Chicago and landed in Newark, then the major eastern endpoint for most airlines. Upon landing, he refused to disembark and loudly demanded that the terms of his ticket be honored and that he be taken to New York. After all, his ticket said NEW YORK not NEWARK.

After many protestations (and lots of picture taking), the airline flew him to Floyd Bennet Field in Brooklyn. The New York papers ran front-page pictures of the indignant mayor sitting in an empty plane proclaiming, "Newark is not New York!"

Five years later, his untiring efforts to make New York City a major player in aviation were rewarded with the opening of North Beach Airport in the borough of Queens. However, public opinion and appreciation were on LaGuardia's side and, shortly after the airport was dedicated, it was renamed "LaGuardia."

Airports have been named for:

Leaders in aviation—Lindbergh Field in San Diego, California, and Yeager Airport in Charleston, West Virginia.

Presidents—John F. Kennedy International Airport in New York and Harry S. Truman Regional Airport in Bates City, Missouri.

Actors—Jimmy Stewart Airport in Indiana County, Pennsylvania, and John Wayne/Orange County Airport in Santa Ana, California.

and for a host of senators, congressmen, and mayors. However, there is no public airport named Wilbur, Orville, or Wright for those brothers who were the first to successfully build and fly an airplane! The airfield closest to Kitty Hawk, North Carolina, where this all took place is called, very simply, First Flight.

Airports

The world's major airports are international centers and handle thousands of passengers every day. Seven of the world's busiest airports are in the United States and, Chicago's O'Hare—the busiest—handles over 60 million passengers a year! In the early 1990s, the world's ten busiest airports were:

Chicago O'Hare	59,900,000
Dallas-Fort Worth	48,198,000
Los Angeles	45,700,000
Tokyo Haneda	42,000,000
London Heathrow	40,500,000
Atlanta Hartsfield	37,900,000
Frankfurt	33,400,000
San Francisco	31,800,000
Denver Stapleton	28,300,000
New York JFK	27,400,000

Source: Airports Association Council International. Figures rounded to nearest thousands.

Not making the big ten are many, many national, regional, and city airports that also serve thousands of passengers every day! The United States has almost 600 airports that offer scheduled air carrier transportation to the general public. At the far end of the list of airports are the numerous private airfields with no scheduled service, limited facilities, and very little daily activity.

Airports are owned by local communities and these communities often vie with other communities for airline landings. The hub and spoke system has been great for some airlines and disastrous for others. In North Carolina, Charlotte (a USAir hub) and Raleigh (an American hub) have thrived under the new system while Greensboro, which is not a hub, has struggled to attract airlines and lost passengers to Charlotte and Raleigh which offer more competitive fares and are within reasonable driving distance.

The hub and spoke pattern means that more and more passengers spend time waiting for connections, and airports try to attract connecting passengers with extra services such as banks, gift shops, lounges, restaurants, health clubs, business centers, meeting rooms, tour group assembly areas, children's areas, and so forth.

Travelers do not, of course, choose their destinations because they like certain airports and want to visit them, but they may select connecting points based on their preferences of airports. How far they must walk between flights, how confusing the airport is, the existence of airport lounges, how crowded the airport is, and how often there are flight delays will influence travelers' decisions. You will often hear travelers speak of their "favorite airports" or talk about which airports have the best private lounges, or the best shops, or even the best hot dogs. The frequent traveler knows them all!

Keeping the Bad Guys Out

A major downside to the glamour of travel and the popularity of tourism is the fact that anything having to do with it is front-page news. This makes airplanes and airports attractive stages for terrorists and the not-so-mentally stable who are looking for a dramatic, world-stopping way to get their messages heard and their stories told.

Since the late 1960s when hijacking planes seemed to be an international pastime, all airports have been equipped with security guards, metal detectors, and baggage-screening devices. In some airports, security is so tight that only ticketed passengers may enter the concourse. Even though the nations of the world may disagree about many things having to do with tourism, such as open skies and competition, they do not disagree on the importance of keeping the airways and airports safe. Therefore, international security measures are widespread and comprehensive.

Many travelers have concerns about being targets for terrorist groups as they travel throughout the world and, despite sound reasoning, they are also not likely to be comforted by the statistical probabilities (they are far more likely to be hit by lightning). Travel professionals have offered the following suggestions for nervous travelers so they will feel as though they are doing something to thwart the unseen enemy:

- Move quickly through airports—arriving and departing.
- Proceed directly through customs, immigration, and baggage claim.
- Leave the airport as soon as possible upon arrival.
- When departing, check in and go to the security check point.
- Report any unattended luggage—and stay away from it.
- Wait in a club lounge rather than in an open area.
- Blend in by adopting the style and mannerisms of the local people.

Domestic versus International Airports

Domestic Travel *Travel between two points in the same country, territory, or possession. Travel within the continental United States, Hawaii, Alaska, Puerto Rico, and U.S. Virgin Islands is defined as U.S. domestic travel.*

Domestic travel differs from international travel: it is more complex and makes more demands of the travelers and the suppliers who serve them. The airports of the world that accept international arrivals and departures are designed and organized to handle these demands and complexities.

An airport that has international arrivals and departures is known as an *international gateway*. Airports that handle flights that operate only within their own country are known as *domestic airports*. Clearly, an international airport, such as Dallas-Fort Worth International Airport, serves both as a domestic and international facility.

The Differences

U.S. Domestic Airports	International Airports
Similar types of physical structure and design.	Great variety in size and quality.
Jetway access to flights common in all but smallest facilities.	Jetways, bus, mobile lounge, and stairway access to flights.
Signs in English.	Mulitlingual signs and international symbols.
U.S. carriers dominate at hubs.	National carriers dominate in home country.
Airline agents check for correct documentation for international departures. International arrivals are not allowed.	Government officials operate passport/documentation checks and customs clearance.
Security checks varied in strictness.	Security strict, presence of armed guards, military personnel. International carry-on and checked baggage examined and departing passengers questioned.
No duty-free shops.	Duty-free shops.
No currency exchange facilities.	Foreign currency exchange common, many facilities in major airports.
Advance boarding passes and curbside baggage check common.	No advance boarding passes; curbside baggage check-in not allowed.
Schedules based on demand, creating peak and off-peak times.	Schedules based on international factors and noise control laws.
Visitors and people without tickets allowed in boarding areas.	Only ticketed passengers allowed in international boarding areas.

UP CLOSE

Frankfurt Main International Airport

As one of the world's ten busiest and largest airports, Frankfurt Main in Germany, serves as a gateway to Europe, the Middle East, Africa, and Asia. It is a world-class airport—virtually a city unto itself! Frankfurt is

Germany's largest airport and is the second largest in Europe in numbers of passengers handled each year. Only London-Heathrow handles more air travelers.

Frankfurt Main is the only one of the world's busiest airports that guarantees minimum connecting times of forty-five minutes. Amazing though that might be in a world of delays and aggravations, it is only the tip of the iceberg of what Frankfurt has to offer!

Scheduled Airlines:	85
Charter Carriers:	200 (Unscheduled, some infrequent)
Air Cargo	Number 3 in the world (after New York and Los Angeles)
Employees:	Over 36,000
Facilities:	Restaurants/catering (over 100), hotels, train station, car rental, conference rooms, clinic providing medical and dental care, pharmacy, duty-free shops, theaters (offering films in English and German), travel agency, post office, grocery store, banking facilities, florist, hairdresser, skittles alley (German bowling), gift shops, chapel, disco, baby/child-care rooms

Explorations

1. What is your city code? If you live in a very small town, give the code of the nearest major city.
2. What is the airport code for the nearest commercial passenger airport?
3. Are there other commercial passenger airports within a 150-mile radius of your town? If so, give their codes as well.
4. What is the name of your local airport (or closest commercial airport)? Explain how it got its name.
5. If your airport is a hub, is it a natural or artificial hub? For which carriers?

Enrichments

Do an Up Close report on your airport. Include facilities such as short-term and long-term parking and the costs; valet parking services and the cost; limousine services, and indicate the names of the airport hotels, car rental companies, travel agencies on site.

Air Fares: It's Not How Far You Fly!

In the travel industry there is much talk about classes of service. The term *class* refers in one sense to the quality of the service. The rule of thumb is the more you pay, the more you get. Hotels, cars, tours, cruises, and airlines all divide their products into low-, medium-, and high-priced items. That way, they have a broad range of products that appeal to a greater number of travelers.

As a travel professional, you have to understand the classes of service so you can explain to customers what quality of product they can expect to receive for the price they are paying. It would be nice if all travelers wanted always to pay "top dollar," but that isn't going to happen. You will most likely be selling from every price range, and most frequently from the very complicated and confusing budget ranges, so you will need to be familiar with the full range of products a supplier has to offer.

When you look at a seating chart for an aircraft, you will see that it is divided into compartments:

First class is the smallest and is located in the front of the plane. The seats are wider and more comfortable than those in the coach compartment, there is more leg room, and they may have footrests like lounge chairs and recline into an almost bedlike position. Meals are more elaborate and are served with linens and china. First-class passengers also receive free alcoholic beverages and headsets for in-flight movies and, for international flights, may also have separate check-in counters and special boarding lounges.

Business class is common on international flights and occupies a separate compartment between first and coach classes. The amenities are similar to those in first class, but not quite so elaborate. Business class was originally created to serve business travelers who wanted more comfort than coach class offered but who could not justify the expense of first class.

Coach class occupies the largest compartment on any commercial passenger airplane. All passengers flying on discount fares sit here. The jumbo aircraft have several compartments devoted to coach seating, and smaller aircraft may offer only coach seating. Meals and soft drinks are served at no charge, but passengers generally have to pay for alcoholic beverages and headsets for movies. The seats in the coach compartment are narrower and offer far less legroom than the seats in first or business class.

Sometimes clients complain that seats in coach are less comfortable than they once were. They are correct, but they probably don't realize that seat space is determined by airline policy, not by the companies that manufacture the planes. Seat space is determined by the width and pitch of the seat and the configuration of the aircraft. The pitch is the distance from the back of your seat to the back of the seat in front of you.

Our 747SP LuxuryLiner

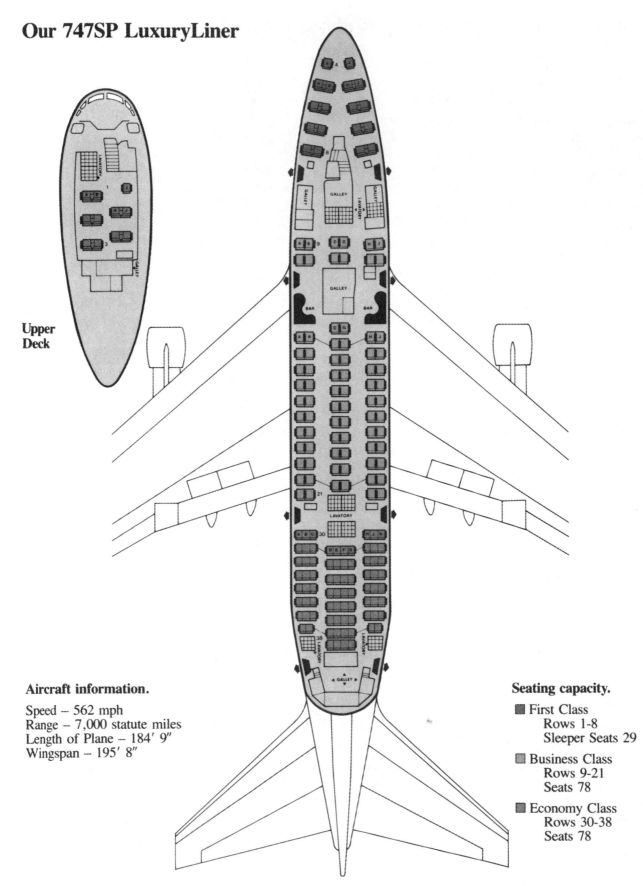

Upper Deck

Aircraft information.

Speed – 562 mph
Range – 7,000 statute miles
Length of Plane – 184' 9"
Wingspan – 195' 8"

Seating capacity.

■ First Class
Rows 1-8
Sleeper Seats 29

■ Business Class
Rows 9-21
Seats 78

■ Economy Class
Rows 30-38
Seats 78

Courtesy of American Airlines.

Modern planes are equipped with seat mounting tracks that permit the airlines to position the seats where they want them. Seat pitch for the planes on domestic routes is generally between thirty-one and thirty-three inches. On transatlantic flights, it is slightly more. Compare this with typical first-class seat pitch at forty inches, which, on a wide-body, can go up to sixty inches! In recent years, the airlines have responded to the intense pressure to improve their profitability by cramming as many seats as possible into the coach compartment. The seat space can vary from airline to airline and from flight to flight even when the same type of aircraft is being used.

It's Just Not Fare!

Whether a traveler sits in first, business, or coach depends upon the fare he or she pays. This may sound fairly simple, but within a given compartment—especially the coach compartment—there may be many different classes of service and hence many different fares. To further complicate matters, within a given compartment, the class of service doesn't actually change the level of "services rendered."

For example, among the passengers seated in the coach compartment there may be those who have unrestricted tickets (known as *full coach* fare tickets) for which they have paid as much as $1,000.00. They could be seated next to passengers traveling on discounted, restricted tickets (also known as *excursion fares* and *supersavers,* or even *ultrasavers*) who have paid less than $200.00. All the passengers will get coach service: their seats will look alike and be the same distance from each other; they'll all pay for drinks and headsets and eat the same sandwiches; and they'll be served by the same flight attendants. The *services rendered* will be substantially the same, only the amounts they paid for specific *fare classes* will be different.

To change the services rendered—meaning to get larger, more comfortable seats, better meals, free drinks, and so on—the passenger must change to a class of service in a different compartment of the aircraft. That is, a coach passenger must change his or her ticket (i.e., pay more) for business or first class. If you think this is confusing, you are absolutely right!

It may not seem fair that a full-coach passenger paying a very high fare sits in a smaller seat, eating a sandwich, and paying extra for his beer, while a first-class passenger who has not paid much more for her ticket is enjoying champagne and a hot meal, complete with hors d'oeuvres! All we can say is, that's the way it goes! There has to be a cutoff somewhere and, as long as air fares are structured this way, the flying public will be expected to grin and bear it!

Once fares were based primarily on distance flown: the further you flew, the more you paid. This was easy to accomplish since the CAB controlled routes (which limited the actual competition between carriers) and set fares. With deregulation and increased competition, that notion bit the dust!

After deregulation, the airlines were given the authority to set their own prices for tickets rather than have the government do it for them. They figured out very quickly that people who had not previously been air travelers would fly if the price were right. Hence, the **promo-**

Promotional Fare *Lower than normal fare offered by a carrier to promote travel to new cities on its route or to promote travel during off-season or slack periods.*

tional fare was born. Its purpose was to promote travel between certain cities at times when traffic was light.

The carriers wanted to attract travelers who previously got where they were going by bus, train, or car and also to create desire to travel in those who simply stayed at home. It worked! By 1986, the Air Transport Association (ATA) reported that 90 percent of all passengers on major scheduled carriers flew on discounted fares. But, make no mistake, the airlines do not want everyone flying at lower fares! The problem the airlines faced when they began offering promotional fares was how to get the new folks flying without losing money on the people who, in the past, paid full fare.

The initial solution to this problem was the "restricted" ticket. Quite simply, the lower the fare, the more *rules* the traveler must adhere to. Discount tickets must usually be booked and paid for in advance, be for travel during a certain time or period, and, in some cases, cannot be refunded or changed without substantial penalties. Typical restrictions are:

- Required Saturday night stay or required length of stay such as seven or fourteen days.
- Advance booking of seven, fourteen, or twenty-one days.
- Advance ticket purchase, sometimes within twenty-four hours of booking.
- Penalties for change or nonrefundability.
- Fares offered only on specific flights or specific days.

Clearly, a businessperson can't work within these parameters. He or she can hardly spend seven days in New York when one is all he or she needs to conduct a meeting! Furthermore, a business traveler often needs the flexibility to change or completely cancel reservations, so penalties and nonrefundable tickets could prove to be counterproductive.

Our "Fare" Weather Friends!

In offering low-cost seats that are purchased in advance, the airlines clearly do not want to fill up their planes with bargain seekers and then not have a seat available for the full-fare passenger at the last minute. That being said, the airlines also don't want seats going empty. What if full-fare passengers don't materialize at the last minute and the opportunity to sell more seats at discounted rates has passed? Early in deregulation, these were the questions that kept airline executives up at night chewing antacids.

To deal with this ever-present dilemma, the carriers developed sophisticated computer systems for estimating passenger numbers on any given flight, including how many people will show up to fly at the last minute, paying full price. They get these estimates by tracking bookings and ticket purchases day by day, season by season, and year by year for each flight in their schedules. The airlines call it *capacity control*, or *yield management*. Very simply, yield management means that the airlines want to be very careful not to sell seats at a discount when there may be a business traveler who needs that seat at the last minute and is willing to pay a much higher price.

This system means there will be different numbers of lower priced seats available on every flight. Only airline executives know how many discount seats will be allocated on a given flight or route, and, for them, this is "TOP SECRET" information! However, you don't have to have a fancy computer or be an airline executive to figure out that flights operating in popular business routes (such as Los Angeles to Chicago) and at popular business times (early morning and late afternoon) and on popular business days (Monday through Thursday) probably won't have very many discounted seats allocated for sale at discounted rates! All in all, there is a very simple principle to airline pricing:

Airlines will not discount seats when they believe they can fill their planes with passengers who are willing to pay top dollar!

Charters and Consolidators

Chartered transportation refers to the exclusive hire of a vehicle or other mode of transportation. Any vehicle that is licensed to transport passengers or cargo can be chartered; you can **charter** a plane, a bus, a car, a train, a ship, and so on.

There are companies that offer only chartered transportation—that is, they are not scheduled carriers. Transportation may also be chartered from scheduled carriers. Companies that specialize in charter transportation arc known as *supplemental carriers* because they tend to go when or where scheduled carriers do not, that is, thcy supplement scheduled service.

A charter flight operates under different rules than those for scheduled flights. A company that leases planes to individuals or groups will impose certain rules and conditions to protect itself and the passengers.

For the sake of clarity, it is easiest to divide air charters into two separate categories: private charters and public charters. Private charters are those whose seats are not available to the general public for sale. Companies, the government, schools, and other organizations may arrange for private charters to move groups of people from one destination to another.

The seats on a public charter may be sold to the general public and are often promoted and sold through travel agencies. Public charters are less expensive than scheduled transportation, but there is more risk involved for the traveler who chooses this type of transportation:

Charter *Exclusive hire of a carrier: airplane, ship, or motor-coach.*

1. Should there be a delay or cancellation, the traveler must wait for the charter operator to make other arrangements. His or her charter ticket will not be accepted by another carrier.

2. The charter ticket is good for one flight on a given day. Passengers will find it difficult, if not impossible, to make changes in their travel plans once they commit to charter transportation.

3. There have been incidences of charter carriers going out of business and leaving passengers stranded far from home. Many times these passengers did not travel with enough money or credit to purchase a ticket for a scheduled flight home.

The Future of Air Charters

The future of charters is somewhat "up in the air." Since deregulation, the charter business has been up and down. There are more scheduled carriers operating flights to foreign destinations and there has been rigorous competition for passengers, especially for the discretionary, or vacation travelers. The lower prices offered by scheduled carriers make charters less attractive to the traveling public.

Charters operated a booming business to Europe in the mid-1980s when the entire travel business was doing well. Then, terrorism hit and travel to Europe declined. With fewer people traveling, scheduled carriers lowered their prices and competed with the low-cost charters for business. Recession and stiff competition among international carriers kept scheduled carrier ticket prices low, further eliminating the need for lower cost competitors. The scarcity or proliferation of air charters is closely tied to the air fares of the scheduled carriers.

Jax Fax

When a client requests information about a charter, an agent does not look at any of the scheduled airline references. Charters are not listed in the *Official Airline Guide*, nor will they appear in any computerized reservation system.

One of the best sources of information about charters is found in *Jax Fax Travel Marketing Magazine*. This publication lists airline charters and scheduled group tours along with the names of the operators and their telephone numbers and addresses.

Consolidators

Consolidator A travel business that purchases airline seats at discounts from airlines that have seats they expect to remain unsold. The consolidator then re-sells the tickets at a mark-up to travel agencies or travelers.

Known as "bucket shops" in Great Britain where they originated over twenty years ago, **consolidators** offer deeply discounted fares for international flights. These fares are offered on many different airlines to destinations throughout the world. Consolidators are able to offer these discounts because they negotiate with airlines to take seats that the airlines know, or can safely predict, will be empty.

The consolidators market these seats, usually through ads in newspapers that list destinations and prices, but no airline names. Traditionally, consolidators have worked directly with the traveling public and not through travel agents. However, as the practice has spread throughout the United States and as more consolidators have sprung up, selling through agents has become more widespread. In some cases, consolidators pay commissions on the sale; in others, they quote a rate to the agent and the agent marks up the cost according to what profit the agency wishes to realize.

Purchasing deeply discounted seats may sound like the only way to fly, but there are some negatives!

- No travel advice or counseling is available.
- Available schedules for your chosen destination may be inconvenient; they may not operate at the times you prefer or may involve many connections.

- It is not always possible to select an airline, and the airline offering seats to your destination may not be at all familiar.
- Stiff penalties apply for changes or cancellations.

Employment Opportunities in the Airline Industry

When most people think about jobs with an airline, they first picture a pilot or flight attendant, then possibly a ticket counter agent or gate agent at the airport. This is perfectly understandable because these airline employees are the most highly visible to the public. However, there are many, many employment opportunities with the airlines ranging from top executives to reservationists to building maintenance crews.

Some airlines require their employees to have a college degree, some college education, or specialized training. In the cases of pilots, flight engineers, and cabin crew, highly specialized training is necessary and strict licensing requirements or government standards must be met. Airlines can be very selective in hiring because airline industry jobs are so highly prized and there are often many applicants for each position offered.

Airlines also generally promote from within. Except in the cases of hiring professionals such as lawyers or accountants, airlines begin their employees in entry-level jobs and move them up according to their ability and flexibility. To move ahead in an airline career, you are often required to move many times. If you begin as a reservationist with the desire to move into training, sales, or management, the next job up the ladder may well be in a field office, reservation center, city ticketing office or airport in another part of the country. Flexibility and the ability to relocate are two key elements in airline work!

Pay levels in the airline industry range from minimum wage (unskilled labor) to six-figure incomes (for executives). Promotability within the industry is generally excellent, benefits are good—including free and reduced rate travel—and the pay can also be excellent. Depending on the airline you work for and the job classification you have, you may be required to join a union.

Following are some positions in the airline industry:

Flight Crew

Pilot, Co-Pilot
Navigator, Flight Engineer
Flight Attendant

Ground Crew—Airport

Station Manager
Maintenance/Mechanics
Gate/Ticket Agent
Customer Service Agent
Baggage Handling, including lost luggage assistance
Private Lounge: Agent, Host/Hostess, Bartender

Reservations Centers

Reservation Agents:
   General Reservations
   Group Reservations
   Meeting and Conference Reservations and Services
   Tour Desk Agent
   International Reservations
Faring Specialists
Trainers
Managers, Supervisors
Customer Service
Clerical Support

Headquarters/Main Office

Executive Level
   Management
   Marketing
   Business Development
   Financial Analysts
Professional
   Lawyer
   Accountant
   Computer Programmer/Systems Analyst
Marketing, Public Relations
Clerical and Support

Field Offices

Management
Sales
Public Relations
Clerical

UP CLOSE

The Flight Attendant

Flight attendant positions are some of the most sought after in the travel industry. Many see the life of a flight attendant as glamorous and fun. Certainly, those aspects do exist, but there is more to the job than flying around the world serving passengers meals and drinks and staying in exotic places. There is a reason the profession is attractive: travel and, in time and with experience, good pay. One major airline reports that only one of every 100 applicants for flight attendant positions are actually hired!

History

The concept of the flight attendant has changed dramatically since its earliest times. The first flight attendants were all male. Flights were noisy and rough and were considered too unpleasant and unsafe for a woman!

In the 1930s, Ellen Church, a nurse, and Steve Stimpson, a passenger agent for United Airlines, tried to convince the airlines that having nurses stationed at large airports would be helpful in the event of an emergency. The idea didn't "take off" at first, but, later, it was decided that having a nurse on board the flights could help the fledgling industry by showing the public that it was safe to fly and that they would be well cared for.

Therefore, one of the first requirements for early flight attendants, or stewardesses as they were called, was to be a registered nurse. Although the medical training was seldom needed, a nurse's skills and training in handling people was a real plus. Other requirements for the early flight attendants were:

1. Female
2. Single
3. Under twenty-seven years old
4. 20/20 vision without glasses (there were no contact lenses back then!)
5. Very specific height and weight restrictions
6. Mandatory retirement at age thirty-two

If you got married, gained weight, had a growth spurt, or developed a need for glasses you were out of a job!

The early flight attendants pitched in and did a little of everything. They assisted in refueling the aircraft, transferring baggage when passengers changed planes, and mopping floors. Other duties included:

- Winding the cabin clocks and resetting them when the aircraft entered a new time zone.
- Putting away the "No Smoking" signs after take-off and landing.
- Checking the floor bolts on the wicker seats to make sure they were securely fastened to the floor of the plane.
- Dusting cabin window sills.
- Carrying the picnic baskets on board so that they could later serve the meals.
- Making sure the passengers opened the correct door when using the washroom.

The flight attendant profession has come full circle in its short sixty-plus year history. Males are now among the ranks again and, even though flight attendants are no longer required to be nurses, many of the current flight attendant methods of dealing with passengers are adaptations

Flight Attendants Today

Being a Flight Attendant

The Pluses

1. The opportunity to meet new and interesting people every day.
2. The chance to make new and lifelong friends.
3. A flexible schedule—not 9 to 5!
4. More time off than in most other jobs.
5. The possibility of living in or being based in a variety of cities.
6. Frequent travel to many places.
7. The opportunity to travel for free or at deep discounts.
8. Paid vacations, good benefits, attractive salaries.
9. Attractive uniforms that eliminate the necessity for an extensive wardrobe for work.
10. Increased benefits with seniority and experience.

The Minuses

1. No guarantee of where you will be assigned to work/live.
2. Reserve status from six months–five years.
3. Work days that may be fourteen-plus hours.
4. The necessity of dealing with all kinds of people (both the nice and the very demanding and rude), yet having to maintain a positive, friendly attitude at all times.
5. Absolute demand for punctuality and good attendance. Personal emergencies and needs must take second place.
6. Need to maintain good health regardless of exposure to extremes of weather and irregular hours.
7. Very strict regulations on appearance, including hair style, make-up, weight, and attitude.
8. Being away from home during holidays and on weekends.
9. "Time off" may actually be away from home.
10. Free travel is on a stand-by basis only. Available seats are given to personnel in order of seniority. A junior flight attendant might have to stand by for several flights before actually getting on a plane!

of nurses' techniques in dealing with patients. The primary role of flight attendants has not changed—that is, they are on board to help insure passenger safety and comfort.

Travel is a service business, and, for the airlines, merely providing safety and comfort in an efficient manner is not enough. In addition to a working knowledge of first aid and emergency procedures, flight attendants must also possess certain technical, psychological, and social skills to do their jobs well. Flight attendants must be quick thinkers and good leaders!

Today's flight attendants:

1. Work primarily for commercial passenger airlines.

2. Are directly responsible for insuring passenger safety and comfort.

3. Insure that the cabin is in order before flight begins by

    a. Verifying that emergency equipment (oxygen bottles, life vests, first-aid kits, mega phones, etc.) is in place, secured, and functional.

    b. Checking galley supplies to be sure there is enough and that all is in order.

    c. Checking the working condition of lavatories, cleanliness of aircraft, magazine selection.

    d. Greeting passengers as they board, assisting them in boarding and finding their seats, stowing carry-on baggage, arming doors (engaging escape slides attached to doors), and counting passengers.

4. Instruct passengers before take-off about location of safety information cards, location and type of emergency exits, location of exit lights and pathway lights, location and use of oxygen masks, location and operation of flotation devices, location of lighted signs, smoking/nonsmoking regulations, seat belt usage, and so forth, that is, covering all Federal Aviation Administration (FAA) regulations regarding passenger safety while on board.

5. Serve meals/beverages.

6. Aid in child care and assist the infirm, elderly, or handicapped.

7. Distribute reading materials and provide pillows and blankets as requested.

8. Deal effectively with medical emergencies and emergency evacuation procedures.

9. Stay qualified for emergencies and keep up with advances for every type of aircraft in the carrier's fleet. United, for example, has six different types of aircraft, the 737, 727, 757, 767, 747, and DC-10, all of of which have different configurations.

Explorations

Check your newspaper for airline advertisements. Are any special fares being offered? If so, answer the following:

1. What destinations are involved?

2. What is the fare quoted?

3. Does it indicate that "restrictions" apply? If so, what are the restrictions?

(If the restrictions are not specifically defined, call the airline and ask what they are.)

or

If you do not find any airline advertisements, select a domestic destination and call an airline to request information on lowest fares and their restrictions. *Example:* Your home city to New York City, Atlanta, Chicago, Denver or Dallas.

Enrichments

If you know someone who works for an airline, "interview" him or her to find out the following:

1. Position held.

2. How did he or she get a job with the airlines?

2. How long he or she has worked for the airline.

3. What was his or her first position and, if he or she has a different position now, how that evolved.

4. Is this person a union member and, if so, what does that mean to him or her.

5. Did this job (or any other position held with the airline) require special or on-going training?

6. What are the travel benefits offered by this airline to its employees?

or

If you do not know anyone who works for an airline, do the following:

1. Contact a major or national carrier for information on job opportunities and the process for applying for jobs.

2. Consult references at the public library or in your school and list what you believe would be the best steps to take in seeking airline employment.

Answers to U.S. Map Airport Codes

1. SEA	22. OMA	43. JAX
2. GEG	23. RAP	44. ATL
3. PDX	24. BIS	45. CHS
4. SFO	25. MSP	46. GSP
5. LAX	26. MKE	47. CLT
6. SAN	27. DSM	48. GSO
7. PHX	28. CHI*	49. RDU
8. TUS	29. DTW	50. ORF
9. LAS	30. CLE	51. DCA*
10. RNO	31. CVG	52. BWI
11. BOI	32. IND	53. PHL
12. GTF	33. SDF	54. PIT
13. SLC	34. BNA	55. EWR
14. DEN	35. MEM	56. JFK*
15. ABQ	36. LIT	57. BUF
16. DFW*	37. MSY	58. ALB
17. IAH*	38. JAN	59. BDL
18. ELP	39. BHM	60. PVD
19. OKC	40. TPA	61. BOS
20. MCI	41. MIA	62. PWM
21. STL	42. MCO	

Associated City/Airport Codes: *16. DAL   17. HOU   28. ORD
51. WAS/IAD   56. NYC/LGA

Aweigh We Go!

Where Are We Going?

After completing this section, you will:

1. Know how cruising as a vacation came to be and who cruises today.
2. Know why cruising is one of the most popular vacation choices.
3. Be able to explain why cruising is considered such a great value.
4. Understand the basics of cruise vacation pricing.

Industry Terms and Jargon

Air/Sea Package

Cruise Lines International Association (CLIA)

Deck Plan

Fly/Sail Package

Port Taxes

Shore Excursion

Stateroom (Cabin)

Ship Talk

It's impossible to discuss a cruise ship or even a rowboat without resorting to nautical terms. Learn these so you won't sound like a landlubber when you talk about cruising!

- *Aft:* Near, toward, or at the rear (stern) of a ship.
- *Amidship:* In or toward the middle (between bow and stern) of a ship.
- *Beam:* The breadth of a ship at the widest point.
- *Berth:* A bed.
- *Bow:* The front of a ship, also known as the prow.
- *Bridge:* A crosswise platform above the main deck of a ship from which the ship is controlled.
- *Bulkhead:* A vertical wall or partition that separates a ship into compartments.
- *Bulwark:* The part of a ship's side above the upper deck.
- *Companionway:* A stairway between decks.
- *Crow's Nest:* A small lookout platform located near the top of a ship's mast.
- *Debark:* To disembark.
- *Disembark:* To go ashore from a ship.
- *Dock:* The area of water alongside a pier or between two piers where a ship is stationed for loading, unloading, and repair.
- *Draft:* The distance from the waterline to the lowest point of the ship under the water.
- *Embark:* Board a ship and depart from port.
- *Fathom:* A unit of six feet in length used in determining the depth of water.
- *Fore:* Near, toward, or at the front of a ship.
- *Freighter:* Primarily a cargo ship, with some accommodations for passengers.
- *Galley:* A kitchen on a ship.
- *Gangway:* An opening in the bulwark of a ship through which passengers may enter and leave.
- *Gross Registered Tonnage:* A guide to measure the size of a ship based on the enclosed square footage of usable passenger space (100 cubic feet = 1 gross registered ton). GRT is a measure of size, not weight.
- *Hatch:* An opening in the deck of the ship leading to a cargo hold.
- *Helm:* The steering gear of a ship.
- *Hold:* The lower interior area of a ship where cargo is stored.
- *Hovercraft:* A high-speed boat that rides on a cushion of air over the waves.
- *Hull:* The body of a ship exclusive of masts, sails, yards, and rigging.
- *Hydrofoil:* A high-speed boat whose entire hull is supported by fins or foils so that it is raised clear of the water when moving.
- *Knot:* A nautical mile per hour, 14 percent longer than a land mile. A unit of speed, not distance.
- *League:* Three nautical miles.

- *Leeward:* The direction away from the wind.
- *Log:* A record of a ship's speed, progress, and shipboard events of navigational importance.
- *MS:* Motorship.
- *MV:* Motor Vessel.
- *Port:* The left side of a ship when facing the bow. Also, the places and cities where ships may dock.
- *Porthole:* A small circular window in a ship's side.
- *Prow:* The bow of a ship.
- *Ship's Registry:* A ship's registered nationality.
- *SS:* Steamship.
- *Stabilizer:* A retractable fin that extends from the underside of a ship to reduce rolling and swaying.
- *Starboard:* The right side of a ship when you are facing the bow.
- *Stern:* The rear of a ship.
- *Tender:* A small boat used to transport passengers between ship and shore when the ship cannot dock.
- *TS:* Twin-Screw (ship).
- *TSS:* Turbine Steamship.
- *Tug:* A small boat equipped with heavy engines for towing ships.
- *Wake:* The waves churned up by a ship's passing.
- *Windward:* Direction facing the wind.

Bon Voyage, Dahling!

No aspect of the travel business has a more illustrious and romantic past than the cruise industry. Many of our forefathers came by ship to America in the seventeenth century, but the passage on the *Mayflower* could hardly be called a cruise. During the late nineteenth and early twentieth centuries, millions of European immigrants traveled like cattle in the crowded, filthy steerage areas of the transatlantic liners. This wasn't cruising either. Even the great "crossings" of the Atlantic by the fabulously rich and the merely well-to-do on ships of astonishing luxury did not exactly constitute cruising as we know it today.

When one traveled by sea in the past, the emphasis was on getting to the destination, and the way to do that was by *ocean liner*—an ocean-going vessel that followed a fixed route and schedule. Just as passengers could look up train schedules between cities, they could also look up the schedules of the arrivals and departures of ocean liners to and from the ports of the world. While the ports of call, or destinations, are still important, modern cruise lines have shifted the emphasis to the journey or the ship or, more simply, the "cruise" is why you go!

When jet airplanes made crossing the Atlantic a trip of a few hours, rather than a journey of a few days, the demand for transportation by ship dropped sharply. By 1958, almost as many people crossed the Atlantic by air as by ship. One year later, the balance shifted, and over 60 percent of all travelers heading across the Atlantic traveled by air.

Some ship lines tried to convince the would-be air traveler that "getting there" was half the fun. That was a fairly desperate attempt to hold on to passengers since travel across the Atlantic could be rough and cold; business travelers didn't need to have several days of "fun" in reaching their destinations; and most tourists decided that it would be far better to spend more time on land and their money on souvenirs! By the early 1970s, planes had replaced ships as the basic means of getting from the United States to Europe and beyond, and scheduled ocean liners had become a thing of the past. Today, only Cunard Line's *Queen Elizabeth II* and a few other ships that are being repositioned from one cruise area to another (i.e., Europe to the Caribbean) offer transatlantic sailings.

The ship lines that survived the advent of the Jet Age gave up their point-to-point passenger transportation services in favor of pleasure cruising. Of the many lines that existed, only a couple such as Cunard and Holland America Line exist today, and Holland America, although operating under the same name, is actually now a subsidiary company of a relative newcomer, Carnival Cruise Lines. Some of the ships still exist, of course, but they have been refitted or renovated and operate with new owners, names, itineraries, and crews. Those that did not survive as cruise ships were scrapped, turned into freight vessels, or docked as tourist attractions.

Prior to the Jet Age, a few ship lines had already begun developing a cruise market to help carry them through the transatlantic off-season from Christmas through March. Cruises departed from New York to Bermuda and the Bahamas with great fanfare. Newspaper reporters and photographers recorded the glamorous departures of the rich and famous. For the affluent, the cruise vacation offered individual attention, extensive amenities, service, and haute cuisine. Some of the wealthiest had their staterooms prepared before departure by their own private decorators and even supplied their own mattresses and linens!

These early cruise passengers came mainly from the major metropolitan areas of the Northeast as they had easy access to the port of New York. As transportation from all regions of the United States to the port cities improved, cruise companies with an eye on the future began to look beyond the limited seasonal travel of the socially elite for a larger market among the vast American middle class.

This was no small task since many people had preconceived notions about travel by ship. There were objections to be overcome then that are still raised by would-be cruisers today. Former soldiers and sailors recalled the unpleasant conditions on troop ships during wartime; weather watchers were frightened of hurricanes and other adverse conditions; many prospective passengers were concerned about seasickness; and still others worried about being "outclassed" in the formal shipboard atmosphere and presence of wealthy "society" passengers.

But the survivors in the passenger ship business did their jobs well! They eliminated the classes of service, fitted all cabins with air conditioning and private baths, added recreational facilities, and equipped their ships with stabilizers and radar. The stabilizers helped to reduce the pitch and roll that causes some people to experience seasickness and the radar allowed them to make itinerary changes to avoid bad weather conditions. The shiplines also bid farewell to New York City as their major port and headed their luxury vessels south to Miami so they could more quickly deliver their passengers to the sunny playgrounds of the Caribbean.

From Slow Boat to Love Boat

So, as you can see, the most successful of the cruise lines have managed to overcome customer objections, and middle America is putting out to sea in droves! In fact, cruising is the fastest growing segment of the travel industry and represents over $60 billion in sales each year!

By the end of the 1970s, demand for cruise vacations was strong, and the existing cruise lines had reached maximum capacity. In the years 1980–1986, over $3 billion was spent in new cruise ship construction—and they're still building! Here are some of the new arrivals of the 1990s:

Line	Ship	Passengers	Launched
Costa Cruise Line	Costa Allegra	800	1992
Club Med	Club Med 2	400	1992
Crown Cruise Line	Crown Jewel	798	1992
Norwegian Cruise Line	Dreamward	1,246	1992
Holland America	Statendam	1,264	1993
Carnival	Sensation	2,040	1993
Holland America	Maasdam	1,264	1993
Costa Cruises	Costa Romantica	1,296	1993
Crown Cruise Line	Crown Dynasty	820	1993
Norwegian Cruise Line	Windward	1,200	1993
Carnival	Fascination	2,040	1994
Holland America	Ryndam	1,264	1994
Silversea*	Silver Cloud	314	1994
Silversea*	Silver Wind	314	1994/95
Princess Cruise Line	Sun Princess	1,700	1995
Carnival	Imagination	2,040	1995
Carnival	"The Ultra Mega Ship"**	2,600+	1996

*Silversea Cruises Ltd., a new line of the 1990s, entered the cruise market with 300-passenger, all-suite ships. In addition to having much larger cabins than their competitors, Silversea ships also offer private verandas in most cabin/suite categories.

**Yet to be named. This ship will be the largest passenger ship ever constructed!

When passenger capacity is quoted, it is usually based on the number of people the ship can accommodate in single and double cabins. If single cabins are filled (with just one person, of course), and all the other cabins are filled with two people, the ship is said to be operating at full, or 100 percent, capacity. Since some "double" cabins often have berths for three and four passengers, it is possible for a ship to operate at over 100 percent occupancy. A cruise ship with a capacity of 2,600 may actually be able to accommodate as many as 3,000!

Although new ships add to cruise passenger capacity, it's not all "plus" berths. Ships do get old and outdated and are sometimes retired from service. Also, in the early 1990s, new Safety of Life at Sea (SOLAS) regulations required ships to meet new safety standards that involved expensive refurbishing, and many of the older ships were taken out of service because undertaking the expense of the procedures simply just didn't make economic sense!

In 1980, the industry reported 1.4 million cruise passengers. By 1990, that number had grown to a whopping 4 million, the vast majority of whom were U.S. citizens! The cruise industry has stated a goal of 10 million passengers by the turn of the century. Sounds incredible, but when you consider that only 5 percent of the population has ever cruised, it's readily apparent there's plenty of room for growth!

Love at First Sail!

Does everybody love the Love Boat? It would seem so. Cruise lines report an impressively high level of customer satisfaction, and repeat cruisers seem to be the rule not the exception! Why is cruising so popular? Because the modern cruise industry offers travelers just about everything they could hope for in a complete prepaid vacation.

Cruises vary in length from a few days to several months. You can travel nowhere—just out to sea and back again—or to any of the exotic ports from Antarctica to Zihuatenejo. You can select cruises for relaxation or education. You can gamble, shoot skeet, or listen to lectures by your favorite professional athlete or investment analyst. You can eat until you can't stand the sight of food. You can enjoy Broadway shows and Las Vegas-style entertainment. You can swim, sun, dance the night away, and then sleep until noon. You can be waited on hand and foot and only be encouraged to ask for more! You can find almost anything on a modern cruise ship—perhaps even your heart's desire. Cruises, for all their modern itineraries and technological advancement, have lost none of their romantic promise!

UP CLOSE

Carnival: A Major Cruise Line

In 1972, Israeli businessman Ted Arison, a co-founder of what is now Norwegian Cruise Line, established Carnival Cruise Lines. With the Boston-based tour operator, American International Travel Service

(AITS), he negotiated a $6.5 million financing package to purchase the eleven-year-old, 900 passenger cruise ship, *Empress of Canada*.

The ship was renamed the *Mardi Gras* and was rushed into service with nearly catastrophic results! The ship ran aground on its maiden voyage and stranded 300 travel agents. Luckily, no one was injured in the mishap, but it was a very embarrassing beginning!

Over the next three years, Carnival suffered heavy losses, and the fledgling company teetered on the edge of bankruptcy. In 1975, Ted Arison bought AITS for $1.00 and took on the responsibility of the $5 million debt incurred in starting the cruise line. The company made a profit within a month, and the *Mardi Gras* finished the year with a passenger occupancy of over 100 percent! By the end of 1975, Carnival bought a second ship, the *Empress of Britain* and renamed her the *Carnivale*. In 1978, Carnival added the *Festivale* (formerly the *Transvall Castle*) to its fleet and has never looked back!

Through its novel concept and marketing of the "fun ships," Carnival single-handedly changed consumer perception of the cruise vacation from formal, stuffy, and expensive to affordable, exciting, and fun for all ages! Today, Carnival is the world's largest and most profitable cruise company. With its subsidiaries Holland America and Windstar Cruises and its affiliate Seabourn Cruises, Carnival will, by the year 2000, offer cruises on at least 25 ships and have a total passenger capacity in excess of 30,000!

In early 1993, Carnival, clearly no stranger to novel concepts and creative marketing, announced the addition of yet another cruise line to its growing family—Fiesta Marina Cruises. This line was established to cater exclusively to the Latin American market. Carnival's second ship, the *Carnivale*, was renamed the *Fiesta Marina*, and the on-board cruise experience was designed to appeal to the Latin American way of life.

On the *Fiesta Marina*, all staff members are Spanish-speaking; the ports of call are predominantly Spanish-speaking; entertainment is selected to appeal to Latin American tastes; and dinner hours are 7:30 P.M. (early seating) and 9:30 P.M. (late seating) to reflect the Latin American and European preference for later dining.

Carnival is a U.S. owned and operated company, but you would not necessarily know it to look at the ships' flags. Most Carnival ships are registered in Liberia and fly its flag—a "flag of convenience." Ship lines often register their ships in countries other than their ownership to avoid strict controls, high taxes, and crippling labor costs.

Here's just a sampling of what Carnival offers today:

Ship	Route
Jubilee	Los Angeles to the Mexican Riviera
Celebration	Miami to eastern Caribbean ports
Ecstasy	Miami to the Bahamas
Fantasy	Miami to the Bahamas
Holiday	Miami to western Caribbean ports
Festivale	San Juan to southern Caribbean ports

Tropicale	San Juan to southern Caribbean ports
Sensation	Miami to eastern and western Caribbean ports

Add to these the ships of Holland America, Windstar, and Seabourn, which offer itineraries in the Caribbean, through the Panama Canal, up the Alaskan Inside Passage, throughout the Mediterranean, and around Southeast Asia, and you have a very impressive list of destinations and ships to suit most any traveler's tastes.

The Modern Cruise Ship

A Look Under the Hood, Behind the Doors, and in the Closets

And what are the modern ships like? Just take a look at the following list of statistics for Royal Caribbean's *Sovereign of the Seas,* a ship with a capacity of 2,282 passengers and a gross tonnage of 73,192. She is as long as three football fields and as tall in the water as the Statue of Liberty is on land. In addition, she has:

- 14,000 tons of steel—twice that of the Eiffel Tower, 70 times that of the Statue of Liberty.
- 807 miles of electrical cable—enough to stretch from Washington, D.C., to Miami.
- Forty-three miles of piping and four miles of corridors.
- 20,000 electrical fixtures, 2,000 telephones and 18 elevators.
- 150,700 square feet of open deck—as much as fifty tennis courts.
- 16,146 square feet of galley area and 56,500 cubic feet of cold storage area.
- 710,415 square feet of interior space—one-tenth the size of the Pentagon.
- Its engines generate 13,000,000 watts of power—enough to supply the needs of a town of 10,000 people.

We've come a long way from the *Pinta,* the *Nina* and the *Santa Maria!*

A Walk Around the Decks

Deck Plan *The layout or "map" of a ship's decks that shows cabin locations, lounges, dining rooms, swimming pools, and so on. In cruise brochures, the cabins are generally color coded in the deck plans to indicate price category.*

Cruise lines are very careful to provide detailed **deck plans** for each of their ships so both the booking agent and cruiser will have an understanding of the ship's layout prior to sailing. Deck plans can be found in their brochures and in the *CLIA Cruise Manual.* The deck plans in the cruise line brochures are easier to read and understand because cabin categories, special areas, and so on are color coded.

There are a few standard deck names, such as the *bridge deck,* from which the captain and officers perform their duties (and where their own cabins are often located); the *boat deck,* where the lifeboats are kept with their supplies of life preservers and emergency equipment; the *sports* or *sun decks,* where putting, skeet shooting, aerobics classes, shuffleboard, sunbathing and so on take place; and the *promenade deck* which has a circumferential walkway for strolling or jogging.

Ships today do not necessarily use the standard deck names. Deck names can be as plain as "Main" deck or as evocative as "Lido," "Caribe," or "Riviera" deck. What a deck is called is not important, but what goes on there is! In the deck plan that follows for the *Sovereign of the Seas*, taken from the *CLIA Cruise Manual*, you will see that there is a genuine promenade deck with a walkway around the ship's entire perimeter, a bridge deck, a sun deck, and a main deck. And, as you can see, there are also other decks with more fanciful names, such as Mariner and Show-time, and decks with very plain names, such as "A" Deck and "B" Deck.

Other aspects of life on a cruise ship are also readily apparent from a glance at the deck plan. There is a card room and a library for those who favor quiet indoor activity, two cinemas, and a casino. There is a beauty parlor, shops, kid's and teens' room, two swimming pools, saunas, and a gymnasium so passengers can stay "shipshape"! There are also numerous restaurants, bars, lounges, a discotheque, and even a medical center should you throw your back out with all that prome-nading, exercising, and dancing.

While a deck plan provides quite a bit of information, there are also written descriptions in the brochures to fill in additional details. Fol-lowing the deck plan of the *Sovereign of the Seas* is the outline from the *CLIA Cruise Manual* that lists the ship's specifications. By the time you have studied all this information, you will know almost as much about the *Sovereign* as if you'd recently done a shipboard inspection yourself!

But, if you want to know even more, there are numerous refer-ence materials to help you out! Here is just a sampling:

- *Berlitz Complete Handbook to Cruising*
- *Cruise Views Magazine*
- *Fieldings Worldwide Cruises*
- *Ford Guides*
- *OAG Worldwide Cruise and Shipline Guide*
- *Official Cruise Guide*
- *OHRG Guide Book—Cruise Directory*

A Room of One's Own on the High Seas

As you have discovered, a difference in air fares does not necessarily imply a great difference in the size or quality of the seats within a given compartment on a plane. On a cruise ship, there can be quite a differ-ence in both price and configuration between one cabin category and another, and, on a given deck, there may be several categories of cab-ins from which to choose. The same deck that has suites and large deluxe outside cabins may have some small inside cabins with upper and lower berths.

The vertical configuration of a ship is as important as the horizon-tal. To determine whether a particular cabin is worth the price, travel-ers will want to know not only how big it is and how many and what kind of beds it has, but they will also want to know its exact location.

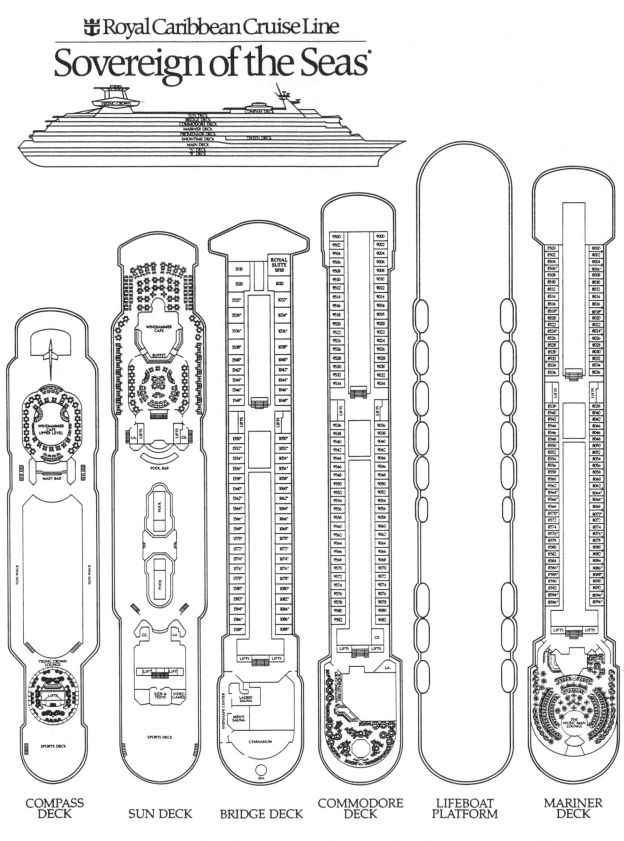

⚓ Royal Caribbean Cruise Line
Sovereign of the Seas

COMPASS DECK

SUN DECK

BRIDGE DECK

COMMODORE DECK

LIFEBOAT PLATFORM

MARINER DECK

Key: *Stateroom has third berth available (Pullman upper or convertible sofa).

**Stateroom has third and fourth Pullman berth available. In most staterooms, two lower beds can be combined to form a queen-size bed.

Courtesy of CLIA.

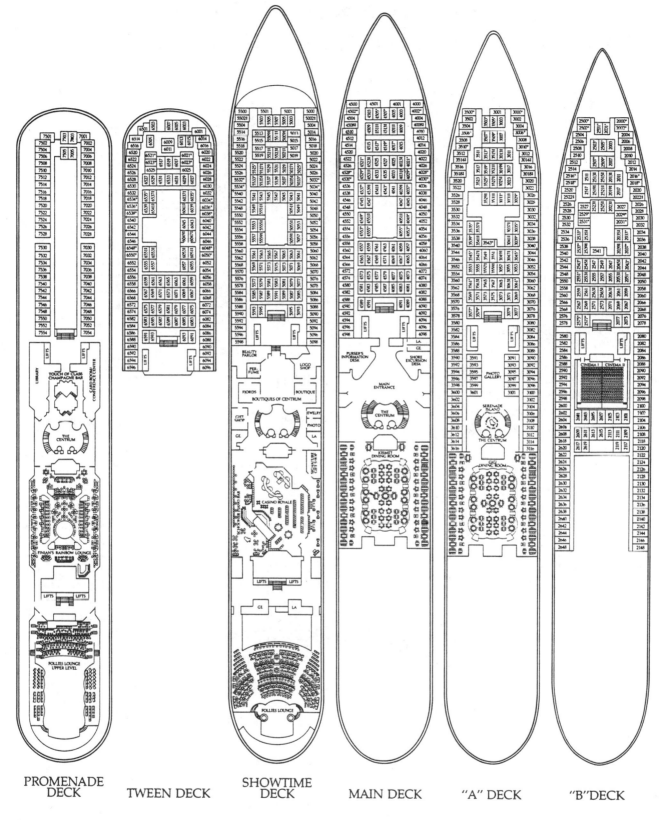

PROMENADE DECK   TWEEN DECK   SHOWTIME DECK   MAIN DECK   "A" DECK   "B" DECK

↕ Connecting staterooms.

Courtesy of CLIA.

CLIA Description

PUBLIC ROOM CAPACITIES

NAME	CAPACITY
KISMET DINING ROOM	650
GIGI DINING ROOM	650
FOLLIES LOUNGE	1050
THE MUSIC MAN LOUNGE	675
FINIAN'S RAINBOW LOUNGE	450
ANYTHING GOES NIGHTCLUB	330
SCHOONER PIANO BAR	100
TOUCH OF CLASS CHAMPAGNE BAR	50
FRENCH CAFE	50
VIKING CROWN LOUNGE	275
CASINO ROYALE	300
CARD/CONFERENCE ROOM	20/100
CINEMA (2)	146
WINDJAMMER CAFE	900

NAME: SOVEREIGN OF THE SEAS

COMPANY: ROYAL CARIBBEAN CRUISE LINE
ORIGINALLY BUILT: 1988
COUNTRY OF REGISTRY: NORWAY
SPEED: 19 KNOTS
RADIO CALL LETTERS: L.A.E.B.
NORMAL CREW SIZE: 825
NATIONALITY OF CREW
      OFFICERS: NORWEGIAN
      HOTEL STAFF: INTERNATIONAL

SIZE/CAPACITY

GROSS REGISTERED TONNAGE: 73,192
LENGTH: 880 FEET   BEAM: 106 FEET
TOTAL CAPACITY (Incl. uppers): 2,690
NORMAL CRUISE CAPACITY (Basis 2): 2,280
SPACE RATIO: 30.76

AMENITIES

COMPLIMENTARY DECK CHAIRS	FULLY AIR CONDITIONED
2 OUTDOOR SWIMMING POOLS	MASSAGE/SAUNA ROOMS
WHIRLPOOL	SHIPSHAPE FITNESS CENTER
NON-SKID JOGGING SURFACE	PING PONG
SHUFFLEBOARD	BASKETBALL
GOLF DRIVING	CASINO
MEDICAL FACILITY	DUTY-FREE GIFT SHOPS
BOUTIQUES	VIDEO ARCADE
PHOTO SHOP	CENTRUM SHOPS
PHOTO GALLERY	PRINT SHOP
LAUNDRY/DRY CLEANING	BARBER SHOP/BEAUTY SALON
WIRELESS SERVICE/FAX SERVICE	SHORE EXCURSION DESK
CLOSING STOCK QUOTATIONS	POSTAL SERVICE
SAFE/DEPOSIT BOXES	SHIP-TO-SHORE TELEPHONE
LIBRARY	DAILY NEWS UPDATE
RELIGIOUS SERVICES	BABYSITTING SERVICES
CHILDREN'S CENTER	

ACCOMMODATIONS

TYPE	NO. OUTSIDE	NO. INSIDE
ROYAL SUITE	1	
SUITES	3	
DELUXE	58	
W/2 LOWERS	722	273
QUEEN-SIZE BED	712	ALL
UPPER AND LOWER	66*	146
TOTAL	722	418
TOTAL CABINS	1,141	

*ADDITIONAL 50 DELUXE CABINS ARE UPPER AND LOWER ALSO.

OTHER USEFUL INFORMATION

NO. OF SITTINGS FOR DINNER:	2
USUAL DINNER HOURS:	6:15 PM/8:30 PM
DINING ROOM DRESS CODE:	VARIES EACH NIGHT
SPECIAL DIET & KOSHER MEALS:	LOW FAT, LOW CHOLESTEROL
TIPPING POLICY:	WAITER: $3.00 PER PERSON PER DAY
	BUSBOY: $1.50 PER PERSON PER DAY
	CABIN STEWARD: $3.00 PER PERSON PER DAY

Courtesy of CLIA.

Is it fore, aft, or center? The center is affected less by the pitching and rolling motion of the ship. Is it near the dining room, over the discotheque, or next to the elevator or stairway? Some people want to be close to these for convenience, and others want to be farther away to avoid noise. And, of course, everyone wants to know whether his or her cabin is on the outside with windows or on the inside with none.

Even on a very large ship the **staterooms (cabins)** are relatively small. These floating resort hotels usually have twin beds that can often be arranged to form a double/queen. In some of the more compact cabins, the beds are configured as upper and lower berths, like bunk beds! On the newer ships, double, queen- and even king-size beds are available. Most cabins have bathrooms with toilets, sinks, and showers; tubs may only be available in the more expensive cabin categories.

Stateroom Sleeping accommodations on a ship; also known as a cabin.

Cabins on the outside of the ship generally have porthole windows, and deluxe cabins and suites frequently have larger windows. Very deluxe cabins and suites may even have their own verandas or balconies. There are closets and dressers, but storage space is limited and suitcases are usually kept in a trunk room rather than in the cabin.

At Your Service!

The *Sovereign of the Seas* has a total staff of 825 people to look after the ship and its passengers—a passenger/staff ratio of three to one! The ratio of passengers to staff is an important consideration. A surprising number of cruise passengers have responded in cruise surveys that they consider the level of service far more important than the itinerary, the price of the cruise, or the size of the cabin.

In addition to the following VIPs of a cruise ship's staff, you will also find chefs, waiters, busboys, and a maitre d' in the dining room; deck stewards to serve you on deck; and wine and bar stewards to bring your drinks. There will be a photographer, salespeople in the cruise ship shops, a trainer and masseuse in the gymnasium/healthclub, and a hairdresser. There may also be nursery attendants and a director of childrens' programs. Some of these people may do double duty as entertainers in the shows, but there may be extra singers, dancers, and musicians on board as well.

And, although you may not see them or have contact with them, there are also the very important members of the maintenance crew. They are responsible for keeping things "shipshape"—from oiling the engines to sweeping the floors!

Who's Who in the Crew?

Captain: The master of the ship who guides and directs it and its crew.

Chief engineer: The supervisor and director of the engine room.

Chief purser: The director of services relating to banking, mail, ship-to-shore telephones, general information, and accommodations.

Chief steward: The director of all cabin services, responsible for the cleanliness of all public areas.

Ship's doctor: Provider of treatment for routine medical problems as well as emergencies.

Cruise director: Coordinator of social activities and entertainment; also offers advice, assistance, and information to passengers—sometimes in lectures and seminars.

Cabin steward: Cleans cabins and attends to passengers' room needs.

Love Boat or Gravy Boat?

Just a quick glance at a cruise brochure or a deck plan with its many restaurants, dining rooms, and cafes will tell you that food plays a major role in cruising. If you are determined to eat every time food is served on a cruise ship, you will be eating six or seven times a day. If that's not enough, you can also order room service, as you would in a hotel, and most cruise lines have food and beverage managers who can assist you in planning a private party.

The following dinner menu, which is typical of cruise fare, will give you an idea how extensive and elaborate dining on a cruise ship can be. If you dined on a package or independent tour the way you can on a cruise, it would increase the cost of your trip considerably . But, on a ship, the cost of all your meals is included in the one price you pay!

Dinner Menu

Cold Appetizers	Fresh Fruit Cup, Oysters on the Half Shell, Smoked Norwegian Salmon
Hot Appetizers	Stuffed Shrimps, Sauteed Baby Eggplant with Tomatoes and fresh Mozzarella
Soups	French Onion, Crayfish Bisque, Chilled Borscht
Salads	Caesar Salad, Tossed Garden Salad, Chilled Asparagus Vinaigrette
Entrées	Swordfish Steak with Maitre d'hotel Butter
	Roast Leg of Lamb with Fresh Herbs and Garlic
	Filet Mignon with Bernaise Sauce
	Veal Scaloppine Lightly Breaded and Sautéed in Lemon Butter
Vegetables	Green Beans with Almonds, Wild Rice, New Potatoes, Asparagus with Hollandaise
	Imported Cheeses
	Fresh Fruits
Desserts	Cheesecake with Strawberries, Baked Alaska, Chocolate Cream Pie, Lemon Sorbet
Beverages	Coffee, Selection of Imported Teas, Milk, Soft Drinks

---

On most cruise ships, dinner is served at two seatings: early and late. Passengers decide prior to cruising what seating times they prefer and have their agents confirm their dining assignments in advance.

You can go just about anywhere in the world on a cruise, and you don't have to be content spending time only in the port cities. Cruises generally include optional **shore excursions** to interesting sites within reasonable driving distance. Shore excursions, along with alcoholic beverages and gratuities, are among the few items not included in the price of a cruise.

Sometimes, passengers like to make arrangements for their own shore excursions. Travelers should be forewarned that, while this might work in some locales, in others the available taxis, buses, and guides might already be taken by the ground operators who will be handling the excursions for the cruise lines. It may also be true that the packaged excursion is a better value than the one that is individually negotiated.

On longer cruises, shore excursions can be more elaborate and may take several days. Increasingly, cruise lines are offering land packages that can be added on before the cruise begins or after it ends. Premier Cruise Lines, the Official Cruise Line of Walt Disney World®, offers vacation packages in Walt Disney World with each of its cruises. Not surprisingly, Premier also bills itself as a "family" cruise ship and offers special pricing for families, expanded children's activities, educational programs, and Disney characters on board.

All Ashore Who's Going Ashore!

Shore Excursion *A tour of a port city or area usually by bus, which departs from shipside. Shore excursions are available for purchase in advance or on the ship.*

Up a Lazy River

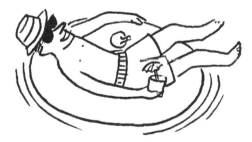

Whatever sea-loving vacationers may want, they can probably find it afloat somewhere in the world. And, furthermore, it certainly isn't necessary to be on the high seas to take a cruise! There are excellent cruises available on the world's major rivers, such as the Mississippi, the Danube, the Amazon, the Nile, the Rhine, the Seine, the Thames, and the Yangtze.

Equally interesting are the barge cruises of the smaller rivers and canals of France, Holland, and England. These barges have been converted to small luxury passenger vessels, specializing in personal service and gourmet cuisine. Because the barges are small, they can also offer their passengers specially planned excursions and activities such as private tours of chateaux and wineries or ballooning over the countryside.

Yacht charters and scheduled cruises on sailing ships are becoming increasingly popular in the Caribbean, Mediterranean, and the Greek Islands. Charters are available both with and without crews. Passengers who like lending a hand and hoisting a sail, but don't want to do *all* the work, can sail on Windjammer Barefoot Cruises and enjoy an informal atmosphere and some "light" sailing activity! Most of the masted vessels are much smaller than the traditional cruise ships and can navigate areas that the "big ones" can't consider. Passengers on these cruises can enjoy a more intimate setting and visits to little known islands, beaches, and bays.

Passengers who are adventurous and have very flexible schedules can also travel by freighter. *Ford's Freighter Travel Guide*, published twice a year, is a good source of information. While the few passenger cabins are comfortable and the passengers are made welcome, they are always secondary to the cargo. Scheduled stops are abbreviated or extended to suit the demands of the businesses that are supplying the cargo, even if the passengers are inconvenienced. Despite these shortcomings, the limited cabins fill up far ahead of time, so advance planning is essential.

The last of the waterborne vessels that passengers may prebook is the humble ferry. *Thomas Cook European Timetable* and the *Thomas Cook Overseas Timetable* are essential reference texts for schedules. Islands are generally linked by ferry services, so it's no surprise to find them plowing back and forth in Japan, the British Isles (linking Britain to Ireland and the Continent), the Philippines, Greece (around the islands), and Italy.

Ferries are also common in Alaska, the Maritime Provinces of Canada, and in the Scandinavian countries. Some take passengers only, some take cars—even railroad cars!—and some even have cabins for overnight passage. One of the most famous and economical is the Star Ferry that travels back and forth, day and night, between Hong Kong Island and Kowloon.

The Dollars and Sense of Cruising

Why take a cruise? Because it is fun *and* an exceptionally good value! Cruise vacations offer a tremendous amount for the money, but they aren't necessarily cheap! But, before talking about the final dollar amount, first it's important to know how cruises are priced. Basically, the price of a cruise is determined by four factors:

1. *The ship (or cruise line) chosen.* There are ships and lines that are priced to attract all income levels—from budget to ultra-expensive.

2. *The length of the cruise.* It only stands to reason that, the longer the cruise, the higher the cost!

3. *The time of the year.* Each cruise destination has its "season"—that is, the time of the year that promises the best weather and is most popular with vacationers. Obviously, not many people would be interested in cruising to Alaska in mid-winter, and it would make no sense to offer cruises at that time of the year. However, cruises to Alaska are offered in the spring and fall when it is much cooler than the summer, and those cruises are traditionally priced less than those offered in the warmer months.

4. *The cabin category selected.* The location and size of the cabin are key in cruise pricing. Outside cabins are always more expensive than comparable inside cabins. Deluxe cabins and suites are, of course, more expensive than standard or unusually small cabins. Many people feel that the size and location of a cabin is irrelevant and that travelers should select the most economical. The reasoning is that most cruisers spend very little time in their cabins, so why spend more money? This point of view was probably more defendable in the past when destinations were all-important and virtually all cruise cabins were minuscule. On today's pleasure ships, where the ship and the actual cruising are often as important as the destination itself, the argument for larger, outside cabins is certainly valid!

Cabin location is also a key factor in pricing. As a rule of thumb, the higher a cabin is above water, the more expensive it will be. Outside cabins on the higher decks have better views and, of course, all cabins on the higher decks are closer to the public areas and activities. Cabins located amidship are also more expensive than their forward and aft counterparts because the pitch and roll of the ship are less pronounced. However, when deciding on the perfect cabin, remember that even the traveler being tossed about in the least expensive, farthest-away cabin enjoys the same food, service, entertainment, and activities as does the passenger enjoying the view from his or her suite!

Once ship, cabin, date, and length of cruise have been decided, figuring the cost is pretty easy. Cruise lines print their prices in their brochures and prices are given *per person, not per cabin.* It is very difficult to give an estimate of the cost of a cruise, because, as we have seen, there are so many different types of cruises! A seven-day cruise on Norwegian Cruise Line's *Dreamward* to the Caribbean may cost anywhere from $1,300 to $3,000 per person!

That may sound pretty expensive for a week, but, consider all that is included in that price! Virtually all cruises include the following in their per person costs: cabin accommodations, all meals, and entertainment such as evening shows, dancing, and movies. Use of the gym and sports facilities is also usually included.

What's not included? It's important to know because no one likes surprises, especially when they involve unexpected expenses! Alcoholic beverages, gambling, shore excursions, purchases at on-board shops, hairdressing, photography, and tipping are not included in the cost of the cruise. **Port taxes,** which can run as high as $75.00 to $ 100.00 per

Port Tax *Fees levied by a port on each arriving or departing passenger.*

person are not included in the quoted per person rates. However, port taxes do have to be paid in advance, so they are generally added on to the amount due the cruise line prior to sailing.

Nonincluded on-board expenses can always be paid for in cash. In the early days of cruising, credit cards were not accepted on board, and unsuspecting cruisers could find themselves in a real bind if they left home thinking that their credit cards would be welcome on board. Today, most cruise lines accept at least one of the major cards for on-board purchases, and a growing number accept credit cards for deposits and final payments. Even in today's credit crazy world, the wise cruiser will check before leaving home to see if the cruise line he or she has booked cares whether or not he or she "left home without it"!

Air/Sea Package A vacation package that includes air fare and cruise accommodations. Also known as a fly/sail package.

Unless the cost of the cruise includes air transportation—known as **fly/sail** or **air/sea packages**—transportation from your hometown to the departure port is not included in the cost. If you fly to the port city, and you are not on a fly/sail package, you will also have to pay for your transportation between the airport and the pier. If you drive to the departure port, you will, of course, have to cover the cost of gasoline, parking, and so on, yourself.

Ready to Go?

It is very rare for a passenger to call up a cruise line and book a cabin. In fact, many cruise lines do not publish their reservation numbers or offer toll-free numbers to the general public. Over 95 percent of all cruises are booked through travel agents—the largest percentage of agency sales for any travel supplier! Because cruise lines are so dependent on agencies for their bookings, they offer great discounts to agents to sail on their ships, joint advertising programs, training in selling cruises, and trips to the major ports to see many vessels at one time. The more an agent knows about a particular ship, the better he or she will be able to recommend it to clients!

Safety at Sea

One major concern of many would-be cruisers is safety. The idea of being on board a ship in the middle of the ocean can make many people uneasy. What happens in case of a fire, a major storm, or damage to the ship?

The question of weather is not as tricky as it once was. Advances in weather predicting and radar for scanning the areas a ship will enter make it possible to reroute a ship to avoid potential problems. When Hurricane Andrew hit Miami in 1992, cruise lines were forewarned. To protect their ships, they sent them out to sea—out of the path of the hurricane—and cancelled cruise departures for that week. Certainly, having a cruise cancelled is a disappointment for those booked to sail, but no one questioned the reason or wisdom in making such a decision.

The United States Coast Guard acts as enforcer of all U.S. government safety requirements. Construction plans for each ship built in the United States first must be approved by the Coast Guard. U.S. safety standards for ships are some of the strictest in the world, which means that American ships are exceptionally safe.

However, these standards are so strict and labor costs are so high that it makes ship building far more costly in the United States than in other countries. For that reason, virtually all cruise ships being built today are built outside the United States, usually in Scandinavia, the Netherlands, or Italy. But, this doesn't mean that the ships being built are unsafe!

All cruise ships that pick up passengers at U.S. ports, regardless of the country of registry, must meet U.S. safety requirements as well as the international standards set by the Safety of Life at Sea (SOLAS) Convention. Furthermore, agents of the U.S. Public Health Service also regularly inspect ships calling at U.S. ports to make sure they meet their established standards of hygiene and sanitation. Safety and sanitation ratings of the ships calling at U.S. ports are made available to the travel industry each year.

However, when it comes to regulating prices, itineraries, and so forth, the cruise industry is one of the least regulated members of the travel industry. While there may be some government intervention and regulation in those markets where they sell and sail their cruises, the lines are largely left alone to set their schedules, itineraries, and prices.

The Cruise Lines International Association (CLIA)

The **Cruise Lines International Association,** more commonly known as CLIA, is a trade association of cruise lines, founded in 1975. CLIA's main purpose since its founding has been to promote cruise vacations, assist its members in marketing their products, and educate travel agents about its member lines and selling cruises.

While the governments of all countries involved in cruise tourism have regulations regarding safety and health standards, CLIA functions as a regulatory body for its member lines by setting rules and standards for the agents who sell cruises on CLIA member lines. CLIA approves the agencies who wish to sell cruises on its members' ships.

Today, CLIA has thirty-five member lines which represent 99 percent of the cruise capacity marketed from the United States. Twenty thousand travel agencies are CLIA affiliates and over 2,000 educational institutions offering programs in travel and tourism use its manual in their teaching.

The *CLIA Cruise Manual,* which is published every year, provides travel agents with a wide range of information about its member lines, including the following:

- Names, addresses, and phone and fax numbers for member lines and their sales staff.
- CLIA member listing by ship and by line.
- Embarkation port maps.

Cruise Lines International Association (CLIA) An organization offering promotional materials, training guides, reference books, and seminars on behalf of cruise lines.

- Cruise guide for honeymooners, singles, children, active adults, and the handicapped.
- Credit card acceptance by cruise line.
- Checklist for shipboard inspections.
- Cruise data and reservation sheet.
- Checklist for hosting an agency "Cruise Night" promotion.
- Glossary of nautical and cruise booking terms.

CLIA, like ICTA, offers continuing education programs to travel agents through local seminars, ship inspection tours, on-board seminars, and training videos. Agents can work toward a CLIA certification as an Accredited Cruise Counselor or Master Cruise Counselor through CLIA.

CLIA also sponsors NCVM—National Cruise Vacation Month—every February. This "media blitz" is designed to increase awareness of the cruise product and create more demand for cruise bookings. Radio and television ads and programs are scheduled throughout the month, major newspaper advertising is run, and specially produced "advertorials" are included in both national and regional magazines.

Cruise Forever! Employment Opportunities in the Cruise Industry

Although it is a fact that cruising represents the fastest growing segment of the travel industry and, although it is also a fact that the vast majority of cruisers are from the United States, cruise lines actually employ very few U.S. citizens—less than 20,000! And, most of those positions are on the land in reservations and sales offices, not on the ships.

As we mentioned earlier in this section, U.S.-owned cruise lines sail their ships under foreign registry to avoid onerous labor costs, taxes, and business restrictions imposed by the U.S. government. Virtually all cruise lines in existence today hire most of their on-board staff outside the U.S.

Prospects for U.S. citizens are best for jobs "on land," especially in reservations and sales. Even foreign cruise lines have sales offices in the United States and hire U.S. citizens as sales representatives. Other exceptions to "foreign hiring" are the positions of social/cruise director, purser, sports and medical staff, entertainer, and lecturer.

Also, a number of positions may be "contract"—that is, you sign on as a professional and receive a contract fee for the services you provide—either from the cruise line itself or through sales to the passengers. Typically, contract workers are:

- Photographers
- Hairdressers
- Shopkeepers
- Entertainers
- Lecturers

But, don't lose heart! Many people dream of working on a cruise ship because they love to cruise. Working on a cruise ship is quite different from vacationing on one! If your dream is to enjoy as much time as possible cruising the world, perhaps your best bet would be to enter a field (such as travel agent) where cruise discounts are plentiful and spend your leisure time being "the pampered" instead of being "the pamperer"!

There are also agents who specialize in selling cruises either within a department in their agency or as employees of cruise-only agencies. These agents spend time inspecting ships and cruising on the different lines because it is important to know all facets of the cruise vacation if you make your living selling cruises! Other travel professionals may specialize in organizing and escorting cruise groups. Known as "cruise hosts," they accompany cruise groups and take care of everything from air tickets to transfers to documentation to special group programs on board to handling problems or emergencies that group members might experience.

Working on board a cruise ship can be fun and can certainly be a low-cost way to see the world. But, take these facts into consideration before signing on for the next ten years:

1 Quarters for staff can be very cramped and are most often shared with others.

2. Working hours can be extremely long—ten- to eighteen-hour days.

3. While the passengers are off "touring the exciting ports of the world," you will probably be "shipbound" cleaning cabins, preparing meals, or practicing for the evening's entertainment.

4. You will be away from home for weeks, probably months, at a time. Holidays are "high season," so you can probably forget spending them with your family and loved ones.

5. Your time off may well be in ports where you know no one and when none of your favorite co-workers can be with you.

However, if, all things considered, you still believe that a life at sea is the life for you, then your first steps should be to contact all the cruise lines to determine what qualifications you must meet and to investigate what other reference and resource materials are available to you, such as the book *How to Get a Job with a Cruise Line*, by Mary Fallon Miller.

Cruise Director

The television show "The Love Boat" glamorized cruising and many of the jobs "on board": One job that was highlighted through the character "Julie" was the position of cruise director. If you ever watched the show, you probably developed some notion of what a cruise director's job was all about—Hollywood style. Let's take a look at the *real* Julies!

Cruise directors are responsible for all social activities on board the cruise ship. Depending on the size of the ship and the number of its activities, a cruise director's jobs can range from calling bingo games to setting up single's programs, to conducting morning exercise programs, to giving safety instructions, to performing in the evening's entertainment. On larger ships, the cruise director may have assistants who help with the responsibilities, but, whether acting on his or her own or with a staff of several people, the cruise director is responsible for participating in social activities and making sure that the passengers have lots of fun! Being "up" every day is a *must* and showing any impatience or aggravation with passengers is never tolerated.

It's a big job and requires many skills. In addition to the obvious need for good people skills and a willingness to "ham it up," a cruise director should also have foreign-language abilities, be well organized, and have the ability and good health to withstand eighteen-hour work days! The majority of cruise directors are male and the average "life on the job" is two to eight years. Although there are no degree requirements for the position, there are some areas of experience and study that can be helpful:

- Management
- Sales
- Public relations
- Public speaking
- Recreation management
- Language courses
- Prior experience as recreation manager, resort activities coordinator, and the like.

Most cruise directors begin in other jobs on board, such as host (or hostess), assistant to the social coordinator or cruise director, children's program director, and so on. Some cruise directors come via "land" jobs at resorts, hotels, or country clubs where they were responsible for social and sports activities.

Explorations

How are cruises marketed in your area?

1. Check the travel section of the Sunday paper for cruise advertisements and answer the following questions:

   a. How many and which cruise lines are represented?

   b. Which cruise ships and destinations are being featured for the lines advertising?

c. Are the lines offering any specials or discounts?

   d. Which agencies are advertising with the cruise lines?

   e. How do the cruise lines instruct you to get additional information or make bookings?

2. Now, check the Yellow Pages of your telephone book for the following:

   a. How many cruise lines are listed under Cruise/Cruising?

   b. How many travel agencies are listed under Cruise/Cruising?

   c. How many agencies specifically indicated "cruise specialist" or "cruise only"—check both Cruise/Cruising listing and Travel Agency listing.

   d. Are there companies listed that advertise discount cruise rates?

Enrichments

If you have cruised before, write a critique of the ship and the cruise experience, including your impressions of the entertainment, food, staff, on-board facilities, activities, ports of call, and so on. Also, give a profile of the passenger(s) you feel would be happiest with the cruise selection.

or

If you have not cruised before, obtain a copy of a cruise line brochure from your instructor to review. If your instructor does not have brochures on hand, most travel agencies have a very large supply and would not mind parting with one or two. From reading through the brochure, answer the following:

1. Based on the descriptions in the brochure, what type of passengers do you see enjoying this particular line?

2. Which ship and itinerary would you choose for your own vacation and why?

3. Which cabin category do you think represents the best value?

A Room of One's Own

Where Are We Going?

After completing this section, you will:

1. Know the importance of hotel selection in travel planning.
2. Know the different categories and classifications of hotels.
3. Know the resources available to you in researching hotels.
4. Understand what influences the pricing of hotel rooms.
5. Know the basics of making a hotel reservation.

Industry Terms and Jargon

Bed and Breakfast
  (B&B)
Concierge
Corporate Rate
Full American Plan
  (FAP)

Hotel Chain
Hotel Representative
  (Rep)
Modified American
  Plan (MAP)

Occupancy Tax
Service Charge

Gimme Shelter

The basic needs of all travelers who venture far from home are food and shelter. The earliest travelers were merchants taking their goods to other countries and people to trade. Thus, overnight shelters were most commonly found along the trade routes and were very simple—a tent or simple structure offering protection from wind or cold.

Close on the heels of the merchants were the religious travelers—pilgrims who journeyed to worship in holy places and missionaries who made their way to "heathen" lands to convert others to their faith. In the Middle Ages when religious pilgrimages and crusades were all the rage, hospitality was considered a Christian's duty and was more an act of charity than a business. Monasteries frequently served as inns and offered travelers free shelter and food.

The most important influence on the development of shelters and inns as businesses was improved transportation. As road systems developed and more people moved about the world, providing overnight accommodations and food became a viable business. Inns sprung up along the highways and stagecoach routes. However, these inns were a far cry from hotels and inns as we know them today! There was little privacy: travelers ate family-style around a large table; there were few, if any, private rooms and no private baths; and travelers were expected to share beds with strangers if the inn was crowded!

Today's traveler would be shocked at the lack of privacy and communal living of these early inns. Today's guests expect and receive, at the very least, their own room with a bed, closet, television, radio, telephone, and private bath with towels and soap. And, as they move up the scale from budget to luxury accommodations, they may even get a private sitting area, desk, bar, hairdryer, bathrobe, scented soaps, shampoos, lotions, conditioners, a little sewing kit, whirlpool tub, and chocolates on their pillows!

Today, there are over 65,000 hotel properties in the United States alone, and new construction adds to that number every year. These 65,000 properties represent over three million rooms for sale every night. Worldwide, there are more than ten million hotel rooms—enough for every person in New York City with a couple of million left over for others! Competition among hotels is often fierce, and the choices for travelers seem almost endless!

The sale of hotel accommodations is a major part of the travel industry. It is a multibillion-dollar industry that provides job opportunities for thousands of people around the world. Seventy percent of leisure travelers and nearly 50 percent of corporate travelers request their travel counselor's assistance in selecting and reserving hotel accommodations.

The Basics

A hotel must meet the basic requirements of providing shelter, security, and food. Additionally, the accommodations chosen should meet the particular needs of the individual guest: convenience, luxury, economy, entertainment, relaxation, excitement, privacy, and so on. If all a traveler wanted was "a roof over his or her head," any hotel or motel would do. But, that is usually not the case. A simple request for an economical, clean, and conveniently located hotel can be a challenge for even the most experienced traveler or his or her travel agent.

Where there may be two or three—even seven or eight—airlines that serve a particular city, there may be, by comparison, dozens, even hundreds, of hotels from which to choose. The selection of accommodations is often far more complex than the transportation!

Selection of an airline schedule and seat is, after all is said and done, quite simple. The choices the hospitality industry offers are fascinating: they range from very simple to extravagantly plush, from roadside to mountain top, from city high-rise to jungle thatch roof, from full-service resorts to kitchenettes. They are as different and as interesting as the travelers themselves.

A traveler's comfort on a flight is certainly important, but having an uncomfortable flight probably won't affect the entire trip. Where a traveler stays has the potential to greatly enhance his or trip—or ruin it! A 1,000-room hotel may be the perfect choice for a sales group and a miserable choice for honeymooners. Where one person will be thrilled with a quaint bed and breakfast inn, another might find it "old" and "depressing."

Assisting with hotel selection is far more exacting, particularly for the vacation traveler, but it is also far more interesting. Travel professionals, like their clients, develop strong feelings about "properties" around the world. Comparing hotels and hotel experiences is a topic of conversation among the world's travelers. Everyone has a favorite hotel and interesting hotel experiences. Learning about the world's hotels is truly one of the most interesting parts of travel and travel planning.

Who Owns This Place?

A hotel can be individually owned, a member of a franchise operation, a subsidiary of a larger corporation, a member of a management group, or part of a "chain." Chain hotels are probably the most easily recognized because they have properties worldwide.

The largest **hotel chains** are Holiday Corporation, Sheraton, Quality International, Hilton Corporation, Ramada Hotel Group, Days Inn of America, Hyatt Hotels, and the Marriott Corporation. A hotel that is part of a chain may be owned and directed by the parent corporation or may be independently managed and permitted to use the hotel name under a franchise agreement with the parent company.

Hotel Chain Hotels operating under the same name or designation.

Best Western is also one of the largest hotel groups, but it operates as a membership organization rather than as a chain. Best Western properties are all individually owned and operated. They join the Best Western group to take advantage of its centralized reservation system and joint advertising and marketing programs. Through an organization like Best Western, individually owned hotels can compete more effectively with the large chains.

Hotels that are members of a chain or group such as Best Western represent an easily accessible room inventory through centralized reservation numbers, participation in airline/agency reservation systems, and a predictable quality and standard of operation. Travel agents and reservationists know what they are selling and travelers know what they are buying when they book chain hotels.

There are chains offering hotels and accommodations of every size, description, and price! Days Inns, Red Roof Inns, and Motel 6 are familiar budget names, and, at the top of the price ladder, there are the deluxe Four Seasons and Ritz Carlton Hotels. Some chains run the gamut and offer accommodations in every price range. Marriott is an excellent example.

Luxury Properties (Very Expensive)	J. W. Marriott Hotels
	Marriott Resorts
	Marriott Marquis Hotels
First Class Properties (Expensive)	Marriott Hotels
	Marriott Suites
Midrange Properties (Moderate)	Courtyards by Marriott
	Residence Inns
Budget Properties (Inexpensive)	Fairfield Inns

Management Contracts. Who owns the hotel may not be nearly as important as who *runs* it! A variation on the chains and member organizations is management contracting. Today, nearly all hotels with 300 rooms or more are owned by one company and managed by another under specially negotiated contracts. This concept evolved when foreign investors wished to develop hotels and use U.S. marketing and management expertise. Unfortunately, foreign governments either prohibited U.S. investment outright or levied extremely high taxes on outside investors. To get around this problem, major international hotel developers created "contract arrangements" with major U.S. chains. The foreign hotels are managed and marketed by the chains and bear their names—however, they are actually owned by the foreign investors and their companies.

Management contracting worked extremely well, and, in the 1970s, Hyatt began using the concept in the United States. Under management contract agreements, the operator has the right to manage the property without the interference of the owner, and the owner is responsible for operating and financing costs. If the hotel management team does not perform to set standards, the owner can "fire" them; if the owner does not offer adequate financing to operate the hotel to the chain's standards, the chain can "retire" from the contract, and the owner will have to change the hotel's name and find some other firm to manage it.

Individually Owned Properties (also known as independent properties). The privately run hotel does exist today. Some of the world's finest hotels operate independently. Individually owned hotels operate more in keeping with their country's culture and, as a result, can be far more interesting than the more homogeneous chain hotels. They can also be far less predictable in standards and quality—particularly at the budget level. The larger and more deluxe hotels may have toll-free numbers direct to their reservation office or use the services of "rep" firms that have toll-free numbers and automated reservations centers.

What Kind of Place Is This?

A hotel by any other name might just be a motel, a resort, a spa, a suite, or a B & B—the list goes on. In recent times, the hospitality industry has worked with a saturated market by creating specialized types of accommodations. Price categories range from budget to expensive. Service levels range from full-service luxury to cook-your-own-meals-in-kitchenettes. Rooms range from huge (furnished with priceless art and antiques) to very basic (the size of a large closet). To help the travel professional and his or her client sort through all this, the industry has created broad classifications.

Motels, Motor Hotels, and Motor Inns

Motels are fairly recent additions to the hospitality industry and evolved to serve the needs of the motorist. They are built near highways for easy automobile access and designed to be no-frills operations. They do not have bellmen, room service, or other amenities available in the traditional hotels. As travel patterns have changed and become more sophisticated, motor hotels and motor inns have evolved. These offer more amenities and services than the motel but still cater to the automobile traveler.

Motels are budget to midrange properties. You would be hard-pressed to find a deluxe motor inn or motel. Since they cater to motorists, they are rarely booked for more than one night and cannot be of the size or in the location to be appealing to groups or resort-bound vacationers; there is simply no call for luxury surroundings and impressive amenities. Reservations in motels and inns are most commonly booked direct by the traveler. Since travel agents and airline reservationists (who also book hotels) rarely deal with motorists, it makes perfect sense that advertisements, promotions, and selling materials would be directed primarily to the traveler.

How do you know if it's a motel or a hotel? Basically, if the access to the room is from a parking lot, it's a motel. If the access to the room is through a lobby and down a hallway, it's a hotel. Some properties have both types of entrances, and no one seems to know what to call them!

Hotels

Within the hotel classification, there are several distinct subgroups.

Commercial hotels provide meeting space and services for the corporate traveler and shopping, sightseeing, and local transportation services for the leisure traveler. Some hotels are built to cater primarily to the business traveler and, while restaurants, lounges, and exercise facilities may be nice, there isn't much in the hotel or its surrounding area to draw the vacationer. Commercial properties compete for corporate meetings and conventions to insure occupancy and maintain profitability.

Airport hotels are commercial hotels, but they serve such a distinct group that they are classified separately. Obviously, their market is the air traveler. Occupancy rates are high and there is rapid turnover. Most guests stay only one night. These hotels are often quite large and usually offer good restaurants, lounges and live entertainment, swimming pools, and exercise areas. All major airport hotels offer complimentary shuttle bus transportation to and from the airport. In some cities, airport hotels are actually located in the airports.

All-suite hotels represent one of the fastest growing segments of the hospitality industry. Typical all-suite hotel units have a living area, kitchen area, and one or more bedrooms and baths. They are not unlike the popular condominium properties found predominantly in resort, beach, and ski areas. These all-suite accommodations appeal to the executive who needs extra meeting or work space; the executive who may need to conduct meetings in his or her room, the employee who is relocating, the employee on a long-term project, or the leisure traveler who wants cooking facilities and more space. These types of accommodations often have great appeal to families.

Budget hotels, also known as economy hotels, experienced rapid growth in the 1980s. The demand for lower cost accommodations caught the attention of the big chains, and they have entered the market to compete with those whose focus has always been lower cost rooms. The attraction to developers and owners is that these facilities are more profitable than the expensive full-service hotels. Budget hotels do not have to provide expansive lobbies, meeting rooms, convention services, room service, bars, or restaurants and, as a result, their operating and personnel costs are much lower.

Resorts

Casa De Campo
La Romana, Dominican Republic

An outstanding, self-contained resort complex created by Oscar de la Renta. Casitas and villas with designer furnishings and fabrics, views of golf courses and gardens.

Facilities Include:

9 Restaurants

7 Bars

Executive Conference Center

3 18-Hole Golf Courses

13 Tennis Courts (10 Lighted)

Health Club / Spa

Equestrian Center

Snorkeling, Scuba Diving, Windsurfing, Sailing, Deep Sea Fishing

Skeet and Trap Shooting

Gift Shops

Private Landing Strip

Although resorts are definitely hotels, they are also lots, lots more and deserve a classification unto themselves. In the 1950s, resorts catered to families who came for long summer stays. These property owners were not interested in group or convention business. In fact, they actively discouraged such business because it ruined the family atmosphere. When groups or conventions prevailed upon them to accept their business, management would often require that group or convention name badges not be worn in the public areas in order to minimize the effect of their presence in the hotel!

The situation today is radically different. The traditional resorts of yesterday now actively seek corporate meeting and convention business. Larger, fancier, and more deluxe resorts are built every year and commit thousands of square feet to meeting and convention space. The resorts also offer state-of-the art sound and video systems and convention staffs dedicated to assist a group in planning everything from arrival cocktail parties, to special entertainment programs, to children's events, to fashion shows and sports tournaments for the spouses.

Elaborate recreation facilities are also a main feature of resort life. Golf courses, tennis courts, fabulous swimming pools, exercise rooms, saunas and hot tubs, world-class restaurants, and night clubs and designer shops vie for the attentions of the prospective guests.

The resort hotel is designed to attract clients who stay longer. They are nearly always located in popular vacation destinations and are often designed to be a vacation unto themselves. Resorts that offer comprehensive services and extensive recreation facilities are known as "self-contained" resorts; that is, the resort itself "becomes" the destination and, hopefully for resort management, guests will see little or no reason to venture to other spots to spend their money!

Self-contained resorts are often *all-inclusives*. That is, like the cruise ships, their prices per person include virtually everything: meals, sports, and resort activities; transfers to and from the airport; and taxes and gratuities. Many vacationers like all-inclusives because they know in advance what the price of the vacation will be, and they do not feel nickle-and-dimed to death when they want to take advantage of the resort's many facilities and activities. And, when it comes to family vacations, it looks like all roads lead to all-inclusives. Mom and Dad don't have to worry about money on vacation since everything, including the kids being entertained all day, is included.

Many families want to vacation together but also want the option of "playing" apart Single parents find all-inclusives especially appealing because they can take their children with them and know that, even without another adult in the party, they, too, can relax and have some time to themselves!

The similarity between all-inclusive resorts and cruise ships is not lost on the marketing offices of all-inclusive properties. They understand they have three formidable competitors in the vacation market: other all-inclusives, self-contained (but not all-inclusive) resorts that can appear cheaper, and cruises. All-inclusives actively promote their similarities to cruises such as one price for everything and gourmet dining. And, they are quick to point out their differences, such as how many golf courses or tennis courts can a cruise ship claim?

Vacationers and travel counselors alike must be very careful to determine how all-inclusive the all-inclusive resort really is! All-inclusive is not a set term in the industry and where one resort may define all-inclusive as everything except alcoholic beverages and personal purchases, another may define all-inclusive as being room, meals, and no charge for poolside lounge chairs and towels. When unsuspecting guests go to play golf or tennis, they may be hit with everything from astronomical greens fees to equipment rental add-ons to charges for locker room towels!

Some resorts also market themselves to specific groups, creating subgroups in the classification that require some additional explanation.

Golf and tennis resorts are common in many parts of the United States. While the resorts may offer other facilities and activities, golf and/or tennis are key to the resort's existence and figure prominently in marketing programs and advertising. These resorts offer world-class courses and courts. Golf courses are usually planned and built by "name" course designers such as Robert Trent Jones, and well-known golfing and tennis professionals are often on the resort staff for teaching and conducting clinics. Many of these resorts play host to the famous tournaments held throughout the year.

A *spa* is a resort with mineral springs. At least, that is what the word *spa* means and is the case in Europe. Many European spas were built on the sites of ancient Roman spas. These provide physical and other therapies and are considered more suited to an older, wealthy, and sometimes infirm clientele. The spas in the United States are different. They emphasize fitness, exercise, and diet. Increasingly popular, they attract a much younger clientele than their European counterparts.

Ski resorts were developed in popular ski areas and often encompass entire communities of lodges, hotels, condominiums, guest houses, and restaurants. The entire city of Aspen, Colorado, is considered to be the resort—not the individual hotels or lodges. In recent years, ski resorts have added other seasonal activities and facilities such as swimming pools, tennis courts, hiking trails, and horseback riding to attract off-season business.

Dude ranches are an interesting resort subgroup. They began as working ranches that accepted summer guests. Today, these ranches have expanded to include swimming pools, children's programs, and other activities. Some dude ranches advertise that each guest gets his or her own horse! Dude ranches usually operate seasonally and generally require a minimum stay of one week.

Gaming Hotels

Las Vegas! Reno! Atlantic City! What pops into mind when you hear these names? Why, gambling, of course! And, where does most of this gambling take place? In the casinos located in the major hotels, of course!

Although they may have many resortlike facilities, such as elaborate swimming pool areas, golf courses, tennis courts, and so on, these hotels are not really resort hotels. If it weren't for the gambling, how many visitors would actually be drawn to vacation in the desert city of Las Vegas? Although they may have vast and state-of-the-art meeting

facilities, they are clearly not commercial hotels, unless, of course, your business is selling playing cards and dice.

These hotels exist for one reason: the income that playing games for money brings to them. As a result, room rates tend to be very reasonable, food costs are low, and the entertainment is top-name and far less expensive than in New York or Los Angeles. Gambling brings in the money and the shows and activities that abound in the hotel are simply there to entertain the guests when their arms have gone stiff and their eyes have glazed over from playing the slot machines.

Everything in gaming hotels revolves around the casinos. They never close, their lights never dim, and no distractions are allowed—no children, no music, no loud talking, no flashing lights, no cannon-rolls or cheers when you hit the jackpot, and no running through the room when you are late for the show or special rendezvous. Getting somewhere quickly can be a problem because the casinos are usually located in the center of the hotel and designed so that guests have little choice but to go through them no matter what their destinations may be!

The casino and the hotel are most often under separate ownership or management. The hotel allocates a certain number of rooms to the casino, or the casino owns them outright, so that they can always invite their favorite high rollers over for a couple of nights and not worry that the hotel has been sold out to a national association of tire dealers or dental hygienists.

Another group of hotels/inns that has claimed its own distinction is the **bed and breakfast** inn. In the United States, these small inns are most likely to be older homes that have been converted to handle overnight guests (i.e., all bedrooms with private baths) or small, older inns that have been upgraded to offer modern amenities (once again, private, modernized baths). The furnishings are often antiques (or reproductions), and the rooms are decorated to create an air of intimacy, friendliness, and home.

In Europe, bed and breakfast hotels are simply that: small hotels or homes turned into guest houses that offer a bed and breakfast for a set price. All rooms may not have private baths, and the furnishings may be economical and very simple. In some countries, you are literally stay-

Bed and Breakfast Inns (B & Bs)

Bed and Breakfast   A room rate, in a very small hotel, inn, guest house, or private home, that includes sleeping accommodations and breakfast. The term is also used to classify the establishment: A "Bed and Breakfast Inn"; "B & B" is also common.

ing in a bedroom in someone's house and may be privy to the day-to-day goings on with the family!

The bed and breakfast inn as a classification is more specifically American. They may be located in cities or in the country (and called country inns). They are generally less expensive than the major deluxe hotels, but not necessarily less expensive than first-class properties, and rarely less expensive than moderately priced motels and budget operations. They appeal to couples, seasoned travelers who like more intimate and interesting surroundings, and, in metropolitan areas, to single, female business travelers.

Clearly, a lone bed and breakfast inn would be hard pressed to come up with the large amount of money it takes to have national advertising, reservation centers, and toll-free numbers. They rely on guide books, regional advertising, word of mouth and affiliations, like *Bed and Breakfast Inns of America*, to promote their properties.

Condominiums, Apartments, and Homes

Short-term rentals in private, homelike facilities is a fast growing market throughout the world. Apartments and homes have long been advertised through realtors and in the classifieds of major city newspapers and internationally published magazines. However, in recent years, representatives of rental properties have formed alliances and published brochures that are distributed to agents. In the past, agents were not sought after as booking resources because the owners or realtors did not want to pay commissions on long-term rentals and were satisfied with the markets they could reach through advertising.

However, as the number of people traveling has grown, the number of people seeking advice from travel agents has mushroomed, and the numbers of condos, apartments, and rental cottages have multiplied, representatives have turned to the travel professional to help sell their properties. Condos are more commonly associated with resort destinations such as Hawaii, apartments with large cities such as London, and homes with rural areas such as the south of France.

Vacation rentals usually range from one week to a month or more. The appeal for these types of accommodations is usually to the more sophisticated traveler who has tired of hotels and traditional vacations and to families who want more space and a homelike atmosphere for the kids. Some rental properties come with full maid service, a cook, a nanny, and even a gardener—just in case you want to grow something the week you are there or because you want the lawn mowed or the roses pruned!

Country inns of America, chateaux of France, Scottish castles, paradores of Spain, cottage colonies of Bermuda, the gasthaus of Germany, chalets of Switzerland, posadas in Portugal, ryokans of Japan, hostels of Europe, and the guest houses of the world are the interesting, out-of-the-ordinary places to stay that the leisure client who is looking for unusual accommodations may often request. They are fascinating to research and fun to recommend. They may be very expensive or remarkably cheap. They are not for everyone—certainly, the business traveler who has only two days to conduct an important meeting in London would wonder at your taking his or her time to talk about castles in Scotland.

Just when you think you've covered most every type of accommodation, your client requests a room with a view of a fish! And, it's possible! The Undersea Lodge in Key Largo, Florida, is actually under water.

Club Med—An All-Inclusive Resort Chain

Originally called Club Mediteranée, today's Club Med is one of the largest resort chains in the world. In 1950, Club Mediteranée, a French company, opened its first "resort"—a tent village on the island of Majorca in the Mediterranean Sea.

Today, Club Med still refers to its locations as "villages," but they are now sophisticated, permanent properties with modern buildings, first-class rooms, and recreational facilities such as swimming pools, tennis courts, and golf courses. Club Med properties are designed to be self-contained, and their French management works to make each resort as unique as its locale.

Club Med was a leader in the concept of "all-inclusive." Meals and sports activities are included in the per person price at almost all locations. In addition to "all-inclusive," Club Med also promotes the "cashless" resort so that their free-spirited guests don't have to carry around reminders of the "real world" such as wallets and purses. Early Club Med guests were given a supply (and could buy extra) "pop beads" to use as currency in the village. A beer at the beach bar might cost three beads and a bottle of wine at dinner ten. When your pop-bead necklace began to choke you, it was time to cough up some real cash to buy more!

The original target for Club Med was single swingers. In fact, the resort had, and reveled in, a reputation of constant fun, parties, and meeting and dating new people. Activities were geared to the tastes of the young and free, so much so, that they quickly became known as young adult "summer camps."

But, Club Med moved with the times and grew up with the market, and today, Club Med appeals to singles, honeymooners, couples, and families. The Club Med resorts at Sandpiper (Florida), the island of St. Lucia in the Caribbean, the island of Eleuthera in the Bahamas, and the Mexican resorts in Punta Cana and Ixtapa offer comprehensive children's programs. At Sandpiper, there is even a"Baby Club" that offers programs and child care for children as young as four months!

Club Med is very proud of its GOs—Gentil Organisateurs—or congenial hosts. Very much like a cruise director, the GO functions as the social and activities focal point for the resorts. The Club Med GOs represent all ages and nationalities and are hired to be key figures in promoting harmony, camaraderie, and fun in the resorts.

As the Club Med organization moves toward its fiftieth year in operation, it is far from middle-aged or set in its ways! There are Club Med resorts throughout the Caribbean, Europe, and in French Polynesia. They even have "moving resorts"—the sailing/cruise ships Club Med I and Club Med II. What is the philosophy that keeps them young and popular? In their own words from their resort brochure: "When you choose to spend the most precious time of your year under our sunshine, our goal can only be to make it absolutely perfect from start to finish."

How Could We Possibly Know?

Armed with a basic understanding of hotel types, your next logical question might be: "Once I know what type hotel the traveler wants, how do I assist with the selection of the best individual property?" As you move ahead in your career, you will undoubtedly have the opportunity to participate in familiarization trips and will most likely also travel on your own. You will never look at a hotel in the same way again! Things that might have made a small impression on you in the past, or slipped your notice entirely, will now stand out.

When you visit hotels, you will look for answers to questions such as:

- Are the employees friendly?
- Is the property clean and in good repair?
- Are restaurants and public areas easy to find, accessible, and pleasing?
- Are the rooms nicely decorated? Are they too hot, too cold, too sunny, too dark?
- Is the closet space enough for more than a one-night visit?
- Is room service dependable?
- Is the housekeeping staff efficient or was your room not cleaned until four o'clock?
- Is the hotel too noisy?

Hotel inspections and personal experience are invaluable, but it doesn't take a genius to figure out there is no way to be familiar with all the properties of the world, not even the major ones. Your coworkers' experiences and recommendations will be an excellent resource, and *don't forget to solicit traveler recommendations and feedback!*

There are also many resources, references, and guides to hotel selection:

- *The Hotel and Travel Index*
- *The Official Hotel Guide (OHG)*

- *The Business Travel Planner (North American Edition)*
- *The Travel Planner, European and Pacific Editions*
- *Sloane's Travel Agency Reports (STAR Guide)*
- Guidebooks and specialized hotel reference publications such as *Country Inns, Romantik Hotels & Restaurants, Michelin Guides (Red-Book), Mobil Guides, AAA Guides, Zagat's Surveys,* and the chain publications and property listings.

Some reference material is biased; that is, it is produced by the hotels or "critics" paid by the hotel and will, of course, present the property in its best light. Others, such as the *STAR Guide* are impartial and highly critical and were created to give travel professionals as honest a picture as possible about the properties reviewed.

Check the Ratings!

✔✔✔✔

With so many properties in each category, further distinction is sometimes necessary to make recommendations on hotel selection. There are independent groups who rank hotels according to quality and, in many countries of the world, governments also have established hotel rating systems.

There are no worldwide standards or guidelines for those who undertake this job; however, there are reliable and often quoted services. The *Star System of the Mobil Travel Guide Rating Service* is the best known in the United States. Mobil has been rating hotels since 1958, and the decisions on the coveted five-star ratings are anxiously awaited by deluxe hotel and resort managers every year. AAA Automobile Clubs also publish ratings using the "diamond system."

Mobil rates properties according to the "look of the place," overall service, maintenance, and prices, but, when it comes to the restaurants, *not the food.* They leave food ratings to others such as *Zagat's Restaurant Surveys.* Mobil selects a cross-section of properties that will give the traveler a good idea of what is available at all price levels: luxury, first class, moderate, and economy. Mobil makes every effort to be unbiased in its reports and ratings, and there is no charge to any establishment to be included in its publications.

The ratings * through ***** apply nationally, and each is subject to annual review. Mobil strives to insure that each property that receives a "star" rating is clean, well maintained, well managed, and above average in its category. If a property is undergoing major refurbishment, managerial changes, ownership changes, or has been in operation less than one year, Mobil will designate it as "unrated"—code NR.

Here's how they do it:

Good, better than average	*
Very Good	**
Excellent	***
Outstanding	****
One of the Best in the Country	*****

AAA diamond awards follow a similar pattern. They also offer a ✔ designation that indicates "good value."

The AH & MA

The American Hotel and Motel Association, founded in Chicago in 1910, is the trade association that represents the hospitality industry in the United States. The AH & MA operates as a federation of lodging associations in the fifty states, District of Columbia, Puerto Rico, and the U.S. Virgin Islands.

Over 10,000 individual properties belong to the AH & MA, and the membership represents nearly 1.5 million rooms—60 percent of the total room availability in the United States. The AH & MA provides leadership and guidance in developing programs for its members and addressing the problems and issues that face the hospitality industry today.

Through its subsidiary, the American Hotel Association Directory Corporation, the AH & MA publishes a number of resources and references: *Lodging*, an industry magazine; the *Directory of Hotel and Motel Companies*; the *Business Travel Planner/Hotel & Motel RedBook*; and *Who's Who in the Lodging Industry*.

The AH & MA also supports educational and institutional research for the lodging industry through The Educational Institute, another subsidiary. The Educational Institute has been used by over 500,000 individuals, making it the largest hospitality educational resource in the world.

What About Everybody Else?

In the United States, we are lucky to have so many nonbiased guides and rating systems. But what about elsewhere? In Europe, you can rely on the *Michelin Guide* (Redbook) for hotel ratings similar to Mobil's, and they actually go them one better. Michelin "star ratings" for restaurants are highly prized, and they don't just look at the place, they eat and rate the food as well. A meal in a Michelin three-star-rated Paris restaurant could cost you nearly as much as your ticket across the Atlantic!

There are other good sources of information about international hotels, but, unfortunately, there is also lots of confusion. Following are some examples:

Switzerland: The Swiss Hotel Association does the ratings, but only for member hotels, which leaves out about 15 percent of the lodging establishments in the country.

Hong Kong: There are no official ratings, and some hotels simply rate themselves.

Mexico: The Ministry of Tourism decides who gets what: one, two, three, four, or five stars, and the even more cherished Gran Turismo and Classe Especial ratings.

Germany: Like Mobil Guides, the private-sector publication, *Varta Guide,* is considered to be the closest to an official rater and awards properties one to four stars.

Greece: The tourist office decides who gets what—ratings from A through E.

Great Britain: Ratings are all over the place. The English, Welsh, and Scottish Tourist Boards award one to five crowns, but only when the hotelier asks to be rated. If hoteliers don't want to be rated, they won't be. Ratings of one to five stars are also assigned by two private organizations, the Royal Automobile Club and the Automobile Association, and they rate whether the hotelier wants it or not.

If all that doesn't frustrate the discriminating international traveler, consider that many hoteliers actively discourage rating because the classifications of their hotels determine the tax rates they must pay. In Italy, many of Rome's deluxe hotels are looking for ways to lose one of their five stars because such a come-down will decrease their tax rates from 19 percent to 9 percent!

In some markets where competition is fierce, such as Asia, a three-star hotel might well be a four- or five-star property in the United States. Conversely, in underdeveloped areas, a five-star hotel might only merit a three-star rating in a more sophisticated market. So, it's pretty clear that international hotel ratings simply are not consistent. What should the poor traveler do?

1. Enlist the help of a professional travel counselor.
2. Check the ratings assigned by the country (or its designated rater).
3. Consult guidebooks and international rating sources.
4. If all else fails, look for a hotel with a recognizable chain affiliation.

How Much Is That Double with a Window?

Room rates are quoted per night. It is generally expected that a guest will arrive at the hotel in the afternoon or evening and depart the next morning. Even resorts that require minimum stays of three, five, or seven nights will quote nightly rates. If meals are included in the price, the rates will be quoted per person, per night. If meals are not included, the rate is generally quoted per room, per night.

Hotel costs vary from city to city and country to country. The following comparison of lowest rates for Marriott hotels was taken from the *Business Travel Planner:*

Salt Lake City, Utah	$69
Perimeter Center, Atlanta, Georgia	$112
Puerto Vallarta, Mexico	$120
Toronto, Canada	$185
San Francisco, California	$205
New York City	$270

If that didn't confuse you, then consider that room costs vary within the hotel itself. This may be because the quality and size of the various rooms differ: a spacious room on the top floor with an excellent view will cost more than a small room on a lower floor that overlooks the garbage cans. And, a single room always costs more per person than a double room.

Cost variances may also be caused by season or date changes. In Washington, D.C., rooms often cost less on the weekend, unless it is Cherry Blossom time, and then hotel rooms always cost more. Or, just imagine what a hotel room might cost during the inauguration of a new president!

Hotel rooms are priced on supply and demand. If demand is great, as it is in St. Thomas in February or during Mardi Gras in New Orleans, the room rates are high. If demand is low, as it is in Phoenix in August or Stockholm in January, the room rates are lower. These rate fluctuations are referred to as "high season," "low season," and "special event" rates.

Further complicating giving an answer to "How much will this room cost?" are other pricing factors such as corporate rates, group rates, family rates, relocation rates, convention rates, senior citizen rates, weekend rates, and an overwhelming number of association and group membership discounts.

Corporate Rate   A special rate negotiated between a supplier (most commonly a hotel or car rental company) and a corporation or business. Corporate rates are widely used throughout the hotel industry, but the definition can vary with the individual hotel or chain. Traditionally, a corporate rate represents 10 percent or more off the hotel's regular room rate.

Corporate rates are the most common "special-case" rates. Some large corporations negotiate directly with hotels and hotel chains to obtain special low rates or guaranteed costs for their business travelers. In order to be competitive in the industry and to offer services that will attract new clients, many travel agencies become members of groups or participate with national services (at a cost) to offer corporate rates at a wide selection of hotels to their clients.

The term *corporate rate* can create confusion, because it does not necessarily mean the room rate will be the lowest a traveler can receive.

Corporate rates are frequently guaranteed not to change for a period of time and, once they are confirmed by the hotel for a specific reservation, they cannot be changed even if the guest must be placed in a room that would normally be much more expensive. Other rates may be available, such as an advertised promotional rate or a budget room rate, that are lower than the corporate rate. Determining what a hotel room will cost and whether or not it is the best rate can be quite a challenge!

What Affects the Price of a Room?

*Hotel location	*Special conditions
*Room location	*Group rate
*Type of hotel	*Meeting rate
*Type of room	*Convention rate
*Day or season of stay	*Family rates
*Number of people	*Foreign currency fluctuations
*What is included	

Some hotels have meal plans that can be optional or required. European hotels often include breakfast in their rates, and resort hotels may require that some or all of a guest's meals be taken at the hotel.

Sometimes, hotel rates can appear quite high in comparison to others, but if you look closer and see that **Full American Plan (FAP)** is written by the rate, you know that all meals are included, and it might not be such a bad deal after all! And don't worry that you won't like what the hotel is serving; the menus for resorts with meal plans offer as many choices as those on cruise ships.

In most cases, three full meals are not a mandatory part of the rate except when the hotel is an all-inclusive resort where clients would normally expect to spend all their time. A more common meal plan requires the guest to take two meals, usually breakfast and dinner. This is called the **Modified American Plan (MAP)**. Once again, this plan is used in resort and vacation properties and would never be a requirement at a commercial property.

In figuring hotel rates, remember that the base rate is rarely ever the total cost. **Occupancy taxes,** state taxes, county taxes, city taxes, and service charges are often added to the bill. The average total tax rate added to a hotel bill in the United States is about 11 percent, which makes a $100.000 a night room really cost $111.00. Most people wouldn't be too upset about an additional $11.00, but consider what a traveler's reaction might be in the larger cities where taxes are considerably higher.

As a percentage of travel costs, federal, county, and city government taxes really take their toll. A "guest" in a Chicago hotel pays over 14 percent in taxes and surcharges and, in New York City, a staggering 21.25 percent! Since larger city hotel rates are higher than those in the rest of the country, the tax bill becomes even more shocking.

A Warm Bed and a Full Plate

Full American Plan (FAP) *All meals are included in the price of the hotel room.*

Modified American Plan (MAP) *Two meals, usually breakfast and dinner, are included in the room rate.*

How Taxing!

Occupancy Tax *The tax levied by many cities on a hotel stay. In addition to local taxes, there may be a set tax per room or per person added to the hotel bill.*

New York, the most expensive city in the United States in which to sleep, eat, and get around (i.e., taxis, rental cars, limos, etc.), far exceeds all other U.S. cities in the tax burden imposed on the visitor. Just consider that a "guest" would have over $50.00 a night added to a $250.00 a night room rate, and its not hard to see why many corporations and associations think twice about sending their travelers and groups to the Big Apple!

A Word of Warning

Quoted hotel rates don't include all the costs a traveler will have to pay once he or she arrives at the property. The nightly rate is just the beginning, but it should be an accurate beginning! When researching hotel rates, you should never accept as firm a quote from one of the published reference books. Those who compile these reference sources give rates as *guidelines only.*

A hotel rate cannot be considered *definite* until it has been confirmed by the hotel or its representative. Any guide or reference book you use will issue many disclaimers and warnings about quoting rates from their publications, *and do take heed!* Hotel rates change frequently and relying on rates from a guide published in January could cause you considerable embarrassment in March!

Very few hotel reservation offices or centers will give you the *full* price, including taxes and service charges, when you ask for a room rate. If you ask for a quote with taxes included, they will probably give you the rate and then tell you what tax percentages would be added on, leaving you to do the figuring. They may also forget to mention **service charges** and special surcharges such as the energy surcharges that crop up from time to time in the Caribbean and other seasonal resort areas.

Service Charge A fee added to a bill, usually in a hotel or restaurant, to cover the cost of certain services as a substitute for tipping.

Making the Reservation

There are four basic ways to make a hotel reservation:

1. Correspond directly with the property either by phone, letter, telex, telegram, or fax.
2. Make the reservation through a travel agent who will either call or use a computerized reservation system.
3. Call the reservation center operated by the chain.
4. Call the reservation center operated by the hotel representative.

Calling a hotel reservation office direct may well be the safest way for any traveler or travel planner to make a reservation. Little room is left for doubt or error if the hotel itself says a room is available and accepts the booking. However, long distance calls are expensive, and, depending on the time of day, the hotel reservation office may not even be open.

More and more properties around the world now have fax machines, and they offer an excellent, fast way to correspond in writing and an equally satisfactory way of receiving confirmations. However, with the wide range of rates, room types, specials, and so on available in most hotels today, faxing does not give the reservationist the opportunity to discuss with the hotel what might be available in a range of rooms or rate options.

Reservations made through computer systems are quick and response time from the property is usually very good. However, not all rates are promoted through the computer systems, and questions about room type, location, and special needs can be handled only in the briefest form. Furthermore, smaller properties may not be in the system at all.

Reps and Res Centers

Many hotel chains have reservation centers for their properties just as the airlines have res centers for their customers. Holiday Inns was the first to automate its reservations process with its Holidex system. Other chains followed suit, and, with improved technology, these systems have become more efficient and extensive.

Firms that represent hotels, or **hotel reps,** provide reservation systems and sales and marketing support for their member hotels. The individual hotels or groups of hotels that employ the services of a hotel rep pay for its services. It does not cost an agency or a traveler more to work with a hotel rep. Many hotel reps have established excellent reputations and, by being selective about the hotels they sell, have earned the confidence of travel professionals.

Hotel Representative (Hotel Rep) *Person or company retained by one or more hotels to serve as reservations and marketing outlets, usually with toll-free telephone service.*

Most hotel reps have toll-free numbers, and because of centralized operations and better control of room allotments, more property owners or managers are willing to release rooms to the rep. This means the agent has better access to *last room availability.* Confirmations are often immediate or available within twelve to twenty-four hours.

More Alphabet Soup!

Hotels, like airlines, have their own system of abbreviations and codes. Unlike the airlines, however, these abbreviations and codes are not always consistent. As more and more hotel chains develop automated systems that interlink with the airline systems, the language will become more uniform.

The following hotel codes can be found in your glossary in the section on abbreviations:

B & B	FAP	STE
BH	GTD, GTY	SUP
BR	MAP	SVC
BRKFST	MP	SWB
CF, CF#, CONF, CONF#	NT, NTS	SWOB
CK-IN	OCC	TRP, TRPL
DBL	OF	TWB
DEP	OV	TWOB
DLX	PP	TWN
DWB	QUAD	WK, WKLY
DWOB	RM, RMS	WKND
EAP	ROH	XL, XLD
EP	SGL	

Employment Opportunities in the Hotel Industry

The outlook for employment in the hospitality industry is excellent for people of every race and ethnic background. Despite the fact that the hotel industry experienced stagnant to negative growth in the early 1990s, jobs remained available and there was little, if any, news of massive layoffs in the business.

Over 1.5 million people in the United States are employed in the hotel industry—more than any other segment of travel and tourism. Predictions are that, by the year 2000, labor demands will have increased to 2 million! In the 1980s, hotel employment grew by 43 percent, which was two times the rate of other U.S. industries.

Young workers aged eighteen to twenty-four have traditionally been the mainstay of entry-level workers in this industry. Because of the lower birth rates in the late 1960s and 1970s, many employers have already begun to feel the pinch of the shortage of qualified, entry-level workers. This shortage has created an ideal atmosphere for quick promotions up the career ladder for hard-working employees.

Is This the Job for You?

For all the promise, careers in the hotel industry are not for everyone, nor are entry-level jobs a guarantee to instant success! The hotel industry is not an eight to five business. Hotels operate twenty-four hours a day, and the busiest times are those when most other people are just getting up in the morning or just sitting down to an evening meal. Low entry-level pay, flexibility in work schedule, and, in many cases, frequent relocation are required of the aspiring hotel executive!

Where Do I Begin?

A hotel of any size is generally divided into fairly distinct areas of management and employment. At the top of the totem pole is the general manager. Don't expect this to be your first job as it takes years of experience and training to qualify. However, if you work in a hotel, you will quickly learn who is the general manager and the position of importance he or she commands. In a nutshell, the general manager oversees and is responsible for everything that goes on under his or her roof! It is a job of tremendous responsibility and, with some companies, requires a degree in hotel management. General managers of very large hotels (700 to 1,000 rooms) may command a yearly salary of six figures!

Following is a description of other areas in the hotel industry:

Administration: Includes accounting and bookkeeping, purchasing, and personnel.

Front Office: This is the most visible and arguably the most important department in any lodging business. Employees are in direct contact with the public and create the first and most lasting impression of the property. Front-office employees include the front-office manager, concierge, reservationists, front-desk staff, and bellmen. In some hotels, security staff is considered front office while in others it may be grouped with housekeeping or maintenance. Switchboard operators, depending on their overall function, may be front office or administrative management.

Sales and Marketing: In some establishments, sales and marketing might fall under the auspices of the administrative wing. However, the function is so important to the success of any hotel, it often claims its own designation. Employees in this department include sales managers, sales staff, and clerical staff. Within the sales staff, there may well be distinctions such as meetings and conventions sales, travel agent sales, group sales, and so on. Very large convention hotels may have a separate department just to handle conventions, meetings, and exhibitions.

Food and Beverage: If hotels have restaurants, banquet and meeting rooms, cocktail lounges, and room service, the management of food services will be a major part of the hotel's operations. In a large convention hotel, it is not unusual to have more than half of the total hotel staff employed in this department.

Housekeeping: Guest comfort is a top priority in any lodging establishment. Most hotels employ a large staff whose responsibility is the cleanliness and neat appearance of guest rooms and public areas.

Engineering and Maintenance: The engineering and maintenance crew have little or no contact with the general public, but their contributions are critical to the smooth, day-to-day running of a hotel. This department is responsible for all mechanical and electrical equipment in the hotel and may have responsibility for the exterior grounds as well.

Large hotels, especially resorts, may have additional departments because they offer more comprehensive services and activities. They may have personnel whose jobs are to organize and oversee recreational services, instructional staff such as tennis and golf pros, health facilities staff such as masseuses and exercise coaches, staff to take care of the parking garage, and staff to oversee the shops and other concessions.

UP CLOSE

The Hotel Concierge

To many experienced travelers, a truly professional hotel **concierge** is an invaluable friend in an unfamiliar city. A good concierge is knowledgeable about local customs, attractions, events, and favored restaurants. He or she is also resourceful in obtaining sought-after tickets,

Concierge *In a hotel, the person in charge of special services for guests. The concierge will arrange tours and transfers, obtain theater tickets, and make appointments with hairdressers, doctors, and so on. In Europe, the concierge has been a key employee in hotels for many years. In the United States, the practice of employing a concierge is relatively new.*

special dining reservations, and last-minute appointments and services from hairdressers, dry cleaners, tailors, doctors, and the like. A concierge is tactful, diplomatic, and discreet. He or she is also unflappable—even in the face of highly unusual and difficult requests, such as the one made for the concierge to hire musicians and arrange for studio time so the guest could record a song he had just written!

It is believed that the position of concierge—which in French means "keeper of the keys"—originated in the Middle Ages. The castle doorkeeper was in charge of all keys and made sure that the royal family and any royal guests were locked safely in their rooms at night. When the royalty went traveling, the doorkeeper went along to oversee the travel plans and arrange accommodations. The security and convenience of having doorkeepers and key monitors was important to the grand, deluxe hotels (royalty's "home away from castle") of Europe. The hotel concierge's responsibilities included not only the keeping of the keys and the greeting of guests at the door, but also seeing that all guests were well cared for during their stay.

In most European hotels, the concierge desk is located in the lobby. In addition to maps, tourist brochures, guidebooks, and other local information resources, the concierge may also have a computer for guest messages, a ticket printer or direct line to a travel agency, airline, or rail company for making travel reservations, and a fax machine.

But, no matter how high tech the European concierge's desk might be, he or she could not function without a logbook and diary. Here, entered by hand in meticulous detail, are the preferences and idiosyncrasies of every guest who regularly uses the concierge's services. Travel professionals who understand the importance of such services for the wealthy and demanding will often write ahead about their clients so that the concierge will already have this special information logged in his or her book and will be ready to greet the new guest as a time-honored customer.

Although the position of concierge has flourished in Europe, it wasn't until the mid-1970s that several U.S. hotels in San Francisco began offering concierge services to their guests. Once introduced in the States, the concept of "concierge" became quickly "Americanized." In Europe, it can take years to become a concierge or head concierge. Once there, the European concierge will probably stay until carried out feet first! Not so in the United States. In American hotels, the position of concierge is often considered just another step up the corporate ladder, and concierges are more likely to move from hotel to hotel and from city to city.

Because European concierges have traditionally been trained through apprenticeships, most European concierges are male. Also not so in the United States. American concierges are hired in much the same way as any other position in the hotel and almost 50 percent of all concierges in the United States are women. Today, there is an International Concierge Institute in Paris and, with this nonapprenticeship training center, more European women are expected to enter the field.

For a concierge—whether in Europe or the United States—the normal list of duties includes making restaurant reservations; arranging local transportation (taxis, rental cars, and limousines); ordering flowers; obtaining theater, sports, or special events tickets; arranging business services, and dealing with minor emergencies. Although it is not a requirement in the United States, most European concierges are multilingual.

Les Clefs d'Or (Golden Keys), the international association of concierges, was founded in 1929 in Paris. Today, there are 4,000 members worldwide, including about 200 in the United States. Their membership insignia, a pair of crossed golden keys worn on each lapel, is a familiar, and welcome, sight to many world travelers.

The real concierges of the world take their positions quite seriously and membership requirements for Les Clefs d'Or are strict. Membership requires a minimum of five years in the hotel industry (three of which must have been as a concierge), a position located in the hotel lobby, and letters of recommendation from two current association members. Concierges who work solely on private VIP floors, in office buildings, in apartment complexes, or in private clubs are excluded from membership.

Explorations

Check your local paper for hotel advertisements. If you live in a particularly small area that does not have representatives of major chains, obtain the newspaper of the closest medium- to large-sized city.

1. Are any special rates being advertised for weekends or special events? Give examples of at least two.

2. Why would a hotel advertise in its *local* paper?

3. Are any hotels or resorts from other areas advertising in this paper? If so, list them (maximum five) and briefly describe what they are offering.

4. Check the Yellow Pages of your phone book under hotels. Are any hotels from outside your immediate area listed? If so, list their names (maximum five).

   Are any chains or reservations services listed? If so, give their names (maximum five).

5. Choose a U.S. resort or major city destination and a weekend. Then, select a hotel chain listed in your phone directory. Call this chain to ask:

   a. If it has a property in your chosen location. (If not, choose another hotel group or destination.)

   b. What the rate for a double room for a Thursday to Sunday stay would be.

   c. Once that rate has been quoted, ask if there are any specials or discounts available.

   What did you learn from this exercise?

6. What do you think are the most important considerations to a traveler in selecting overnight accommodations?

Enrichments

Visit a local hotel. Describe the following:

1. Exterior of the building and grounds.
2. Reception, lobby area.
3. Restaurants, other public areas.

Based on what you saw, how would you classify this hotel?

or

If you have recently (within the last year) visited another city or resort area and stayed in a hotel or resort, write a description of it. See what you can remember about the hotel and its facilities that might not have impressed you at the time, but now has more meaning since you are studying travel and tourism.

Behind the Wheel

Where Are We Going?

After completing this section, you will:

1. Be familiar with the questions to ask prior to making the decision to rent an automobile.

2. Know the standard industry requirements for renting an automobile.

3. Know the basic car classes.

4. Understand the basics of car rental pricing.

5. Be familiar with the differences in, and special considerations of, renting cars abroad.

Industry Terms and Jargon

Car Class

Collision Damage
  Waiver (CDW)

Drop Charge

Kilometer

Loss Damage Waiver
  (LDW)

Mileage Allowance

Mileage Charge

Rental Agreement

Value Added Tax
  (VAT)

How They All Got Rolling

The car rental industry had its beginnings right along with the automobile industry. It didn't take motorists long to figure out that, if having a car was convenient at home, then having wheels at one's destination when traveling by train would be mighty convenient too!

The earliest car rental rates and restrictions would amuse travelers today—ten cents a mile with a three-mile minimum use requirement! Most car renters today would meet the mileage requirement by the time they got out of the rental car lot!

Hertz, the nation's largest rental car firm, wasn't the first on the block when it began in 1918, but it has outlived its earliest competitors. Today, Hertz has over 200,000 cars in 1,400 U.S. locations, making them still number one in size.

Avis, which actively marketed its number-two position to Hertz for many years with its "We Try Harder" slogan, began operating in 1946. It was this company's founder, Warren E. Avis, who first put car rental counters at airports. Today, Avis counters, along with many others, are found at virtually every large and midsized airport in the United States.

National Car Rental was the third of today's major companies and entered the market in 1947. Budget, another well-known name to travel professionals and car renters alike, opened its first car rental location in 1958 and focused its advertising on the cost-conscious traveler. The Budget philosophy and pricing worked because, along with Hertz, Avis, and National, Budget ranks as one of the four largest rental car companies in the United States.

Dollar, another relative newcomer to the industry, is pushing the top four in size and number of locations. Of the top seventy-five airports in the United States, Hertz, Avis, and Budget have rental counters at all seventy-five, National has counters at seventy-four, and Dollar has counters at sixty-nine. The closest competitor after that is Alamo with only twenty-one rental counters located in the top seventy-five airports.

Although the rental car companies got rolling fairly early on in the automobile age, the industry really took off right along with commercial air travel. Air travelers were not "deposited" in the center of the city as were train travelers. Airports, by necessity, were located farther from town. Car rentals often made more sense to the businessperson traveling on a tight and important schedule than depending on taxis or local mass transit.

Who Wants to Drive?

Travelers can get to a great many places on earth by air, but how will they get around once they are there? A lot of them will want to rent cars and will need assistance in doing so. Arranging for a rental car is usually quite easy by phone or through the computer, and it generates a few dollars of commission for the travel agency professional. Some travelers are more likely to get the benefits of a car than others, so you will need to consider a few things before saying "yes" to car rental. A positive response to any of the following questions leads logically to the addition of a rental car to business or leisure travel arrangements:

- Will your business in the city require you to make several expensive trips by taxi?
- Is this a city in which you would be comfortable driving?
- Do you need to visit sites in areas that have no easy access by air or mass transit?
- Do you wish to tour an area at your own pace?

The rental car is frequently the most satisfactory answer to all of these questions. The car allows clients to be both mobile and independent. There are, however, considerations that could make renting a car an undesirable alterative. If the answer is "no" to the following questions, a rental car may not be the best transportation choice:

- Will you drive the car enough to justify the cost of the rental plus parking, tolls, and so on?
- Will the area be sufficiently safe for a driver unfamiliar with the terrain?
- Will you be comfortable with the language, laws, and customs of driving at this destination?
- Are you between the ages of twenty-five and seventy-five and in possession of a valid driver's license?

We Americans love our cars, the images they project, and the freedom they provide. Driving one's own car is one thing, but driving someone else's is quite another, and the rental car supplier has certain constraints and considerations unique to his or her business.

A car rental company must have good reason to entrust a traveler with the expensive automobile he or she plans to drive off the lot. A car might not only be stolen, it could be an instrument of destruction or death. Furthermore, once the car pulls away, the company loses all control over its product.

When you fly, cruise, or stay in a hotel, company representatives are all around you. Should a traveler run amuck and start ripping up seats or breaking things, there is usually someone nearby to intervene on behalf of the supplier company. Not so with rental cars.

Rental companies protect themselves and society by requiring that renters be of age, be duly licensed to drive, be personally responsible, and have good credit. Here are some of the most common requirements and restrictions in renting cars:

Age: If your travelers are under twenty-five they may have difficulty renting a car. Drivers in this age group are statistically at greatest risk of being involved in traffic accidents. A person between the ages of eighteen and twenty-five may be allowed to rent if he or she holds a credit card recognized by the car rental company, if his or her business sends a purchase order or letter of authorization, or if his or her parent or legal guardian completes a "Guarantee of Rental to a Minor" provided by the rental company. Each company has its own policy, and some even charge a higher rate for the driver under twenty-five. The older driver can present a problem as well. While rental car companies in the United States are apt to rent to an adult as long as he or she has a valid driver's license, some foreign countries have a maximum age of sixty-five, seventy, or seventy-five.

License: All renters are required to present a valid driver's license. Only licensed drivers may rent cars and only those drivers whose names and signatures appear on the rental contract are authorized to drive the car. An international driving permit is required for U.S. citizens in some countries and is generally recommended where it isn't required because it provides a translation of the license into several languages. A traveler involved in an accident in a foreign country will want his or her credentials to be readily understood by the local police. The American Automobile Association (AAA) provides the international driver's permit and the photos that must accompany them for a nominal fee. As with most transactions in foreign countries, the renter will be expected to show his or her valid passport.

Credit: This is only one of many times when a credit card will make life easier. Even if a company will accept them (and many don't!), both cash rentals and prepaid vouchers are complicated and time consuming, requiring the renter to provide adequate evidence that he or she is personally responsible. For many rental car companies, possession of a valid, major credit card is a *requirement.*

Who's Renting What

Having decided to rent a car, the next decision is which car to rent. Most car companies provide an extensive selection, but they may not keep all the car types in the fleet at every location. You may be able to get a four-wheel-drive vehicle, a van, or a convertible at some locations, but not others. You may also be able to get a station wagon or a subcompact at some locations, and yet not be allowed to take them one way (pick up in one city and drop off in another).

Car Class The size, type, or price range of a rental car, that is, economy, compact, midsize, full-size, luxury, and so on.

Car rental companies will provide a list of **car classes** (full-size, midsize, compact, etc.) and even of the makes it carries (Ford, Chrysler, etc.), but unless there is only one make per class, they will not guarantee you will get the car of your dreams. For example, if the car company offers Fords, Buicks, and Oldsmobiles in a certain class, and you prefer Buicks, the company will note the preference, but they won't guarantee you will drive away in a Buick.

The only thing a rental car company will guarantee is the size of the car. If, when you arrive to pick up your economy-sized car, an economy-sized car is not available, the rental company will give you a larger car at the same price. Most drivers are thrilled with this unless, of course, they were budgeting gas costs on what the smallest car will consume. For the cost-conscious driver hoping for economy transportation, the standard-sized car offered as consolation for not having any economy cars available might look a lot more like a gas hog than a sleek Thunderbird!

You may have never been particularly interested in cars, but if you are the person responsible for helping a traveler with rental decisions, you will need to know the makes and models and their general characteristics in order to give the most sensible advice. You won't get to be employee of the year by suggesting that a party of four with luggage and skis try to travel over rough mountain roads for a week in a little Ford Escort.

Even though the actual car type cannot be guaranteed, there are tricks of the trade, and knowing who is aligned with whom is one of them. All the major companies specialize in models from specific manufacturers. American car rental companies show a great preference for U.S. cars, although a few do have foreign models as well. In fact, Detroits's Big Three—Ford, GM, and Chrysler—own pieces of some rental car companies and that interest is, of course, reflected in the rental fleet.

The following lists the major car rental companies and the types of cars they offer:

Alamo: Most of the fleet is General Motors, meaning an abundance of Buicks, Cadillacs, Chevrolets, and Oldsmobiles.

Avis: General Motors owns a stake in this company, and 70 percent of Avis' cars are GM manufactured. The other 30 percent is made up of Chryslers, Fords, Toyotas, and Nissans.

Budget: The company claims that business travelers love the Lincoln Town Car and their fleet proves it—25,000 of them! Their midsize and small cars are mostly Fords and Mercuries.

Hertz: If you are particularly fond of the Ford LTD, Hertz is the place to go; they have thousands of them. The company rents mostly Fords because Ford Motor Company owns 49 percent of the company. At Hertz, you might also see a Lincoln Town Car, Continental, and the occasional Volvo.

National: Like the others, this rental company also favors American-made cars, especially those made by part-owner, General Motors. Chrysler also plays a big role in the company as well, and the range of models from both companies is extensive.

Thrifty: Thrifty is a Chrysler company, so it makes sense that most cars are Chryslers. Some Thrifty outlets are franchises and may exercise more choice in fleet selection, but, if you rent from Thrifty, you can pretty much expect to be handed the keys to a Chrysler of some description!

Choosing a car rental company should not be limited to car selection. Sometimes rental cars are cheaper from companies that are not fortunate enough to have facilities on the airport property (known as *on site*). Space in airports is limited and the newer car companies may have to keep their cars in a lot several miles away (*off site*).

Companies with off-site locations generally pick up passengers in a courtesy van or shuttle bus and transport them between the airport and the lot. The lower prices are an incentive to travelers to overlook the inconvenience of the transfer. Even the companies with lots on airport property may require shuttle transportation; big metropolitan airports are like cities themselves, and the rental car lot may not be just out the door! However, on-site properties are generally only a minute's ride from the airport, while off-site companies may be ten to fifteen minutes away, or even more.

Do You Want an FCAR, or Will an ECAR Do?

Everyone knows that many sizes of cars are available, but choosing the right size vehicle for a trip can be confusing if you don't know your makes. The car companies, in their reservation information and in the reservation computers, categorize their fleet in order to make it easier to know what's what. Basically, in the United States, a renter can expect the following standard features: automatic transmission, power controls, and air conditioning.

It will come as no surprise to you that the car companies use codes to distinguish their car types. Like city/airport codes, these are pretty easy to figure out. Here is a computer list of cars that Hertz makes available:

Code	Translation	Car Selections
EMAN	Economy, manual transmission	ESCORT / CHEVETTE / LYNX
ECAR	Economy, automatic	ESCORT / CHEVETTE / LYNX / TERCEL
CCAR	Compact Car	COROLLA / OMNI / SENTRA / TURISMO
ICAR	Intermediate Car	TOPAZ / ARIES / RELIANT
SCAR-2DOOR	Standard Car, 2 doors	THUNDERBIRD / REGAL / SKYLARK
FCAR-4DOOR	Full-sized car, 4 doors	LTD / TAURUS / CELEBRITY / MARQUIS
PCAR-4DOOR	Premium Car, 4 doors	REGENCY 98 / LTD CROWN VICTORIA
LCAR	Luxury Car	CADILLAC FLEETWOOD
SPCL	Special Types or Special Requests	SPORTY / PSGR VAN / 4-WHL DR / HANDICAPPED / SKI

We Said RENT, Not BUY!

Car rental rates are as varied as air fares and hotel costs. To accommodate the needs of almost all travelers, car rental companies generally offer a number of different "rate plans." At the most basic, cars rent for twenty-four-hour periods or "daily rates." A daily rate may have a **mileage allowance,** such as 100 miles, before **mileage charges** are imposed. Included in all rental rates are minor repairs, oil, public liability and property damage insurance, and the first full tank of gas.

Extra charges the renter will bear are extra gas needed, taxes, collision damage waiver, and personal accident insurance. These charges can be substantial; in some cases, these charges can be equal to (or even greater than) the quoted daily rate. In Chicago, the following taxes are added to the rental rate: Chicago transaction tax, motor vehicle rental tax, municipal auto rental tax, and a Chicago surcharge. If the Chicago guest is doing business at McCormick Place, a McCormick Place tax is also added. Just to drive the point home, a $200.00 rental could have almost $50.00 of taxes added on!

Other rate plans may be:

Unlimited Mileage: No per mile charges are added on no matter how much you drive the car.

Weekend Rates: Often beginning on a Thursday or Friday morning and lasting until Sunday evening.

Weekly Rates: Based on keeping the car a full seven days or more.

Commercial or Corporate Rates: Discounts or special programs offered to volume users.

There are also senior citizen discounts, association or club membership discounts, discounts offered to certain credit card holders, and even seasonal rates in major tourist areas such as Florida or California. Special car rental rates or packages may also be offered with package tour plans.

No matter what the rate or rate plan, all rates will be based on the assumption that the renter will pick up and drop off the car at the same place. One-way rental rates can be considerably higher, and **drop charges** may be added if a car is picked up in one city and left in another. It is expensive for the car companies to have to send someone to a less popular location to pick up cars and drive them back to a more popular location, so the cost is passed along to the renter in the form of drop charges.

Another substantial charge for the car rental client is insurance. The **rental agreement** will indicate the amount the renter must pay in the event the car is damaged. To avoid the charge, he or she can purchase a **collision damage waiver (CDW)** or **loss damage waiver (LDW).** The CDW waives the rental company's right to charge the renter for damages if the car is involved in an accident. The LDW waives the company's right to collect damages from theft or vandalism in addition to collision. Neither of these protects the renter if he or she violates the terms of the rental contract, driving while under the influence of drugs or alcohol, or letting an unauthorized person drive the car.

Insurance, as you might imagine, can substantially increase the daily rental cost. Travelers should check their own insurance, or their company's if they are traveling on business, to see if they already have coverage that includes car rental.

Mileage Allowance The miles a car renter may drive at no additional cost.

Mileage Charge Charge made for each mile a rental car is driven beyond the established limit for the rental rate used.

Drop Charge An additional fee that is often charged by a car rental company when the customer rents a car in one city and returns it to another.

Rental Agreement The contract between the car rental company and its customer which is executed/signed when a car is rented.

Collision Damage Waiver (CDW) Optional car rental insurance that significantly reduces or eliminates the renter's liability or damage deductible should the rental car be damaged or wrecked. Some car rental firms have deductibles equal to the cost of the automobile.

Loss Damage Waiver (LDW) Optional car rental insurance that reduces or eliminates the renter's liability if the car is vandalized or stolen.

Foreign Cars

It's great to know that you can rent a car just about anywhere, but would you really want to? You may have visions of tooling around Rome in your Fiat convertible or taking on the Third World in a Land Rover, but unless you are a trained stuntdriver you may want to let these enriching experiences pass you by.

In addition to the international driving permit, you need to know about a few other things that pertain to car rental abroad:

- The price will probably be in a foreign currency, and just like other purchases, it will be at the exchange rate in effect on the day of posting. You will have to ask specifically if a rate is guaranteed.
- Distances will be measured in **kilometers,** not miles.
- Gas will be in liters, not gallons, and may cost three or four times what it does in the United States.
- **Value-added tax (VAT)** may not be included in the rental rate. It can add from l0 to more than 25 percent to the final cost.
- The car will probably be much smaller than its U.S. counterpart and have an unrecognizable name.
- Automatic transmission and air conditioning may increase the rental price dramatically. Most foreign cars are manual transmission and automatic must be requested.
- A car rented in one country may not be allowed to cross the border into another.
- The charge for picking up a car in one country and dropping it off in another may be quite high.
- Some countries don't allow tourists to drive at all, and in some driving is on the left side of the road.

Most professionals recommend that rental cars be confirmed prior to leaving home. Travelers will probably find that the rates are more reasonable because more packages designed for tourists are available. If you decide to rent a car after you arrive in a foreign country, you are just like anybody else and won't get the good rates the company offered to entice you to make your decision (and, in most cases, your payment) before you left home!

Driving a car gives a traveler lots more freedom than taking trains, taxis, and buses, but it can be a harrowing experience. Although there are now many internationally recognized road signs, others, such as street and regulatory signs, are in that country's native language. Driving habits and styles may also be quite different. By world standards, U.S. drivers are, for the most part, mannerly and well controlled. Even a native New York cab driver would appear sedate in some countries!

Safety standards differ widely throughout the world. You won't find a German car without a functioning seat belt, and stiff fines are imposed for drivers or front-seat passengers who do not buckle up. And

Kilometer A measure equal to 3,280 feet or five-eighths of a mile. The standard measure of distance in continental Europe is the kilometer.

Value-Added Tax (VAT) A government-imposed tax on goods that is common in European countries.

you would certainly want to buckle up in a country that tends to ignore speed limits and where it is not unusual to see Mercedes and BMWs whisking down the autobahns (freeways) at close to 100 miles an hour!

The individualistic Italians, on the other hand, pay no heed to seat belts, and you will often find them broken or missing entirely. Cars that are cheerfully rented in Italy—open sided, missing seat belts, broken locks, and so on—would never pass inspection in the United States. It is also not uncommon for cars to wildly exceed the speed limits on the freeways (autostradas), and, in the cities, the sheer noise of honking horns, yelling drivers, and screaming sirens would put rush hour in our major cities to shame!

Driving in Great Britain, while certainly calmer and slower than in some of its continental neighbors, is on the left-hand side of the road, and the driver's seat, of course, is on the right. Crossing the street as a pedestrian can be challenging to an American; just consider what a thrill driving would be!

Employment Opportunities in the Car Rental Industry

The numbers of rental car companies and cars rented increases each year, and the outlook for employment in the industry is good. The large car rental companies may have central reservations offices and employ reservationists, supervisors, and clerical help. Local rental offices and airport locations have station managers, supervisors, and customer service agents who work directly with the public. There may also be rapid or express return agents who meet the customers as they drive in to return the car and check the car in (and the customer out) with a handheld computer!

On the regional and national levels, there are sales representatives who call on travel professionals and large corporations, airlines, and tour packagers. In the executive offices, there are clerical employees, sales and marketing professionals, and, of course, the officers of the corporation.

Like airlines and hotels, the car rental business is a twenty-four-hour-a-day service. Many customers arrive on the earliest flights and leave on the latest. Busiest times of the day at airport locations are morning and late afternoon/evening. Sales counter representatives are the first, and sometimes only, contact a customer has with the company, and the impression he or she makes is very important!

Some rental car companies are quite progressive in flexible schedules and employee benefits. Most customer service agents and maintenance crew wear company uniforms, thus reducing the money required for a working wardrobe. Some companies provide the uniforms at little or no extra cost to employees and offer a dry cleaning allowance as well.

Like many entry-level jobs in the travel industry, reservationists and customer service representatives may move up the corporate ladder to supervisor, manager, or sales representative. The experience of dealing one on one with the general public is invaluable and, no matter where you go, there is probably always at least one rental car firm who could use your services!

Explorations

Check your Yellow Pages listings under rental cars.

1. If you live in a medium- to large-sized metropolitan area, answer the following:
   a. How many locations are listed for each of the top four companies?
   b. Give the names of other listed rental car firms and the numbers of rental locations they list (maximum 5).
2. If you live in a smaller population area, answer the following:
   a. Which of the top four companies are listed and indicate whether they have local rental locations or just list 800 numbers.
   b. Give the names of any rental car companies which advertise local rental facilities.
3. Give the reasons you recommend or do not recommend renting a car for the following trips:

   New York City theater and shopping weekend: Yes ( ) No ( )
   Why _____

   Colorado winter ski trip (fly into Denver, transfer to ski resort):
   Yes ( ) No ( )
   Why _____

   Business trip to Rome, Italy: Yes ( ) No ( )
   Why _____

   A trip to Las Vegas: Yes ( ) No ( )
   Why _____

Enrichments

Make a visit to your local commercial airport. Answer the following questions:

1. How many rental car counters are located in the airport? (Give their names.)
2. Which of the companies appears to be the largest? (Consider amount of space, number of employees.)
3. Do the companies that have on-site lots have cars within walking distance or must the renter take a shuttle bus?

4. How many off-site companies have counters at the airport? (Give their names.) Also, if possible, give approximate distances or shuttle bus time to their lots.

5. Give your impressions of the rental car counter area at the airport you visited.

6. Based on this visit and visual impression, which company would you be most likely to use or recommend to arriving passengers?

All Aboard!

RESERVATION

Where Are We Going?

When you have completed this section, you will:

1. Know about the limitations and types of train travel offered in the United States.
2. Understand the role of Amtrak in U.S. rail travel.
3. Be familiar with modern advances in rail travel.
4. Know the importance of rail travel in other parts of the world.

Industry Terms and Jargon

Amtrak	Couchette	Eurailpass
Bullet Train	Eurail	Observation Car
Cooks Timetable		

Getting a Leg Up on the Iron Horse

Every day, thousands of trains thunder along the railroad tracks of the world. They are carrying people to vacations, family visits, and business meetings; they are providing daily commuter transportation between the suburbs and the cities; they are carrying mail, food, and freight to the cities, towns and remote villages of the world.

It is passenger traffic that is important in travel and tourism, and trains carry millions of passengers from place to place every day. Trains are the backbone of transportation in European countries; Japan could not do without its "bullet trains"; and the countries of Latin America, Asia, and Africa would be sorely inconvenienced and "set back" in time if rail travel were to disappear tomorrow.

The "iron horse" was the first great transportation achievement of the industrial age. The early locomotives huffed and puffed across the countryside at speeds that a horse could easily outrun. However, these locomotives could could carry heavier loads more rapidly for long distances, and it wasn't long before the newer, steam-driven locomotives could easily outpace their four-footed competitors (hence the expression "iron horse").

Although roads of rails were used in Europe as early as 1550, they were simple wagonways of wooden rails where horse-drawn wagons could be moved more efficiently than over rutted dirt roads. To prevent wear and to offer a smoother surface, strips of iron were attached to the tops of the rails. These early railroads made horse-drawn wagon transport easier, but they really weren't a vast improvement over the horse and coach on the open roads. It wasn't until locomotives began pulling passenger cars that rail travel won the patronage, hearts, and imaginations of people everywhere. Probably more songs have been written about and more pictures painted of trains than of any other mode of transportation.

UP CLOSE

Maglev: Futuristic Rail Travel

With heads turned skyward, constantly scanning the turbulent business of air travel, travel professionals and travelers alike may be missing the most incredible development in transportation happening right here on the ground!

Magnetic levitation—maglev for short—and its commercial application in high-speed ground transportation may be in use before the year 2000! Maglev is based on the suspension, guidance, and propulsion of vehicles by magnetic force. Trains are suspended several inches above a single track, called a glideway, and are capable of traveling at speeds in excess of 300 mph!

Maglev technology was developed in the United States in the mid-1970s, but the federal government concluded through evaluations and

Important Dates and Developments
in Passenger Rail Travel

1769 James Watt of Scotland patented the first efficient steam engine.

1814 Three railway cars were pulled by locomotive in England.

1825 The first regularly operated steam railroad, the Stockton & Darlington of England, ran its first train. In the United States, the first locomotive was run on rails in Hoboken, N.J.

1830 In the United States, the first successful steam locomotive, the *Best Friend of Charleston*, began operating out of Charleston, S.C.

1833 Andrew Jackson became the first U.S. president to take a train ride!
Inauguration of the Orient Express, the train that carried the rich and powerful from Paris to Istanbul over a spectacularly scenic route.

1839 America's first long-distance railway express service began between Boston and New York.

1859 First Pullman sleeping cars were introduced between Bloomington, IL, and Chicago.

1863 First dining cars were used between Baltimore and Philadelphia.

1869 First transcontinental railway was completed in the United States, joining the Central Pacific and Union Pacific railroads in Promontory, Utah. It was now possible to travel by train from the east coast to the west coast in a matter of days—a trip that once took months!

1883 Standard Time, sponsored by the railroads, was adopted throughout the United States.

1931 Air conditioned rail cars were brought into service.

1945 The domed observation car was introduced, making rail travel more scenic than ever!

1955 World's first 200 mph run was made between Bordeaux and Dax, France.

1959 Eurailpass was introduced to promote European rail travel by non-European tourists.

1964 Shinkansen, the Japanese bullet trains, were introduced and offered passenger transportation at speeds in excess of 125 mph.

1971 Amtrak, a government-subsidized rail corporation, is formed to help save financially troubled U.S. rail companies and preserve rail service in America.

1990 The X2000 "speedy tilt train" began scheduled operation in Sweden.

1993 The "Chunnel" opened, enabling passengers to travel by rail under the English Channel between England and France.

Fast Forward

2001 Will the Maglev high-speed train, using electromagnetism to glide over a single rail at 300 mph, change the world of transportation?

studies that there was not a large enough market to justify spending money on high-speed ground transportation. The Japanese and Germans, whose societies are highly dependent on efficient ground transportation, took over maglev research and are working to put it to use in their countries as well as exporting it to others, including the United States, its mother country!

Maglev could be a vital component in short- and medium-range transportation and could link airport hubs and major metropolitan centers. Maglev could alleviate heavy automobile and air traffic congestion in high-density transportation corridors such as San Francisco/Los Angeles, New York/Boston, and New York/Washington. At speeds of 300 mph, travel between Washington and Atlanta would take two hours!

Speed and quiet are two major features of maglev transportation. But they are not the only or even the most important ones. Maglev is pollution free, energy efficient, and doesn't rely on petroleum products. It would not be susceptible to delays and cancellations in bad weather, and early studies indicate that travel via maglev would be dramatically less expensive than air travel. Proponents of maglev say "let the airlines have the long-haul flights, maglev will cover the short- to medium-distance trips!"

Maglev is as revolutionary as the jet and may well bring us all back to earth!

Rail Travel in the United States

By the 1900s, the railroads offered all the conveniences of a modern home or hotel: electric lights, steam heat, comfortable seating, dining cars, sleeping cars, wash rooms, and even parlor cars for socializing and club cars for having an after-dinner drink and a game of cards. Train travel had become a pleasurable, even glamorous, mode of transportation. The rich even had their own luxurious rail cars, built and decorated to their specifications. They could hook their cars to the scheduled trains and ride the rails in private and plush surroundings!

By the 1920s the automobile age had arrived and private automobiles and buses were making a dent in passenger rail traffic. As car ownership spread throughout the United States and more roads were built, the railroads continued in their decline. In the 1950s and 1960s, increased and affordable air travel dealt the final blows, and rail passenger traffic declined to the point that major rail companies went out of business, and many travel professionals predicted that the end of rail travel was at hand.

Amtrak   The National Railroad Passenger Corporation, a government-subsidized corporation that operates almost all passenger train service in the United States.

In 1970, the U.S. government, in an effort to help the ailing railroads and yet not take them over completely, created the National Railroad Passenger Corporation, more commonly known as **Amtrak.** This semipublic corporation is financed through federal subsidies and participation of the private rail companies. Most all major rail companies immediately joined Amtrak and, by 1983, the few holdouts had joined as well.

Although Amtrak continues to be plagued with budget woes, the company has made some advances. While certainly not financially healthy enough to stand on their own, the rail companies have seen positive development, increased stability, growth, and even the promise of future enhancements through the Amtrak organization.

I Think I Can, I Think I Can . . .

Can you get there by train? In many parts of the world, "you know you can!"

In the United States, a qualified, "maybe you can."

When Amtrak took over the nation's railroads, there were many, many unprofitable routes, and, in a necessary cost-saving measure, they were eliminated. Regular rail transportation between the major cities of the East Coast—Boston/New York, New York/Philadelphia, New York/Washington and Washington/Philadelphia—continued pretty much as usual. Millions of business travelers and commuters use these train services every year, and it would have been disastrous to cut them out.

But, many of the longer haul trips and schedules between smaller cities in the United States were drastically cut back or eliminated all together. Until recently, it was not possible to travel across the United States by train without having to make connections. Chicago and the sunny South are not linked by regular rail service, nor can you board a train in Atlanta and travel to Dallas—two of the most important business centers in the lower half of the United States. Train transportation is also sadly lacking in the heavily traveled "California Corridor," the area between San Francisco and Los Angeles.

For vacationers, Chicago still has its scenic departures to the West with domed **observation cars,** sleeping cars and dining cars. These trains are popular with those who want to experience the thrill of traveling across the United States, but not the exhaustion of driving! And, vacationers from the mid-Atlantic states and Southeast can put the family *and* the family car on a train and head for Florida!

Observation Car A railroad car specially designed for sightseeing.

Outside of regular commuter service and the few remaining long-hauls, there isn't much to make the traveler or the travel professional pick up the phone to check the schedules. But, despite its perennial budget woes, Amtrak compiled a short list of new projects and enhancements for the 1990s:

Sunset Limited. The existing Los Angeles–New Orleans Sunset Limited route extended eastward to Jacksonville, Florida, and south to Miami.

Chicago–Florida. Service between Chicago and Florida was terminated in the late 1980s because it was one of the railroad's biggest money losers. However, the original route was circuitous and bypassed Atlanta, the most important city on the route. With track improvements, Amtrak would like to re-open the route, this time through Atlanta, to offer vacationing Chicagoans a route to the sunny South and southerners direct access to Chicago and its popular scenic western routes.

Shorter Haul Routes such as Los Angeles–Bakersfield and Boston–Portland and a rail link to Vancouver from Washington State are also on the list. As air travel becomes more expensive and as airlines cut back on short-haul routes to save money, Amtrak and the iron rails may start humming again!

In the golden years of railroads, train travel was glamorous, exciting, and romantic. Americans loved their trains and, like ships, gave them names and waxed poetic about their virtues. Although the days of the Wabash Cannonball, Empire Builder, and Super Chief may be over, travelers might want, or certainly appreciate, a description of the "Iron Horse" they will be riding.

Amtrak has reduced the definitions and names to a manageable, though not particularly romantic, number. Much like the airlines, the

What Kind of Train Will It Be?

type of equipment depends on the type of trip. Equipment for short-haul, commuter-type runs will be very different from that used on long-haul or scenic routes. Following are some examples:

Turboliner. Used on short-distance commuter routes in New York State, this equipment has single-level coach, parlor, and food service cars.

Amfleet. This equipment class consists of single-level coach, club, and food service cars and is found on short- to medium-distance routes. In this line are the new long-distance cars operating in the East.

Metroliner. This service operates with high-speed electric locomotives in the Washington–New Haven corridor and uses specially painted Amfleet equipment with special comfort features.

Heritage. This group includes single-level coaches, dining, lounge, and sleeping cars and is usually employed on medium- to long-distance routes in the East and Midwest.

Superliner. This group of cars has double-level observation coaches, sleepers, lounges, and diners. Superliners are used on the scenic routes west of Chicago.

Auto Train. This line uses Heritage equipment and special cars, such as the domed observation coach and domed lounge. The train also includes automobile carriers to transport both passengers and their cars on the route between Virginia and Florida.

The New Kid on the Tracks. In the early 1990s, Amtrak began testing the Swedish X2000, a high-speed "tilt" train for use on medium-range routes, such as New York to Boston. Although the train's maximum speed of 150 mph is not a great deal faster than Amtrak's Metroliners, the design of the X2000 allows it to take curves at a much higher rate of speed than its U.S. counterparts. In fact, the manufacturer claims that the train can go 40 to 45 percent faster through curves than conventional equipment.

The appeal of the X2000 is that it was designed to enhance rail travel, not by racing along at amazing new speeds on newly designed high-tech tracks, but by maintaining a constant speed through the twists and turns of existing track. This impressive feat is accomplished by means of a hydraulic tilting system in the wheel base that compensates for strong centrifugal forces. Early test runs in the United States show that curves that now have 75 mph speed limits can be taken at speeds of 90 to 100 mph without spilling the first drink or rattling an ice cube!

Making the Reservation

Reservations for transportation on Amtrak may be made through a travel agency or with Amtrak reservation offices. Amtrak is a member of ARC, and travel agents can issue Amtrak tickets through several of the airline computer reservation systems. Ticketing procedures are similar to those used for the airlines; however, train and air tickets cannot be combined.

Fares for train travel may be obtained from the reservation systems in which Amtrak participates and also from their comprehensive resource guide, *All America Train Fares*. Unlike air fares, Amtrak fares do not fluctuate constantly, and are not subject to severe penalties for change or cancellation. In high-traffic areas, train fares may be lower than air fares.

A standard rail ticket is for a single seat in either first- or second-class compartments. On long-haul routes, private sitting rooms that convert to sleeping compartments may also be available. Special accommodations such as sleeping compartments or **couchettes** must be reserved far in advance as availability is limited. These accommodations carry extra charges that can be substantial.

Couchette A sleeping berth in a publicly shared compartment on an international train. Normally, a compartment has four first-class or six second-class couchettes.

Amtrak offers tour programs that combine rail travel with hotel accommodations and local sightseeing. Amtrak also has special excursion rates and, for the foreign visitor, national or regional USA rail passes. The USA rail passes must be purchased outside the United States and are not for sale to citizens or permanent residents of the United States or Canada.

Special services can be requested for Amtrak passengers, including special meals, special assistance, wheel chair assistance, special assistance for blind or deaf passengers traveling with guide dogs, and so on. Some requests can be confirmed immediately, others may take twenty-four to seventy-two hours to confirm. Unlike the airlines, meals are *not* included as part of the trip, no matter how long. Some train passengers take their own food (box lunches, etc.) on board. Those wishing to purchase meals or snacks on trains that offer food service should be aware that Amtrak accepts only cash or traveler's checks. Credit cards are accepted only in certain club cars and full-service dining cars. If you forget to take along some cash, you may well go hungry!

Foreign Rails

There are rail systems all over the world and most are government owned and operated. The most important rail systems for the beginning travel professional to know outside the United States are VIA Rail Canada, **Eurail,** BritRail, and the Japanese National Railways. In most countries of the world, the passenger rail industry did not face the decline it did in the United States and has remained a very important means of public transportation. There are reasons for this:

Eurail The rail system of the countries of western Europe plus Hungary.

Price of Fuel. Even with regular increases in gasoline prices in the United States, the rest of the world (except of course the Middle East) endures much higher fuel costs, sometimes two to three times higher.

Standard of Living. In many countries, private car ownership is much more out of the reach of middle and lower earning groups than it is in the United States. In some of the larger cities, car ownership is made even more difficult by limited and costly parking, high insurance and tax rates, theft and vandalism, and almost unbearable traffic and driving conditions.

Extensive Rail and Mass Transit Services. Unlike the United States, even small- and medium-sized cities in Europe and Japan have frequent, dependable rail service to the larger cities and reliable local transportation services.

Proximity. Although not the case in Canada, European countries and Japan are smaller and the distances to travel between major cities are much less than in the United States. For British businesspeople, a train trip between Edinburgh, Scotland, in the north of Great Britain to London in the south is a journey of only four to five hours. For the U.S. businessperson, traveling the north-south length of the country (New York/Miami) is a journey of thirty-plus hours!

Price and Availability of Air Travel. Air travel is expensive in foreign countries, and high-speed trains, dependable and comfortable service, and reasonable prices make rail travel a viable alternative to flying. Because rail travel is so widespread and convenient, airlines in Europe and Japan simply don't offer the shorter haul flights that U.S. travelers consider standard fare. In fact, with new developments in high-speed rail transportation, it is only on journeys longer than five hours that new trains in Europe will be outdone by aircraft.

When most people think of foreign rail travel, they think first of Europe, probably because the European rail system is the most famous in the world and also because most international travelers from the United States are headed to Europe. But, railways exist all over the world, and the travel professional who works with itineraries involving rail travel needs to know what his or her resources are!

Cook's Timetable The Thomas Cook Continental Timetable and Thomas Cook Overseas Timetable have routes and schedules for trains outside the U.S., features of each train, national and international rail maps, timetables, and routes for ferries and steamers.

The bible of European rail travel is the *Thomas Cook European Timetable.* Published in England twelve times a year, **Cook's Timetable,** as it is known to agents everywhere, is an essential resource for anyone who sells or schedules trips by rail. *The Cook's Continental* and its companion, the *Thomas Cook Overseas Timetable,* contain routes and schedules for trains worldwide, as well as timetables for ferries and steamers, temperature charts, rail maps, information about documents, temperature and metric conversion charts, and a host of details about the special features of each train.

The *Eurail Guide,* another indispensable reference, describes rail trips in over 100 countries with highlights of European and British one-day rail excursions. Information on nearly 400 one-day trips outside Europe are also included. The *Eurail Guide* also includes information on special rail passes offered throughout the world and ticket prices for more than 700 European train trips.

Rail Travel in Canada

Canada has two major railroads, Canadian National Railways which is government owned and Canadian Pacific Railway which is privately owned. In 1978, somewhat along the lines of Amtrak, VIA Rail Canada, a government-owned corporation, took over the management of Canadian passenger rail services.

High-speed trains such as the new Light Rapid Comfortable (LRC) offer express service between Canada's major cities. Canadian rail is known for its transcontinental trains that connect Central Canada to the Maritime provinces in the east and mountainous provinces in the west. Travel by rail through the spectacular wilderness of the Canadian Rockies, in particular, attracts many visitors from the United States, some of whom can connect directly from Amtrak routes.

There is a fairly high degree of cooperation between Amtrak and VIA Rail Canada. Amtrak's automation system has the schedules and fares for the Canadian VIA rail services and acts as VIA's general sales agent in the United States. VIA reciprocates throughout Canada. In 1992, VIA Rail Canada joined the Airlines Reporting Corporation (ARC), a move that will allow U.S. travel agents to issue tickets on VIA Rail for travel in Canada, rather than ticketing through Amtrak. Eventually, VIA Rail Canada plans to offer its schedules and reservations capabilities through the travel agency automated systems such as Apollo and Sabre.

VIA Rail Canada also offers the Canrailpass, a thirty-day rail pass that allows unlimited train travel throughout the VIA Rail network. There is a choice of Systemwide or Eastern Regional passes and pass holders are eligible for special car rental rates from Hertz. These passes are for non-Canadian rail passengers and can only be sold outside Canada.

Rail Travel in Europe

During the Industrial Revolution, the network of rail systems grew up naturally within the European countries to provide transportation for their rapidly expanding populations. Today, as a result, you can go just about anywhere in Europe by train. There are simple little narrow gauge trains that chug from town to town in the mountains, intercity trains that shuttle commuters back and forth, and superfast trains that go by in a blur and eat up the miles between cities and countries.

All European railroads are government owned, and there is widespread cooperation and coordination among them. An excellent example of this cooperation is the **Eurailpass.** First introduced in 1959, the Eurailpass was created to promote train travel by non-European tourists. It is good for unlimited rail travel through seventeen participating countries in Western Europe and can also be used on on some ferry and bus services.

The Eurailpass

Eurailpass *An unlimited-use rail ticket purchased for a specific period of time to travel by train in the countries that participate in the Eurail system. In some cases, the pass can be used for bus and ferry transportation.*

Eurailpasses must be purchased outside Europe and are not available for use by European citizens or permanent residents. When a conductor in Europe asks to see your ticket and you proudly hand him your Eurailpass, he will want to see your passport as well, just to be sure you are a valid user! Passes are good for first-class travel and can be for a period of fifteen days, twenty-one days, one month, two months, or three months. If your tastes don't run to first-class travel, there is a second-class pass, but its sale is restricted to travelers under the age of twenty-six and is called the Youthpass.

UP CLOSE

The Chunnel

Another example of European cooperation in rail travel is the Eurotunnel, more affectionately known as the "Chunnel," which runs between Great Britain and France under the English Channel. Opened in late 1993, this tunnel enables people to travel by rail between England and France. Prior to the Chunnel's opening, travel across the Channel was by ferry and hovercraft, sometimes over very choppy and uncomfortable seas.

Motorists don't have to leave their cars behind as most of the trains operating under the Chunnel are auto-train shuttles. In fact, passenger rail service is less frequent than the motorist shuttle service. Motorists drive their vehicles directly onto the trains, which are air conditioned and well lighted. Both French and British customs facilities for this high-speed shuttle transportation are located on both sides, and customs formalities are conducted at departure only. All of this means that motorists may drive right off the train without having to so much as wave goodbye!

The Channel Tunnel is actually three tunnels: a tunnel for northbound travel, a tunnel for southbound travel, and a central service tunnel. They are thirty miles long and 81 to 146 feet below the sea bed. Safety features include passages linking the tunnels every 1,200 feet, ventilation and cooling systems, and four independent sources of power with two each on the British and French sides.

Prior to the Chunnel opening, trips between London and Paris were time consuming and cumbersome. They involved long train rides, uncomfortable ferry or hovercraft transportation over the Channel, or wrangling with local transportation and traffic between the airports and the cities. High-speed rail service through the Chunnel reduces London to Paris travel time to an amazing three hours! Such ease of travel is appealing to leisure travelers and a near miracle for business travelers!

Reserving Your Seat in Europe

Obtaining a Eurailpass is actually very simple. Travel agencies can order them through their reservation systems and have them to you in a matter of a week or less. In addition to the various Eurailpasses offered, most European countries offer their own rail passes for travel exclusively within their boundaries. Some of these can be ordered through the agency reservation systems; others have to be ordered direct from the reservation offices of the specific railroad. Virtually all Western European nations have reservation offices or 800-number services within the United States.

Most people, unless they are seasoned travelers and absolutely convinced they do not need the help or want the convenience of working with a travel agent, would be well-advised to call one when it comes to planning rail travel abroad. There are many different types of passes, and costs for tickets can vary depending on the route, class of service, or actual train selected. Some trains, such as the high-speed, first-class expresses, are more expensive than others.

In addition to passes and point-to-point tickets, there are also specials. Britain and France have their special "shrinker" tours by train. From April to October you can take a "Franceshrinker," fully escorted tour of Burgundy, Mont St. Michel, or the Loire Valley and still come back to your hotel in Paris to sleep. In Britain, you can stay in London and take a "Britainshrinker" tour by train to Bath, Dover, and Canterbury or to Stratford-on-Avon. These tours allow you to see some of the most interesting sites in the country without having to change hotels every night. And, finally, there are rail-drive packages that include rail tickets and rental cars.

Some other helpful points about rail travel in Europe:

- Travel light; porters are not always around when you need them.
- Don't lose your rail pass; they are nonrefundable.
- Always keep watch over your possessions. You are your own security guard on a train.
- Verify train schedules locally at each stop.
- Be certain you are in the right car going in the right direction.
- Get seat reservations on busy trains or you may have to stand.

For those who know how to use them, the trains of Europe are an excellent way to conduct a business trip or enhance a vacation.

Rail Travel in Japan

The government-owned Japanese National Railways operates most train service in Japan, but there are a number of privately owned companies as well. All of Japan's privately owned trains are single class and require advance seat reservations. Many of the privately owned trains serve resort areas.

The Japanese Railways Group surpasses all other rail systems in the world in both service and size and is considered to be the finest rail system in the world. Over 26,000 trains operate each day. In 1970, Japan enacted the "Law for Construction of Nationwide High-Speed Railways," and they haven't slowed down since! The law mandated that many routes have speeds of up to 150 mph. Passengers can see how law-abiding their engineers are by checking the speedometers located throughout the trains.

Bullet Train *High-speed Japanese train; also known as Shinkansen.*

The most famous Japanese trains are the Shinkansen, the **bullet trains.** The famous "Hikan" leaves Tokyo every quarter hour and runs the 345 miles between Tokyo and Kyoto in 2.5 hours. The 735-mile trip between Tokyo and Hakata is accomplished in just under 6 hours! The trains are safe, clean and smooth running. The only thing they aren't good for is sightseeing—the speed is so great, everything within 1,000 feet is a blur!

Although there was much to-do about Europe's "Chunnel," the Japanese were way out in front in such high-tech construction. In 1988, the 33.4 mile Seikan Tunnel, the world's longest undersea tunnel, was opened to passenger service. The tunnel connects Tappi and Yoshioka and links Hokkaido by rail with the rest of Japan.

The tunnel reaches a depth 787 feet beneath the surface of the water and 328 feet under the seabed. Like the Chunnel, it is a complex of three tunnels; however, in the Seikan, there is one main tunnel and two service tunnels. The opening of the tunnel allowed the Japanese to suspend service on the hazardous 4.5-hour ferry ride between Aomori and Hakodate, and the sixteen-hour trip from Sapporo to Tokyo was reduced to 11 hours. High-speed train service in Japan has been so successful that domestic airlines have made little progress in offering competing service!

Tickets for rail transportation can be purchased at Japanese railway stations or at major travel agencies throughout Japan. The major city stations have "Green Windows" where English is spoken. There are also rail passes for unlimited travel on the trains, buses, and ferries of the system. Vouchers are sold *only* outside the country. Once the visitor arrives in Japan, he or she must exchange the voucher for the actual pass.

The World Is Out There Waiting

There are also tour programs available through the railways that offer reduced-rate excursions.

Romantic Rides:
The Great Trains of the World

Murder on the Orient Express, the Agatha Christie mystery novel that was later made into a movie, immortalized this romantic train and showed the world why it was considered the epitome of luxury and the ultimate rail travel experience. The Orient Express, which began service in 1833, carried the rich and influential from Paris to Istanbul over a spectacularly scenic route. By 1977, the Orient Express was barely a shadow of its former self and was taken out of service. However, in 1982, the Venice Simplon-Orient-Express was initiated and featured many of the train's original coaches, refurbished to their former elegance. Today's Orient Express travels from London to Venice, and those interested in traveling aboard her must make special arrangements and be prepared to part with a tidy sum as this is a deluxe tour, not a simple train ride!

Other greats around the world are:

- "The Ghan," winner of the 1990 Australian National Tourism Award. This train was named in tribute to the Afghan traders who, in the 1800s, carried passengers and goods on camels between Port Pirie and OOdnadatta, Australia. Today, the train travels between Adelaide and Alice Springs, the ideal jumping-off spot for tours to the Australian Outback.

- Also in Australia is the "Indian Pacific" which travels sixty-eight hours between Sydney on the west coast and Perth on the east coast, a 2,461 mile journey. Considered one of the world's great train trips, it takes in some of the most scenic vistas of Australia.

- "The Royal Scotsman," which offers deluxe travel in renovated Victorian and Edwardian railroad cars, offers itineraries throughout the Scottish highlands. Like the "Orient Express," the Royal Scotsman is a touring train and is considerably more expensive than standard rail travel in Britain.

- "The Trans-Siberian Express" of the Commonwealth of Independent States (formerly the Soviet Union). This train travels from Moscow in the east to Mongolia and is the longest overland rail trip in the world.

- "The Copper Canyon Ride" in Mexico offers some of the most spectacular scenery the country has to offer. Completed in 1981, the rail line crosses thirty-nine bridges, passes through eighty-six tunnels, and climbs to a height of 8,071 feet as it travels through the Sierra Madres. The train stops at Divisadero on the rim of the Urique Canyon for twenty minutes so passengers can take a long look down 6,000 feet into the canyon!

Workin' on the Railroad: Employment Opportunities in the Railroad Industry

The best known jobs are those of the engineer, who drives the train, and the conductor, who yells "All Aboard," takes tickets, and generally makes sure that on-board service is running smoothly. There are, of course, public contact jobs that don't involve riding a train all day. There are reservationists, station agents, sales representatives, and clerical workers.

In the 1920s when rail travel was at its peak in the United States, over two million people were employed by the lines. Today, the employment number has shrunk to under 300,000. The decrease in employment has been caused by the decline in rail passenger traffic which can be attributed to automobiles and air travel.

Although rail travel can be lots of fun to do and interesting for the travel professional to research, plan, and book, it's best to realize that career opportunities within the rail industry itself are limited.

Explorations

1. Determine if scheduled rail travel is available in your area. If so, give a description of what destinations are served.
2. Where is your nearest Amtrak passenger station?
3. If you have traveled on a train in the United States in the last five years, give your impressions of the service, equipment, and overall experience.
4. If you have traveled on a train outside the U.S. in the last five years, give your impressions of the service, equipment, and overall experience.

Enrichments

1. Choose a position "pro" or "con" in the development of maglev transportation in the United States. In one page (no more than two) give your reasons for your position and why you think our country would be better off with/without funding for such transportation.
2. Do you think rail travel has a future in the United States? Tell why or why not.
3. If there is a train station located in your city or close by, visit it and write a report on its services, condition, personnel, and so on.

Tours Are Terrific!

Where Are We Going?

When you have completed this section, you will:

1. Know the basic features of a package tour.
2. Be familiar with the different types of tours available to travelers today.
3. Know the benefits of taking a tour or package vacation.
4. Understand how tours are priced and what affects the cost of a tour.

Industry Terms and Jargon

Guide

Itinerary

Land Arrangements

Miscellaneous
Charges Order
(MCO)

Step-On Guide

Tour Escort/Tour
Manager

Transfer

Tour Beginnings

Package and inclusive tours are a relatively new concept in the travel world. The idea of taking a tour probably began with the Grand Tour, popularized by the British aristocracy beginning in the 1600s. The purpose of the Grand Tour was educational and cultural and could last from one to five years. Traditionally, Grand Tours were taken by young men who traveled with tutors, servants, and enormous amounts of luggage. At the height of its popularity, the "Grand Tour" was made by thousands of young Englishmen.

In the late eighteenth and early nineteenth centuries, wars and international upheaval took their toll, and the idea of the Grand Tour was abandoned. Traveling embattled roads and byways was hazardous and, while dealing with the difficulties and challenges of travel in foreign countries had always been considered a valuable part of the educational experience, getting killed certainly was not!

By the mid-1800s, when touring was again becoming popular, many things had changed and the Grand Tour was replaced by families and groups traveling together—and you didn't have to be a member of the aristocracy to join a tour. As we mentioned in Section 1, Thomas Cook, a Baptist missionary from England, is credited with being the "father of the packaged tour."

By 1856, just fifteen years after his first group excursion to a temperance convention, Thomas Cook had started a travel agency and a tour company and was offering group travel to Europe, on Nile cruises, to India, and to the United States. We can also thank Thomas Cook for creating the first travel brochures, formal itineraries, and travel vouchers.

Packages? Tours? What's the Difference?

A *package* consists of a number of services and accommodations that a traveler buys from a tour operator, or in some cases, a hotel. These services and accommodations, or component parts, are put together and sold to the general public direct or through travel agencies.

If you have ever purchased a computer, you know that there are many different parts or components: the monitor, the processor, the keyboard, the printer, software, and so on. Each component could be purchased separately, but often the manufacturer or distributor will put the components together and offer a "special package price." This type of packaging is not unlike package tours whose basic components—or features as they are called in travel—are:

- Hotel accommodations, including taxes and service charges.
- Transportation from/to airport and hotel—known in the industry as **transfers.**
- One or more sightseeing or entertainment features such as theater tickets, admission to local attractions, meals, cocktails, sightseeing tours, and so on.

Transfer   *Local ground transportation, usually from airport to hotel. Transfers are frequently included in the price of tour packages.*

Transportation from and back to the participant's home city may or may not be included. With hotel packages, transportation is usually not included. Package features offered at the tour destination(s)—that is, exclusive of air transportation—are commonly referred to as ground or **land arrangements.**

Hotel packages are put together by the hotels or their marketing representatives and sold through their reservation services. These packages are advertised to the public and are commissionable to travel agents.

A *tour* is also a "package" of travel arrangements but usually includes more features and offers air transportation to and from the participant's home city. There are four basic types of package tours:

- Independent tours
- Hosted tours
- Escorted tours
- Custom tours

Tours are put together by a *tour operator* or *tour wholesaler* and are advertised to the public. These two terms are often used interchangeably, but there are some distinctions that should be understood by the travel professional:

1. The tour operator may sell to agencies and also directly to the general public. Some tour operators also operate retail travel agencies, such as American Express and the Carlson Travel Group.

2. A tour operator may actually handle the direct operations of a tour and employ personnel (such as drivers and guides) and own motorcoaches and, in some cases, hotels.

3. A tour wholesaler contracts with suppliers to secure space and to operate the tour. The wholesaler simply sells the arrangements.

4. A tour wholesaler does not usually sell to the general public or operate a retail travel agency. Most tour operators sell exclusively through existing agencies.

Both tour operators and tour wholesalers pay commissions on the sales of their tours and packages.

Sometimes, to further confuse the who's who in the tour business, travel agencies also package tours. Agencies may develop tours for special groups on a one-time basis or they may package and sell tours as the operators and wholesalers do and promote them for sale to the general public. However the arrangements are made and the packages sold, all tours fall into the four basic groups just mentioned.

Land Arrangements *Those elements of a trip provided to a client upon reaching his or her destination: transfers, hotels, meals, sightseeing, and so on.*

The Independent Tour

This type of tour is best known as a *package*. It is unstructured and participants may not even know they are on a tour since they do not travel with a group or have a formal **itinerary** to follow. The independent tour or package can be arranged to suit individual requirements. The purpose of a package is to offer a traveler all the benefits of the opera-

Itinerary *The complete schedule of a trip.*

tors' volume discounts and guaranteed rates without sacrificing flexibility and independence.

Independent tour packages offer the traveler a selection of hotels and a choice of extras such as meal plans, rental cars, rail tickets, and entertainment features. In many cases, the purchaser can choose the options he or she wants included. Travel counselors must be careful to analyze the cost of an independent tour package. It is not uncommon for the agent and his or her client to discover that some packages actually cost more than the component parts. However, even at slightly higher rates, a package may be worth the price to the traveler. It offers convenience, prepayment options, and a major tour company to back up the purchaser if something should go wrong.

However, if you are assisting a person with travel plans who feels he or she can do a better job arranging the component parts separately, you can still help. It takes more time to make these individualized arrangements for a client, but it is important for any good businessperson to ensure that the customer gets what he or she wants and gets it at the best value.

A fly/drive tour is a subgroup of the independent tour. This package includes air and a rental car. Accommodations may or may not be included, depending on the operator or specific tour offering. Obviously, a fly/drive is the most independent of the independent tours! There are also rail/drive packages that may include air transportation to the first destination, rail transportation to some destinations, and car rental in others. A good example of where a rail/drive package would be desirable is a tour of England. Consider the merits of this six-night arrangement:

- Air transportation from your U.S. home city to London, tourist class, excursion fare.
- Round-trip transfers between the airport and your London hotel.
- Four nights in London, room, breakfast, and taxes included (three nights at the beginning of the trip, one night on return from Windermere).
- Rail tickets to Windermere in England's scenic Lake District.
- A rental car in Windermere for touring the area.
- Two nights in Windermere, room, breakfast and taxes included.
- Return rail tickets to London.
- One night in London, room, breakfast, and taxes included.

Hosted Tours

A hosted tour is different from an independent tour in that a host is available at each major destination to assist with planning and making arrangements for additional tours or entertainment. Normally, the host has a desk in the hotel lobby and is there certain hours of the day. The host usually does not accompany the participants on sightseeing excursions or travel with them to the next destination on the itinerary. Another host will greet the participants at the next city in the airport or the hotel.

A hosted tour is an excellent choice for travelers who want a certain sense of freedom, but who do not want to be burdened by driving and making all transportation and itinerary decisions on their own. Participants on a hosted tour can decide how much free time they wish to have and then use the services of the host in helping them make plans for the specific tours that appeal to them.

The only time participants of a hosted tour are traveling with a group is when they are on sightseeing tours or transferring between destination points on their itineraries. It's a convenient way to have the best of both worlds—freedom when you want it, assistance when you need it, and group activities when you feel like it.

Escorted Tours

An *escorted tour* is what most people think of when they think of a "tour." It offers a structured itinerary and includes meals, sightseeing, entertainment, transportation, and accommodations. Participants travel together as a group. In many cases, the group members meet at a gateway or major airport and fly together to their chosen destination or they meet at a scheduled time and place at the first destination. From that point, the participants travel together (usually on a motorcoach) and are accompanied by a full-time, professional tour escort.

The job of the **tour escort** is to see that the trip operates smoothly. The tour escort takes care of hotel check-in, handles payment for meals and admissions included in the tour, and takes care of any unforeseen problems such as transportation delays, lost luggage, or itinerary changes. Rarely does the participant have to worry about the details and aggravations of travel; they are taken care of throughout the trip.

Tour Escort *The individual who accompanies a tour throughout and is responsible for its smooth operation.*

A tour escort may also be the **guide** on the trip or there may be local guides. These local guides are referred to as **step-on guides** as they literally step on the motorcoach to conduct the sightseeing tour. Tour escorts are usually qualified to conduct sightseeing tours, but tourism regulations in some cities or countries may require that local guides be employed.

Guide *A professional who is licensed/authorized to conduct local sightseeing trips and excursions.*

Rather than select the price of each accommodation and feature, the traveler who is considering an escorted tour selects a complete price package. Tours may be classified as budget, thrifty, classic, deluxe, top value, and so on. Classifications are not consistent within the industry; they are created by the tour operator and can mean different things from one company to another. The travel counselor must be able to interpret the different classifications of tours offered by each operator under consideration.

Step-On Guide *The guide who steps on a motorcoach at a destination to give a local sightseeing tour. Also called a local or city guide.*

Many people imagine that an escorted tour rushes through a city a day. While this reputation may be somewhat deserved, many tours offer a more relaxed pace and free time for the participants to enjoy destinations on their own. Most tours are carefully paced and are not designed to exhaust the participants. Furthermore, they can be more relaxed and trouble-free than independent or hosted tours. Participants enjoy the benefits of having someone else to look after the details while they enjoy the sights.

Custom Tours

Specially arranged tours, or custom tours, for groups are usually escorted tours specifically designed for a particular group. Tour operators may offer custom planning; tour wholesalers, for the most part, do not. Travel agencies often plan and conduct custom tours for local groups. A truly custom tour is arranged for a specific group—doctors from a certain area, members of a specific arts group, specially arranged study groups, or groups from churches or clubs. These tours may be advertised to club/group members, but they are essentially "private" departures and are not offered for sale to the general public.

The travel dates are selected by the group, and all arrangements are booked according to the group's specific budget, preferences, and interests. A tour for an arts group would be designed to include museums, exhibits, and lectures. A tour planned for a group interested in gardens and country homes would have a very different itinerary from that for a group interested in playing the major golf courses of the world.

Custom tours may not be as economical as regularly scheduled package tours, but the group members still enjoy the benefits of discounted pricing while spending time in activities that appeal to them with people who have similar interests.

Incentive tours are a type of custom, escorted tour. However, the business is so large that there are entire firms who work exclusively on packaging incentive tours. An incentive is a tour that is planned by a company to reward its employees for achieving sales goals or exceeding performance expectations. These tours are planned for a specific group and, since they are rewards, they are nearly always all-inclusive, deluxe, and fully escorted. Programs are often planned to further "reward" the participants; name entertainment, gifts, and special recognition in the form of badges, medals, and trophies are often lavished on participants.

F-Stops, Short Stops, Meal Stops—Tours for Every Interest!

Some tour operators offer tour programs designed to appeal to one specific market. While these are not truly custom tours because they have regularly advertised departures and are open to the general public, they have been "customized" for special interests. Some special interest tours available for general purchase are:

Photography Tours. These tours are planned with the most scenic itineraries in mind. Longer stops for picture-taking are budgeted and there may even be professionals along to instruct and assist enthusiastic shutterbugs.

Sports Tours. These special interest tours can range from tours to special tournament games, to visiting the great stadiums of the world, to watching spring training, to "playing with the pros" in basketball camps. Sports tours may also be arranged around participating in a specific sport, such as one that appeals strictly to fishermen, golfers, or skiers.

Gourmet Tours. Those interested in cooking or just plain eating well will enjoy tours arranged to visit the best restaurants of the world, tour famous cooking schools, and talk with world-class chefs. On some tours, cooking classes are even conducted!

Cultural Tours. Tours arranged to visit museums or attend ballets, operas, concerts, and theatrical performances will have quite a different clientele than tour packages arranged for anglers!

Eco-Tours. These tours are marketed to those who wish to see the world's great natural treasures and help preserve them.

Adventure Tours. Adventure tours such as rafting, camping, trekking, and so on, have enjoyed great popularity with "baby boomers" seeking a thrill, but wanting the comfort of having someone along who knows what he or she is doing!

Religious Tours. These tours promote travel to the religious shrines and holy places of the world. They may be specifically designed to appeal to individual groups, such as Catholic, Jewish, or Christian heritage trips, or may be designed to educate the participants about the world's religions.

Specific Needs, etc. There are tours sold specifically to the handicapped, the retired, or "golden years" travelers, grandparents traveling with grandchildren, families, teens, singles, gays, minority groups, and so on.

The Dollars and Sense of Taking Tours

Many people want to see the world but are not sure about striking out on their own. If the desired destination is a foreign country, the language can be a real drawback. Tours provide a real security blanket: there will be someone there to help should things go wrong or when dealing with a foreign language just becomes too stressful.

Just consider the traveler who wishes to see the Orient. He or she must deal with a distinctly different culture, writing that is indecipherable, and a language in which even the old standards of smiling, pointing, and flapping his or her arms about simply won't work! Such difficulties should never keep a traveler home, but they may well send him or her in search of a fully escorted trip. The escorted trip to the Orient is by far the most popular form of travel for Westerners. Even the traveler who turned up his or her nose at group travel in Europe will seek out the comfort of an escorted tour in the Orient.

In addition to peace of mind, escorted tours the world over offer other benefits to the traveler:

Relaxation. Group tour participants can truly "leave their cares behind." Someone else does the driving, the thinking, the running, and the paying. Tour participants can just sit back and enjoy the ride!

Professional Planning. Itineraries are carefully planned by professionals who know the areas well. While the independent traveler struggles with maps, unfamiliar streets, delays, and long lines for tickets and admissions, the tour group member is never lost and,

Within the Tour Industry

Motorcoach Companies.   Some tour companies own and operate their own motorcoaches. Others do not, and they charter equipment from coach companies for their tours. Motorcoach companies may also offer tour planning services for customers who call them direct.

Travel agencies that plan group tours may charter from motorcoach companies or may request custom itinerary planning from tour companies. There are lots of ways to put a group together and how a company eventually selects the operators, equipment, and the rest is almost always based on price.

Sightseeing Companies.   When a tour operator takes a group into a large city or to visit a special attraction, he or she will often use the services of an independent sightseeing company. Sightseeing companies may operate their own motorcoaches or have step-on guides for hire.

In some cases, local or even national ordinances prohibit a tour escort acting as a guide. In many places throughout the world, guides are licensed and must operate from a local business. In cases such as these, the tour operator has no choice but to use local guides. However, even without such laws, tour operators often employ the services of a local guide service because they are the best versed in the area!

Some sightseeing companies also offer their own local tours which independent travelers may purchase and enjoy on their own. Names that might ring a bell in the sightseeing business are Gray Line Tours and American Sightseeing International.

Gray Line is the world's largest sightseeing company and offers about 1,500 excursions each day! Gray Line is not a single company but an association of over 200 independent companies. American Sightseeing International is second only to Gray Line in size and operates in much the same way. The two companies offer local and long-distance sightseeing programs, charter services, and transfer services (motorcoach and limousine).

Destination Management Services/Receptive Services.   These companies offer services to tour planners and groups which include obtaining special events tickets, charter service, hotel negotiations, special tour planning, gifts, meals, and arranging special entertainment or events (such as dinners held in museums, old homes, and the like). Many incentive planners, travel agencies, and meeting planners use receptive services to assist them in planning for groups which have special requirements or "out of the ordinary" requests.

---

because the escort handles all admissions, breezes to the head of the line at crowded attractions.

Companionship. Travelers share their experiences with other group members and form new friendships. Although the group members are not preselected or known in advance (such as on a custom tour), most travelers can rest assured that the tour participants will be compatible—after all, they chose the same destination, had about the same budget, and saw the same benefits in taking a group tour!

Great Prices. Tour operators send thousands of people to their selected destinations every year. Because of the numbers they represent, they can negotiate exceptionally good hotel, meal, transportation, and sightseeing rates. Although the independent traveler may be able to do it "cheaper," he or she won't be staying in equally nice hotels or eating the same meals!

Known Costs. Before a tour participant ever leaves home, he or she knows what is included in what he or she has paid thus far and what expenses he or she will have to cover. An independent traveler never knows what surprises may lie in wait!

Fall Foliage: A Tour Itinerary

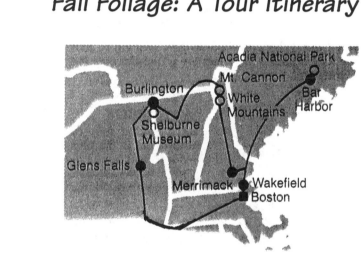

Day 1   Boston. Your tour escort will meet you at the airport and assist with transfers to the Marriott Hotel. For tour participants not flying to Boston, please join your group at the hotel. When you register, you will be given information about the location of the welcome cocktail party and dinner. 7:30 P.M.: Welcome Cocktail Party, followed by a Get Acquainted Dinner.

Day 2   A full and exciting day of sightseeing in the Boston area. Visit Quincy Market, the Old North Church, and Faneuil Hall and admire the lovely homes of Beacon Hill. Lunch on your own in the Quincy Market area. In the afternoon, we will continue our tour of the area to see Harvard, Radcliffe, and MIT, then on to Lexington and Concord. Return to Boston to enjoy dinner at one of Boston's oldest seafood houses!

Day 3 Board your deluxe motorcoach for today's drive north to Bar Harbor, Maine. On the way, we will visit Salem, Massachusetts, famous for its witchcraft trials in the 1600s. Our scenic ride will continue through the New England countryside with a late afternoon arrival at our hotel. Tonight's included dinner is a New England-style lobster bake!

Day 4 Our guide will travel with us into the beautiful Acadia National Park. We'll see Sieur des Monts Springs and the Abbe Museum and overnight in the beautiful White Mountains of New Hampshire. A hearty, five-course dinner is included at our hotel this evening.

Day 5 Another magnificent day of touring through the spectacular scenery of New Hampshire and Vermont. If you think you couldn't possibly see any more, just wait until you take the aerial tram ride to the summit of Mount Cannon. Overnight in Burlington, Vermont. Dinner on your own.

Day 6 Our day begins with a visit to the Shelburne Museum to see the unique collection of American folk art, then off for the beautiful ride across Lake Champlain into New York state. A scenic ride through the Adirondacks will bring our group to the Lake George resort area. We will enjoy dinner together before retiring to our hotel in Lake George.

Day 7 Enjoy a peaceful morning in Lake George before taking a sightseeing cruise of Lake George. After our cruise, we will once again enjoy the New England countryside as we head for Boston and our evening flights home.

Additional nights hotel accommodations pre- or post-tour can be arranged in Boston. This tour operates Monday through Saturday, mid-September through October.

This tour is specially designed for enjoyment of New England's spectacular fall foliage season. Other New England tours focusing on history and visits to coastal resort areas are offered from mid-May through mid-September.

Selecting and Booking Tours

Most tours and packages are sold through travel agencies. It is possible, with some operators, to book direct, but most tour companies find it far less costly to sell primarily through agents and pay them a commission for their sales. Some airlines operate tour desks and offer tour products to the public. In these cases, both the agents and the airlines sell direct to the consumer.

Tour operators design their brochures to be appealing to the traveler and to be a sales tool for the travel counselor. Brochures are characterized by pictures of destinations and people, but they are more than just an album of things to see. The well-written brochure produced by the reputable tour operator also includes detailed information about the itinerary, a listing of all included features, easy-to-understand cost structures, and an accurate description of the accommodations.

The Cost of the Tour

Cost is, of course, one of the main considerations in selecting a tour. However, quoted costs can be deceiving and it is important to compare what is included in each tour under consideration. Factors that will affect the cost of the tour are:

Length. The longer the tour, the more costly it will be.

Accommodations. The type of hotels used by the operator will greatly influence cost. The more deluxe the hotel, the higher the cost. Also, budget tours often use hotels that are not centrally located.

Transportation Provided. Is round-trip air transportation from the participant's home city included? Are transfers between the hotel and airport included? What type of motorcoach is used? Are additional flights required during the tour and is the cost of such transportation included?

Features Included. What type of sightseeing is offered? Are all sightseeing costs included or is sightseeing listed as "optional" (i.e, you pay for it). Does the brochure specify "visit" (you actually go in to see the place) or "see" (you only "see" the place, but don't visit it)?

Meals Included. Included meals can make a tremendous difference in the cost and/or value of a trip. Meals can be very expensive, especially in large cities, and the more meals included, the better the value.

Book 'Em!

When transportation is included in the tour, the agent need only make one call to the tour operator to confirm the space. If transportation is not included, the agent should first confirm those arrangements and then call the operator to book the land package. The agent should advise the tour operator of the client's air travel itinerary.

Brochures are as varied as the tour operators who create them. In many agencies, you may find there are preferred vendors whom you will be expected to promote and sell. The efficient agency of today does not attempt to have brochures for every possible operator. It has, through experience, compiled a list of the vendors (or suppliers) found to be the most reputable and profitable. This list could be a written one or it may be just "understood" by the experienced agents. You should ask your agency manager which vendors the agency recommends and become familiar with their products by studying their brochures and sales materials.

In virtually all cases, the traveler will pay the agency and the agency will then remit payment to the operator. The client will pay the agency by check, cash, or credit card; the agency will then pay the tour company, usually by agency check, but, in some cases, an agent may use special ARC documents such as a tour order or **miscellaneous charges order (MCO).** The agent always deducts the commission owed from the final payment.

Miscellaneous Charges Order (MCO) *A handwritten document issued by a travel agent or an airline as proof of payment for specified travel arrangements. An automated multipurpose document (MDP) is scheduled to replace the MCO in the future.*

Tour Documents

The tour documents are everything the traveler will need to join the tour: proof of payment, vouchers, confirmations, and so on; each tour operator differs in what is included or required. The tour documents also include such things as written instructions and full itineraries to the participants. Most tour participants eagerly await their "documents" and may call their agent several times to check on their arrival as the due date draws near. The operator will not send documents until the traveler has made the final payment. The package the tour participant receives will include:

- Baggage tags to identify the client as a member of the group.
- A printed itinerary.
- The final details outlining requirements for passports and inoculations.
- Information about the destinations and recommendations for free time and optional tours.
- Vouchers to be exchanged for services rendered.
- Air tickets (if transportation is included).

Some operators also include information about insurance, guidebooks, phrase books, passport/document wallets, and flight bags.

No More Tours— Let's Have a FIT Instead!

As you can see from your reading, there are many good reasons to recommend a tour. With the many different types available, it would seem likely there would be something to satisfy even the most discriminating and independent traveler. However, even though tours may offer flexibility and many options, there are always some travelers who will prefer itineraries that are custom made to satisfy their individual requirements. Some people simply enjoy planning their own trips from beginning to end. Others may have requirements that even the most flexible packages cannot accommodate. For example:

Mr. Julian Thomas wants to play golf in Scotland while his wife and daughters visit gardens and country homes. He then wants to drive through the English Lake District on the way to the family's ancestral village in Wales. He probably won't find a tour package to suit his needs and will turn to his agent for assistance in planning.

This type of individual tour is called *Foreign Independent Tour,* although today the term FIT is used for both foreign and domestic independent travel. A FIT is, very simply, a custom tour planned for one traveler rather than for a group.

Some agencies have FIT specialists while others are really not equipped to handle such requests at all. The FIT can be a very time-consuming and unprofitable exercise for an agent without extensive contacts and experience. FITs require extensive research and close attention to detail. Luckily, many FITs are requested by travelers who intend to spend more money than the average tourist and the commissions from the component parts of the itinerary can be large.

On the other hand, the traveler who wants to stay in inexpensive guest houses or hostels and bicycle through the countryside for a month may not be worth the effort. The hotels he or she selects may not even pay commissions and, if they do, the amounts are probably very small—not enough to cover the expense of writing letters or making phone calls. An agent could spend hours planning such a trip for a very small return. Many agencies that offer FIT planning do so for a fee or request a nonrefundable deposit from the client before the planning begins.

Got You Covered!

Most trips go well and according to plan. However, what if something goes wrong? A couple has paid out substantial sums for nonrefundable air tickets, a cruise, or a tour and, at the last minute, one of them falls ill, there's a death in the family, water pipes burst in their home causing damage they must take care of, or they are stuck in traffic and miss the only possible flight.

What happens then? The trip must be postponed indefinitely. Naturally, the travelers are upset and disappointed to miss their happily anticipated vacation, but do they have to lose everything? Or, what happens if they make it on the trip and then must buy an expensive ticket home because one of them becomes ill? What if they should require extra medical assistance such as an "air ambulance" or helicopter transportation to a medical facility? What if their regular insurance won't pay for these extras? And, finally, what about the traveler whose baggage is lost (and never found) or stolen?

All of these eventualities can cost bundles and ruin a trip. But, like most misfortunes, there is insurance to cover it! The most common types of trip insurance are:

- Travel accident and optional sickness coverage.
- Travel baggage coverage.
- Trip cancellation and emergency medical assistance.

Many agencies and tour operators sell trip insurance. It is a good option to offer and it brings in extra revenue for the company. A number of companies offer insurance through travel companies; The Travelers and Mutual of Omaha are two of the largest.

It is important both to offer insurance and to be able to determine if it is really a necessity on a particular trip or for a specific traveler. For trip cancellation/interruption insurance, you must consider the "worst case" scenario and recommend the correct amount of coverage. Trip cancellation insurance can be quite expensive and many travelers decide not to purchase it believing they won't have to cancel, or if they do, they won't lose much. Travelers should *read the fine print* before buying anything; insurance does not cover every eventuality!

Travel accident and sickness insurance can be very important, but many people have personal insurance that covers their medical expenses even when they travel out of the country. Before purchasing an expensive policy, travelers should check with their own insurance agent to determine if they really need this type of coverage.

Travel baggage insurance may also make a traveler feel better about taking along expensive items or clothing. However, carefully read what is covered! There are limits on jewelry, watches, furs, precious gems, and cameras; in other words, the most expensive items a traveler will take along on the trip may not be covered for the full amount of the policy. Understand the limitations and have travelers check their homeowners or renter's insurance to see if their personal belongings are covered away from home.

Tour operators often include travel insurance forms with the final documents. If the tour participant is interested in purchasing insurance, and you are offering it through your agency, you should compare coverages to see which is the best!

Employment Opportunities in the Tour Industry

The tour industry is a growing field and career opportunities abound! There are tour wholesalers, tour operators, sightseeing companies, and travel agencies with large group tour planning departments, all of whom—at some time or another—need good entry-level people! With the exception of the tour manager (also known as a tour escort), employees of tour companies are not always out taking tours. Quite the opposite; they are in the office planning and booking them for others.

- *Reservationists* take the calls (usually from travel agents) and handle the booking requests.
- *Operations employees* rarely talk with agents or travelers. They are responsible for preparing passenger lists, tickets (if air tickets are

included in the tour), rooming lists, preparing document packets, and mailing them out to the agents/travelers.

- *Destination specialists* work in creating new tour programs for the company. Their jobs might involve travel to new destinations to negotiate with hotels, suppliers, and so on.
- *Sales representatives* may or may not be in the main office. Many times sales representatives are responsible for a certain region of the country, far from the operations or executive offices of the tour company. Most often, these sales reps work from their homes and visit the home office on a regular basis as required by their managers.
- *Tour managers* and *drivers* (if the company owns its own motorcoaches) are, of course, the "field" personnel who take full responsibility of the tour and its passengers. They are the ones who travel frequently—sometimes for months at a time!

UP CLOSE

The Tour Manager

Are you . . .

- Free to travel the world?
- Flexible with your time?
- Friendly and independent?
- Fun to be around?
- A good leader and communicator?
- Interested in meeting people?

If your answers to the questions above are "yes," then tour management may be the field for you. A tour manager, also called a tour director or tour escort, has a great job. He or she is paid to see the world, is a "star" to his or her customers, and often stays in luxury hotels and dines in places only the wealthiest can afford.

The tour manager meets interesting people, makes new friends, and tours the world—while getting paid for it! Hotel and meal expenses are paid by the employer while the tour manager is on the road and, with training and experience, the pay is also good.

But tour management is not all glamour. It is demanding work involving long hours and plenty of responsibility, not to mention the extensive destination research often required before a tour begins. A tour manager must be a diplomatic leader, quick thinker, a good performer under pressure, and must have a good sense of humor. While on tour, the hours can be long and a tour manager's time is never his or her own—it belongs to the group!

Every tour operator or group travel planner will differ in this respect, but, basically, the duties of a tour manager may include any or all of the following:

1. Confirming hotels, meals, sightseeing attractions, air reservations, and other special arrangements that the tour may require. (These duties are more commonly required of employees of a small tour company or travel agency.)

2. Making tour payments to suppliers.

3. Studying and becoming familiar with tour materials such as the rooming list and tour itinerary.

4. Greeting and checking in participants at the point of departure; taking baggage counts and making sure all passenger luggage is loaded on the motorcoach.

   a. If conducting an air tour, the tour manager should make sure all passengers are checked in before checking in himself or herself.

   b. If conducting a cruise tour, the tour manager should remain visible until all tour members have gone to their cabins.

5. Working with local guides.

6. Working with the driver of the motorcoach.

7. Advising the group, answering questions, offering assistance, and making special arrangements as needed.

8. Handling hotel check-in and check-out.

9. Handling emergency situations.

10. Remaining visible and available to all tour participants.

Explorations

Construct a tour of your hometown/area.

- Select the places of interest to visit.
- Design a one- to two-day itinerary, including hotel and restaurant (dinner) selection.

See if you can price the tour for thirty people on a per person basis: include hotel costs, taxes, one dinner, sightseeing admissions, and local transportation and tips (gratuities).

Enrichments

Choose one of the following destinations in the United States and design a one-week (seven-night) tour itinerary for the area. *If one of the areas is your hometown region, do not use it!*

San Francisco, CA
New Orleans, LA
Charleston, SC
Albuquerque, NM
Chicago, IL
Denver, CO

Abbreviations Commonly Used in the Travel Industry

AC Air Conditioned

ACCT Account

AD Agency Discount

ADV Advise

ADVSD Advised

AGT Agent

A/L Airline

ALT (1) Altitude; (2) Alternate

ANML Animal

AP American Plan

APT
ARPT } Airport

ARR Arrival

ARNK
ARUNK } Arrival Unknown
ARRUNK

AUTH Authorization, Authorize

AVAIL
AVL } Available
AVLB

B&B Bed and Breakfast

BBR Banker's Buying Rate

BH Baggage Handling

BK Book

BKD Booked

BP (1) Boarding Pass; (2) Bermuda Plan

BR Bedroom

BRDG Boarding

BRKFST Breakfast

CC (1) Continental Breakfast; (2) Credit Card

C CAR Compact Car

CD (1) Code; (2) Corporate Discount

CDW Collision Damage Waiver

CF Confirmation

CF# Confirmation Number

CHD
CHLD } Child

CHG Charge

CHNG Change

CHTR Charter

CK (1) Check, form of payment; (2) Check, verify

CK-IN Check-In

CL Class

COM
COMM } Commission

COMP Complimentary (free)

CONF Confirmation

CONF# Confirmation Number

CONNEX
CONX } Connection, Connecting

CORP Corporate

CPL Couple

CPY Copy

CR (1) Carrier; (2) Credit

CTC Contact

CTO City Ticket Office

CTY City

CTY CTR City Center

CTY CD City Code

CURR Currency

CXL Cancel

CXLD Canceled

CY Copy

DBL Double

DEP (1) Departure; (2) Deposit

DLVR Deliver

DLX Deluxe

DLY Daily

DOCS Documents

DSO District Sales Office

DSM District Sales Manager

DT
DTE } Date

DWB Double With Bath

DWOB Double Without Bath

EAP Each Additional Person

E CAR Economy-Sized Car

EFF Effective

EP European Plan

EQPT Equipment

ERR Error

ETA Estimated Time of Arrival

ETD Estimated Time of Departure

EX
EXCH } Exchange

EXEC Executive

F First Class

F CAR Full-Sized Car

FAM (1) Familiarization; (2) Family

FAP Full American Plan

F/B Fare Basis

FF Frequent Flyer

FF# Frequent Flyer Number

FIT Foreign Independent Tour

FLIFO Flight Information

FLT Flight

FNDS Funds

FOP Form of Payment

FRY Ferry

FQ Fare Quote

GMT Greenwich Mean Time

GP
GRP } Group

GRND Ground

GTD Guaranteed

GTY Guarantee

HK Holds Confirmed

HLD Hold

HR Hour

HRLY Hourly

HTL Hotel

I CAR Intermediate-Sized Car

ID Identification

INCL Includes

INS Insurance

INTL International

ITIN Itinerary

JT Joint

L CAR Luxury Car

LOC Location

LIMO Limousine

LV Leave

M/M Mr. and Mrs.

MAP Modified American Plan

MAX Maximum

MCO Miscellaneous Charges Order

MCT Minimum Connecting Time

MI Mile

MIDWK Midweek

MIN Minimum

MSCN Misconnect

MKT Market

MP Meal Plan

MPM Maximum Permitted Miles

MSG Message

MT Meet

MTG Meeting

MV Move

N/A (1) Not Available; (2) Not Applicable; (3) No Answer

NBR Number

NME Name

NN Need

NR (1) Nonrefundable; (2) Near

NO OP Not Operating

NO REC No Record

NS Nonsmoking

NGT
NT } Night

OJ Open Jaw

OK Confirmed

OP Operates, Operating

OV Ocean View

OW One Way

P Person, Passenger

PAX Passengers

PCT   Percent

PD   Paid

PER   (1) By (OK per sales office); (2) Person

PH   Phone

PK   Park

PKG   (1) Package; (2) Parking

PLZ   Please

PMT   Payment

PNR   Passenger Name Record

PP   Per Person

PSBL   Possible

PSGR   Passenger

PRT   Prepaid Ticket Advise

PTY   Party (as in "party of three")

PUP   Pick Up

Q   Queue

QN   Queen

QT
QTE   } Quote

QUAD   Quad

RE   Regarding

REF   (1) Refer, Reference; (2) Refund

REP   Representative

RL/RLS   Rule/Rules

RM/RMS   Room/Rooms

RMK   Remark

ROH   Run-of-House

RPLY   Reply

RQ   (1) Request, On Request; (2) Rate Quote

RQST   Request

RR   (1) Reduced Rate; (2) Railroad

RT   Round-trip

RTE   (1) Route; (2) Rate

RTG   Routing

RTN   Return

S   Smoking

S/C   (1) Service Charge; (2) Security Charge

S CAR   Standard Sized Car

SCHED   Schedule

SEP   Separate

SGL   Single

SKED   Schedule

SO   Sold Out

SPCL   Special

SS   (1) Sightseeing; (2) Steamship

STE   Suite

SUP   Superior

SVC   Service

SWB   Single Room With Bath

SWGN   Station Wagon

SWOB   Single Room Without Bath

TA   Travel Agent

TCP   To Complete Party

TFR   Transfer

TIX   Tickets

TK
TKT   } Ticket

TM   Time

TKTD   Ticketed

TRN   Train

TRP   (1) Trip; (2) Triple

TRPL   Triple

TTL   Total

TVL   Travel

TVLR   Traveler

TWB   Twin Room With Bath

TWOB   Twin Room Without Bath

TWN   Twin Room

TX   Tax

UM
UMNR   } Unaccompanied Minor

UN   Unable (As in "unable to confirm")

UNAVL   Unavailable

UNK   Unknown

VAT   Value Added Tax

VFR   Visiting Friends and Relatives

VFY   Verify

W   Window

W/   With

WCHR   Wheelchair

WK Week

WKLY Weekly

WKND Weekend

WL Waitlist

WS Window Seat

X (1) Connection; (2) Except (X2 = Except Tuesday)

XL Cancel

XLD Cancelled

XSEC Extra Section

Y Full Coach Fare

YM Military Coach Fare

YCH Child's Coach Fare

Z/ Zip Code

ZT Zulu Time

Glossary

AAA   See American Automobile Association.

Accommodation   Hotel room, suite, cruise cabin, and so on.

Accountable Document   Refers to any form that can be validated and completed in exchange for travel, travel services, or goods. Agency accountable documents include: Airline ticket stock—both hand-writable and automated, MCOs, PTAs, and Tour Orders. The agency is accountable to ARC for the safe-keeping of these documents and the accurate reporting of each sale involving an accountable document.

Access Code   A combination of characters that lets CRS users gain access to the reservation system or a specific field of information.

AD-75   The discount code used on airline tickets issued at the 75 percent discount extended to travel agencies by most major airlines. Agencies receive or are entitled to a limited number of tickets at this rate. Employee use is a matter of individual agency policy.

Add-On Fare   Also called "arbitrary" or "proportional" fare. A fare to be used only in combination with other fares in construction of a through fare. Add-on fares occur most commonly in international travel and are less expensive than regular tourist-class fares.

Adjoining Rooms   Adjacent hotel rooms with no connecting door.

Adult   An airline passenger twelve years of age or older.

Advance Purchase Excursion (APEX)   A discounted fare on international flights. Purchase is required in advance of departure (usually 21 to 30 days) and is subject to length-of-stay requirements and cancellation penalties.

Aeronautical Radio Incorporated (ARINC)   The communication network owned by major airlines that links different airline computer systems with each other.

Aft   Near, toward, or at the rear of a ship or the tail of an aircraft.

Agent (AGT)   One authorized to sell a supplier's products.

Agent Identification Plate   Metal plate provided by ARC to approved travel agencies that contains the agency name, address, and eight-digit code number. It is used in the validation of hand-written tickets and other accountable documents.

Agent's Coupon   Portion of the issued ticket that the agency retains for its records.

AH & MA   American Hotel and Motel Association. A lodging industry association of hoteliers in the United States, Canada, Mexico, and Central and South America.

Airline Code   The two-character code designation of an airline. *Examples:* AA = American Airlines, DL = Delta Airlines, UA = United Airlines.

Airline Pilots Association (ALPA)   The airline pilots' union.

Airlines Reporting Corporation (ARC)   Corporation jointly owned by most of the major United States airlines. It collects payments for tickets sold by travel agents, distributes the monies to the airlines, and supervises the appointment of travel agencies to sell airline tickets.

Airport Code   The three-letter code designation of an airport. *Examples:* ATL = Atlanta/Hartsfield International Airport (Atlanta, Georgia); DEN = Denver/Stapleton International Airport (Denver, Colorado); LGA = LaGuardia Airport (New York City, New York); ORD = O'Hare International Airport (Chicago, Illinois).

Air/Sea Package   A vacation package that includes air fare and cruise accommodations.

Air Taxi   An aircraft carrying up to nineteen passengers and operating with fewer restrictions than scheduled carriers, usually flying within a 250-mile radius.

Air Transport Association (ATA)   A trade organization of scheduled United States and Canadian airlines.

Air Volume   See ARC Revenue.

All-Suites   Hotels that offer only suites: bedroom(s), living area, kitchenette.

ALPA   See Airline Pilots' Association.

Amenity   An added comfort or convenience for travelers. *Examples:* Saunas, beauty parlors, health spas, gourmet restaurants and special soaps and shampoos in hotels; free liquor, headsets on airlines.

American Automobile Association (AAA or "Triple A") An organization offering a variety of travel and motoring services, AAA has regional clubs that own and operate travel agencies, usually under the name AAA World Wide Travel. Unlike the motoring club, AAA travel agencies provide services to nonmembers.

American Plan (AP) Hotel rate that includes lodging and three meals daily. Internationally, American Plan is known as "full pension."

American Sightseeing International (ASI) The business name of the American Sightseeing Association. The association is composed of local tour operators offering sightseeing tours, transfers, and charter transportation. ASI publishes a tariff available to travel agencies.

American Society of Travel Agents (ASTA) The largest organization of independent travel agencies and tour operators with associate members from related travel fields such as airlines, hotels, and travel schools. ASTA offers many services to its members including educational seminars, magazines, newsletters, and government relations committees. ASTA has also established Principles of Professional Conduct and Ethics for members.

AMTRAK The National Railroad Passenger Corporation, a government-subsidized corporation that operates almost all passenger train service in the United States.

AP See American Plan.

APEX See Advance Purchase Excursion.

Appointment Designation as a sales outlet by a conference, association, or airline.

ARC See Airlines Reporting Corporation.

ARC Revenue The official dollar volume for agency airline sales. The size of an agency is usually defined as $ARC Revenue. Example: "ABC Travel is a $4 million ARC Revenue agency."

Area Settlement Bank Banks throughout the country are appointed by ARC as the processing centers for agency ticket sales. Once a week, agencies will send a detailed report of all airline tickets sold to the Area Bank and authorize the Area Bank to withdraw (draft) payment from their company banks. Agencies failing to make this report or failing to make payment to the Area Bank will be found in default by ARC and could lose their authorization to issue airline tickets.

ARINC See Aeronautical Radio Incorporated.

Arrival Unknown (ARUNK) The term used by airlines to indicate surface or land transportation segments in a trip itinerary.

ARTA See Association of Retail Travel Agents.

ARUNK See Arrival Unknown.

ASI See American Sightseeing International.

Association of Retail Travel Agents (ARTA) A trade association for U. S. retail travel agents.

ASTA See American Society of Travel Agents.

ATA See Air Transport Association.

ATB See Automated Ticket/Boarding Pass.

ATB Printer Refers to the printer that issues "cardstock," Automated Tickets/Boarding Passes.

Auditor's Coupon Portion of the issued ticket that an agency submits to the designated area bank with its weekly sales report.

Automated Ticket A computer-generated airline ticket.

Automated Ticket/Boarding Pass (ATB) Refers to the type of airline ticket stock that has both the flight coupon and the boarding pass on the same card. Also referred to as "cardstock" tickets.

Automatic Flight Insurance Flight insurance often provided by a travel agency for each ticket it issues. Also available through certain credit card companies.

Automation Refers to the computerized reservation and accounting systems used by travel vendors, most commonly travel agencies.

Automation Contract The legal agreement, usually between an agency and the provider of the automated reservation system, that stipulates the cost, terms, and conditions of having the CRS in the agency.

Availability Ready for immediate purchase. A CRT shows the availability of a supplier's product. The most important question to ask could be, "Is the seat, hotel room, car, tour, cruise available on the date needed?"

Back Office System Agency accounting/billing systems. Larger agencies often have automated accounting systems that produce statements for clients, generate the ARC report, and compile comprehensive financial and management reports.

Back of the House The parts of a hotel not usually seen by guests: accounting, kitchens, storage, and so on.

Back-to-Back Ticketing Booking overlapping round trips that have opposite origin and destination points. Both bookings will meet the restrictions for discount fares. The passenger uses one coupon from one ticket for departure and one coupon from the other ticket for the return. Considered unethical by airlines. Agents are not supposed to use the practice to reduce fares for their clients.

Baggage   Personal effects transported with a passenger. Checked baggage is stored on an aircraft in the cargo hold. Carry-on baggage is stored in the passenger compartment.

Baggage Allowance   Amount of baggage a passenger may transport without having to pay extra charges. Individual airlines may determine their own baggage allowances. When traveling internationally, it is critical to check each airline's allowance.

Baggage Check   A tag indicating flight number and destination that is attached by the airline to a passenger's luggage. A stub or receipt is given to the traveler as his or her claim check for checked baggage. (See Checked Baggage).

Baggage I.D. Tag   Personal identification attached to luggage by passenger. All U.S. airlines require I.D. tags on checked baggage. (See Checked Baggage.)

Base Fare   The air fare before taxes are added.

Banker's Buying Rate (BBR)   The rate(s) officially set by U.S. banks for the purchase/exchange of foreign currency. Most airlines use the Banker's Buying Rate in computing international fares. *The Wall Street Journal* prints the BBR on a regular basis.

BBR   See Banker's Buying Rate.

Bed and Breakfast   A room rate, in a very small hotel, inn, guest house, or private home, that includes sleeping accommodations and breakfast. The term is also used to classify the establishment: A "Bed and Breakfast Inn"; "B & B" is also common.

Bermuda Plan (BP)   A hotel rate that includes lodging and a full breakfast.

Berth   Sleeping accommodations on a ship or train. Also a space where a ship docks.

Bias   The deliberate programming of flight schedules and availabilities in an airline reservation computer to favor one airline's service over another's. The U.S. government requires all reservation systems to provide agents unbiased displays of air schedules.

Black-Out Dates   A supplier's predetermined dates when travel on specific fares or special hotel promotional rates are not available (usually holiday or peak travel times).

Blocked Space   Group space reserved on aircraft, cruise ships, or in hotels by travel agencies, wholesalers, or tour operators for the purpose of resale. If not sold within a specified time, blocked space must be returned to the supplier.

Boarding Pass   A permit for the traveler to board a ship, plane, train, or other form of transportation. Part of the check-in process. Travel agencies now provide advance boarding passes to air travelers—a very popular service that saves travelers time and frustration and lessens their chances of being bumped by the airlines.

Bond   Insurance to protect against loss due to bankruptcy or default on payments. ARC requires travel agencies to purchase bonds to protect the airlines in case the agency fails to pay for the tickets it issues. Some tour companies are bonded to protect their clients' prepayments.

Booking   v., Making a reservation; n., The reservation. Example: The agent is booking a reservation. The client has a confirmed booking.

Booking Code   The letters used in a reservation to confirm space at a specific fare.

Boutique Agency   A term used to describe smaller travel agencies that have a high concentration of their business in leisure travel or special interest travel.

Bow   The front of a ship; also known as a prow.

BP   See Bermuda Plan.

Bridge   A nautical term referring to the control center of the ship.

BritRail Pass   An unlimited-use ticket that is purchased for a specific period of time for travel by rail in the United Kingdom (England, Wales, Scotland, Northern Ireland). BritRail is the official name of the train system.

Brochure   A printed folder that contains promotional information about hotels, cruises, tours, and so on. It may be a simple flyer or as large as a magazine. Agencies keep brochures on file as aids in selling travel and making bookings for clients.

Budget   (1)The amount of money a client has to spend, that is, "What is your budget for this trip? (2) A pricing category, as in deluxe, superior, moderate, budget; for example, a budget hotel will cost far less than a deluxe hotel.

Buffer Zone   An area 225 miles wide extending beyond the northern and southern United States' borders where special tax provisions apply. Applicable to points in Canada and Mexico.

Bulk Fare   A net fare contract with an airline for a certain number of seats. The purchaser contracts to buy a specified number of seats on a flight. If the seats are not filled, the purchaser does not receive a refund.

Bulkhead A vertical wall or partition that separates an aircraft into compartments. Bulkhead seats usually have more leg room but less storage space. On aircraft, bulkhead seats are frequently reserved for passengers traveling with infants or for those who require additional leg room for medical reasons.

Bullet Train High-speed Japanese train; also known as Shinkansen.

Bumping The practice of removing a confirmed passenger from a full flight to make room for a passenger with higher priority. An industry discount traveler or a free passenger may be *bumped* to accommodate a full-fare passenger.

Business Class A class of airline service between first and coach. Service is geared to the business traveler. Business class is most commonly offered on international flights and is a popular alternative to the greater expense of first class.

CAB See Civil Aeronautics Bureau

Cabana A room outside the main hotel/resort building, situated near the pool or beach area.

Cabin Sleeping accommodations on a ship; also known as a stateroom.

Cancel To void reservations.

Cancelation Clause The provision in a booking agreement that outlines the damages/fees to be paid if one of the parties cancels the arrangements.

Cancellation Fee/Cancellation Penalty The amount due when a cancelation is made after booking or after an established date.

Cancellation Number The verification number given to the agent or client when travel arrangements are cancelled. When guarantees or refundable payments are involved, a cancellation number should always be requested and noted in the client file.

Capacity Controlled The limits placed on the number of airline seats, hotel rooms, and so on, available at a set rate (discounted) or promotional offer.

Car Class The size, type, or price range of a rental car: economy, compact, midsize, full-size, luxury, and so on.

Carrier/Common Carrier Company such as an airline involved in the sale of transportation for people or goods.

Carry-on Luggage Articles that passengers will hand carry on the airplane. Airlines place restrictions on the amount and size of carry-on luggage.

Category The class/classification of hotel rooms, cruise cabins, rental cars, and so on. *Examples:* Hotels—Deluxe, Superior, First Class, Budget; cars—Luxury, Full-Size, Standard.

Cathode Ray Tube (CRT) The computer screen that displays information and permits communication with the central computer's data base.

CDW See Collision Damage Waiver.

Certified Travel Counselor (CTC) A designation awarded by the Institute of Certified Travel Agents (ICTA) to travel professionals with five or more years of industry experience. Candidates complete a two-year graduate level tavel management program.

CH or CHD Common carrier abbreviation for Child.

Charter Exclusive hire of a carrier: airplane, ship, or motorcoach.

Checked Baggage Baggage carried in the cargo hold of an airplane and not accessible to a passenger during the flight.

Check-in The point at which clients must present tickets, vouchers, or confirmations at a hotel, airport, cruise terminal, or tour operator's facility. To "check-in" at a hotel means a traveler registers, shows proof of payment, and receives room keys.

Check-out Formalities, usually including payment, associated with leaving a hotel.

Child (CH/CHD) In air travel, a child aged two to eleven years; under two years, a child is classified as an infant.

Chunnel See Eurotunnel.

Circle Trip Travel that is essentially "round trip" in nature (the client is leaving from and returning to the same city), but follows one route on departure and another route on return, for example, Atlanta/Chicago/Denver—going; Denver/Dallas/Atlanta—return).

City Code Three-letter designation used by airlines to identify cities. Many city codes are identical to the three-letter airport codes. *Examples:* NYC = New York City; ATL = Atlanta (city) and Hartsfield (airport).

City Pair The departure and destination (or stopover) points used in booking a flight itinerary.

City Ticket Office (CTO) An airline ticket sales office whose location is other than an airport terminal.

Civil Aeronautics Bureau (CAB) Prior to 1978, this now defunct federal organization regulated all

U.S. airlines. They controlled routes, fares, designations, and airline growth.

Class of Service   Indicates the type of service a passenger will receive in conjunction with the fare paid for transportation. *Example:* first class, second class, tourist class, and so on.

Clear a Wait List   To confirm a requested reservation from a wait list. *Example:* Mr. Jones was wait-listed for flight #101. A seat becomes available and Mr. Jones now has a confirmed reservation. He *cleared the wait list.*

CLIA   See Cruise Lines International Association.

Client Profile   Complete information on a client: travel preferences, addresses, frequent flyer numbers, billing instructions, and so on. This information is compiled by a travel agency and stored in its computer system.

Coach Class   (1)The section of an air carrier where lower cost seats are located. (2)The actual class of service paid for.

Code Sharing   An agreement where two air carriers use the same two-letter airline codes for their flights. *Example:* DL = Delta Airlines and DL = Comair (commuter carrier).

Collision Damage Waiver (CDW)   Optional car rental insurance that significantly reduces or eliminates the renter's liability or damage deductible should the rental car be damaged or wrecked. Some car rental firms have deductibles equal to the cost of the automobile.

Commercial Account   See Corporate Account

Commercial Airline/Commercial Carrier   An airline that sells its seats to the public.

Commercial Rate   See Corporate Rate.

Commission   The percentage paid by suppliers to a travel agency for selling travel arrangements.

Common Rated   Two or more destinations, near each other, for which air fares are the same. *Example:* Fort Lauderdale (FLL) and Miami (MIA) are geographically close to each other and serve the same areas. Air fares from any city in the United States to either of these destinations are the same. They are common rated.

Commuter Carrier   Carrier that operates smaller equipment and services smaller cities or population areas that cannot support major aircraft or traffic.

Complimentary (COMP)   Free, at no charge.

Computer Reservations System (CRS)   Refers to the automated reservations systems developed and marketed by the airlines and used by most travel agencies to book airline seats, hotels, and rental cars. The major systems are Apollo (Covia Corporation), Sabre (American Airlines), System One (Texas Air Corporation), and Worldspan (Worldspan Corporation).

Concierge   In a hotel, the person in charge of special services for guests. The concierge will arrange tours and transfers, obtain theater tickets, and make appointments with hairdressers, doctors, and so on. In Europe, the concierge has been a key employee in hotels for many years. In the United States, the practice of employing a concierge is relatively new.

Concorde   Supersonic commercial aircraft. Also called SST for supersonic transport.

Concourse   The area in a large airline terminal where the gates are located. The bigger the airport, the more concourses it will have.

Conditions   Section of a transportation or tour contract that states exactly what the purchaser is offered and what responsibilities the supplier may have.

Conducted Tour   See Escorted Tour.

Configuration   A term used to describe the interior seating or cabin plan of an aircraft, ship, motorcoach, and so on.

Confirmation   The acceptance and acknowledgment of a reservation by a supplier. Confirmations are frequently identified by number or the name of the booking agent and the date of the reservation. Confirmation numbers should always be requested for hotel and tour reservations.

Conjunction Tickets   If more than one ticket is required for a trip, tickets are issued for the passenger in sequential numeric order.

Connecting Flight   Air transportation arrangement that requires a passenger to change planes en route to his or her chosen destination.

Connecting Rooms   Adjacent hotel rooms with a connecting door

Consolidation   The practice of concentrating travel purchases with one agency, airline, hotel chain, car rental firm, or other business.

Consolidator   A travel business that purchases airline seats at discounts from airlines that have seats they expect to remain unsold. The consolidator then resells the tickets at a markup to travel agencies or travelers.

Consortium   A group of similar businesses, such as travel agencies, that pool their purchasing power so they can achieve better prices, commissions, and concessions.

Continental Breakfast   A light morning meal, most often toast, rolls, and coffee or tea.

Consulate   An office of one government located in the country of another that provides services to its country's citizens who are living or traveling in the "host" country.

Continental U.S.   The forty-eight contiguous states; excludes Alaska and Hawaii.

Continental Plan (CP)   A hotel rate that includes lodging and a continental breakfast.

Convention Rate   A special air or hotel rate offered to attendees of a convention.

Conversion Rate   The rate of exchange from one currency to another.

Cook's Timetable   The *Thomas Cook Continental Timetable* and *Thomas Cook Overseas Timetable* have routes and schedules for trains outside the United States, features of each train, national and international rail maps, timetables, and routes for ferries and steamers.

Corporate Account   The business/company accounts that a travel agency services. Agencies often perform special services for their corporate accounts: ticket delivery, specialized reporting, individualized accounting, and so on.

Corporate Credit Card   A credit card (such as American Express or MasterCard) that is issued for employees of a company to use for business travel expenses. American Express and Diner's Club offer specialized accounting reports with their corporate cards.

Corporate Rate   A special rate negotiated between a supplier (most commonly a hotel or car rental company) and a corporation or business. Corporate rates are widely used throughout the hotel industry, but the definition can vary with the individual hotel or chain. Traditionally, a corporate rate represents 10 percent or more off the hotel's regular room rate.

Corporate Traveler   A business traveler.

Couchette   A sleeping berth in a publicly shared compartment on an international train. Normally, a compartment has four first-class or six second-class couchettes.

Coupon   Part of an airline ticket. There are valid flight coupons, agent's coupons, reporting coupons, and passenger copy coupons.

Courier   (1) A professional tour escort. (2) A delivery person.

Courtesy Van   A van or bus used by a hotel or car rental company to transport its guests/customers between its facility and the airport.

CP   See Continental Plan.

CRS   See Computer Reservation System.

CRT   Cathode Ray Tube.

Cruise   A pleasure voyage by ship.

Cruise Lines International Association (CLIA)   An organization offering promotional materials, training guides, reference books, and seminars on behalf of cruise lines.

Cruise Only   (1) Cost includes only the price of the cruise. (2) An agency that handles only cruise sales.

CTO   See City Ticket Office.

Currency Code   A three-letter code for the monetary unit of a country. *Examples:* USD=U.S. Dollar; MEP=Mexican Peso.

Customs   A government agency charged with collecting taxes on imported items and preventing the entry of prohibited items. International travelers may not enter a country until they have been "cleared" by a customs agent.

Day Rate   A special rate for use of a hotel room by day only.

Debarkation   Getting off a ship, plane, or train. Also known as disembarkation.

Deck   A level (floor) on a ship.

Deck Plan   The layout or "map" of a ship's decks which shows cabin locations, lounges, dining rooms, swimming pools, and so on. In cruise brochures, the cabins are generally color coded in the deck plans to indicate price category.

Denied Boarding   The practice of refusing to accept confirmed passengers, usually because space is filled by the time they arrive at the check-in point.

Denied Boarding Compensation   The compensation (money, free transportation, hotel accommodations, and so on) given to a passenger who has been involuntarily "bumped" (denied boarding) from his or her confirmed transportation.

Department of Transportation (DOT)   The federal agency responsible for the coordination of air commerce in the United States and the approval of routes and schedules.

Deposit   A down payment that may be required to confirm a reservation; most often, deposits are requested by tour operators, cruise lines, and resorts.

Deregulation   The elimination (by law in 1978) of U.S. government control of airline routings, fares, and schedules.

Destination The place to which a passenger is traveling.

Destination Management Company (DMC) A multifaceted company that offers services to inbound groups that include, but are not limited to, transportation, theme parties, audio-visual, temporary personnel, interpreters, entertainment, flowers, gifts, and so on.

Direct Access Computer term. The capability of moving (by computer key-in) from one airline data base to another.

Direct Flight A flight that does not require a passenger to change planes during intermediate stops; also known as a through flight. A flight to San Francisco from Chicago that makes a stop in Denver is a direct flight.

Discount Fare An air fare that is less expensive than regular full fare. Discounts are calculated off full coach fare; that is, a 25 percent discount means 25 percent less than regular coach.

Distribution The network of branches, subsidiaries, and independent agencies through which a travel supplier sells its products.

DMC See Destination Management Company.

Documents (1) All the confirmations, tickets, itineraries, and so on, a passenger receives for a fully prepaid trip.(2) The forms/papers required by a foreign government to enter its country: passport, visa, tourist card, and other papers.

Domestic Travel Travel between two points in the same country, territory, or possession. Travel within the continental United States, Hawaii, Alaska, Puerto Rico, and U.S. Virgin Islands is defined as U.S. domestic travel.

DOT See Department of Transportation.

Double A hotel room for occupancy by two people. It may have a double, queen-, or king-sized bed(s).

Double Booking Making reservations for two or more virtually identical sets of arrangements as insurance against getting bumped or because a traveler is unsure of exactly what he or she wants in travel plans. Considered unethical by travel agents and carriers.

Double-Double A hotel room with two double (queen or king) beds.

Double Occupancy Rate The rate for a room shared by two people. The rate may be quoted for the room or per person.

Downgrade To move a passenger to a lesser class of service or accommodations.

Downline Space Refers to all segments (legs) of an itinerary after the originating flight.

Downtime Period when a computer is not operable due to technical problems/malfunction.

Driver-Guide A driver (motorcoach or hired car) who is authorized/licensed to act as a guide on tours.

Drop Charge An additional fee that is often charged by a car rental company when the customer rents a car in one city and returns it to another.

Duty The import tax charged on certain goods brought into a country.

Duty Free Purchases exempt from import taxes. U.S. citizens returning from foreign countries may bring home $400 worth of goods, duty free. Tax is charged on amounts over $400. Additional taxes or restrictions apply to cigarettes, alcohol, and agricultural products.

Duty-Free Shop A store in which international passengers may purchase items free of import tax. Most major international airports have a number of duty-free shops. Purchase of an item in a duty-free port or store does not mean that the traveler will not have to pay customs on return to the United States.

Economy Class Also known as tourist or coach class. The level of service below business and first class.

Economy Fare On U.S. airlines, lower cost air fares that may have restrictions.

Economy Hotel A hotel that keeps its rates down (generally in the $20 to $30 range) by keeping rooms simple and offering minimal services.

Efficiency Hotel accommodations with cooking facilities.

Elapsed Flying Time Actual flying time between departure city and destination or stopover point.

Electronic Ticket Delivery Network (ETDN) A network of air ticket printers located in public facilities, such as hotels or airports, that allows travel agencies to send tickets to clients who are not located near, or are away from, the agency location.

Embark To depart; the starting point of a cruise.

Embarkation The process of boarding a ship, plane, train, or coach.

Emigration The process of leaving one country to live in another.

Endorsement An airline's written authorization on a ticket that permits a passenger to travel on another airline or allows certain fare restrictions to be waived.

Endorsement Box   The place on an airline ticket where special conditions or permissions are noted.

English Breakfast   A full breakfast that may include juice, cereal, bacon, eggs, sausage, kippers, toast, butter, marmalade, and coffee or tea.

Enhancement   An new program, format, or information display in a computerized reservation system.

Entrance Fee   Amount charged for touring museums, exhibits, amusement parks, and the like.

EP   See European Plan.

Equipment   Type of aircraft or vehicle for transport. Airlines use three-character codes to indicate the type of plane scheduled to be used on a flight. *Examples:* D10 = McDonnell Douglas DC10 Jet; L10 = Lockheed L1011 Jet

Escort   Travel professional who leads a group; also called a tour escort, tour leader, tour manager, or courier.

Escorted Tour   A prearranged, escorted travel program.

Escrow Account   An account supervised by a bank or financial institution in which funds are placed for safekeeping until the service has been provided. Client payments for charters frequently go into escrow accounts until the trip is completed.

ETA   Estimated time of arrival.

ETD   Estimated time of departure.

Eurail   The rail system of the countries of Western Europe plus Hungary.

Eurailpass   An unlimited-use rail ticket purchased for a specific period of time to travel by train in the countries that participate in the Eurail system. In some cases, the pass can be used for bus and ferry transportation.

European Plan (EP)   Hotel rate that includes accommodations only, no meals.

Eurotunnel   The tunnel under the English Channel connecting England and France. Also referred to as the Chunnel.

Exchange Order   A document issued by a supplier or travel agent to be exchanged for prepaid travel services.

Exchange Rate   The rate used to calculate how much money one country's currency (money) equals in another. See also Conversion Rate.

Excursion Fare   A round-trip fare that is less expensive than two one-way fares. These fares are generally available only for coach seats and, in most cases, have booking rules and travel restrictions.

FAA   See Federal Aviation Administration.

Familiarization Trip (Fam Trip)   A free or discounted trip for travel agents designed to familiarize them with a destination or travel service in order to stimulate travel sales to that area/supplier.

Fare   The fee paid by a passenger in exchange for travel.

Fare Basis Code   The combination of letters and/or numbers an airline assigns to a fare to distinguish it from other fares. These codes appear in fare (tariff) displays and on tickets. *Examples:* F = First class; YM = Military fare in tourist class.

Federal Aviation Administration (FAA)   The government agency that regulates civil aviation in the United States. The FAA's functions include enforcing airline security regulations, airport traffic control systems and aircraft maintenance, and licensing pilots.

Feeder Carrier   Small, local airline that operates between smaller airports "feeding" passengers to major carriers at larger airports.

Fictitious Point Principle   In international faring, the use of a fare to a city to which the passenger is not actually traveling in order to get a lower fare. Fictitious point faring is not allowed in U.S. domestic faring.

Final Payment   The last payment due on a tour, cruise, and so on. Final payment must be received before a traveler can receive his or her tickets and travel documents.

First Seating   The earlier of two meal times in a ship's dining room.

FIT   See Foreign Independent Travel.

Flag Carrier   Any carrier designated by a country to serve its international routes. Most countries have only one official flag carrier. The United States has many.

Flight (FLT)   Regularly scheduled air service from departure point to destination including stops en route.

Flight Coupon   The portion of an airline ticket for travel on a specified flight. The passenger must have one coupon to present to the airline for each flight taken. A passenger whose trip requires four flights must have four coupons in his or her ticket.

Fly/Drive   A vacation tour package including air transportation and rental car.

Fly/Sail   See Air/Sea.

Fortress Hub   An airport that a single airline has designated as a major connecting point for its flights and where that same airline controls most of the flights.

FOP   See Form of Payment.

Foreign Independent Travel (FIT)   A custom-designed, international trip, generally unescorted. It may be partly or fully prepaid.

FORE   See Forward.

Form of Payment (FOP)   How a client will pay for his or her travel arrangements: credit card, cash, check, and so on.

Forward (FORE)   Toward the front of a ship.

Franchise   A contract under which an independently owned business (such as a hotel or car rental company) buys the right to distribute or sell the products and services of another company. The company selling the rights—the franchisor—usually offers marketing and management support. A travel agency franchise purchases a package of services (including start-up and computer contract) from the franchising firm. The agency pays an initial fee and a monthly fee thereafter for support services.

Freighter   A ship designed primarily for carrying cargo. Passenger accommodations, although secondary, are sometimes available.

Frequency   The number of flights offered on a specific route in a given time period.

Frequent Flyer Program   Airline program in which members accrue miles (points) for flights taken. The miles/points are usually redeemable for free travel arrangements.

Frequent Guest Program   A hotel program in which members accrue points for nights stayed/dollars spent during the stay. These points are usually redeemed for free hotel nights or other travel arrangements.

Front Desk   The reception/registration/check-in area of a hotel.

Full Pension   See American Plan.

Galley   A kitchen on a ship, boat, or plane.

Gate   The area in an airport where passengers gather to board a plane.

Gate Agents   Airline personnel who check in passengers at the flight departure gate.

Gateway City   The last city of departure or first city of arrival in travel from one country to another.

GIT   See Group Inclusive Tour.

GMT   See Greenwich Mean Time.

Gratuity   A tip. Optional payment for services, as to a waiter.

Greenwich Mean Time (GMT)   Used for calculating standard time worldwide, GMT is the solar time in Greenwich, England. Also known as Zulu Time.

Gross Registered Tonnage (GRT)   Is not a weight measurement, but a guide to determine size of a ship based on enclosed square footage of "usable" passenger space. (One GRT equals 100 cubic feet of enclosed space.)

Ground/Land Arrangements   See Land Arrangements.

Ground/Land Operator   See Land Operator.

Group Inclusive Tour (GIT)   A prepaid tour with specified minimum size, content, and price in which a certain number of people travel together for an entire trip.

Group Rate   Special rate offered by travel suppliers for a minimum number (usually ten to fifteen) of people traveling together.

Guaranteed Reservation   Lodging reservation secured by the guest's agreement to pay even if he or she fails to arrive at the hotel. Payment may be guaranteed by credit card, a company, or by prior agreement between the hotel and a corporation or travel agency.

Guide   A professional who is licensed/authorized to conduct local sightseeing trips and excursions.

Guidebooks   Detailed destination information can be found in such popular series as Baedecker, Birnbaum, Fodor, Frommer, and Fielding guides. Guidebooks are important sources of information for agents and the traveling public.

Half-Pension   See Modified American Plan.

Hardware   The actual equipment in a computerized reservation (or any automated) system, that is, printers, CRTS, modems, and the like.

Headline City   City listed at the top of an airline tariff page.

Heliport   Landing and takeoff area for helicopters.

Hidden City Ticketing   Ticketing "trick"/technique for obtaining lower fares. Based on faring by certain airlines where the air fare from city A to city C with a stop in city B can be less than for a ticket between A/B. *Example:* The fare from Raleigh/Durham, N.C., to Roanoke, Va., is $200. The flight stops in Washington, D.C. The fare from Raleigh/Durham to Washington is $350. A passenger buys a ticket to Roanoke, but gets off the plane in Washington. Considered unethical by airlines.

High Season   The most popular period for tourist travel to a destination. Rates for transportation and accommodations are more expensive than for other times of the year. January and February are high season in the Virgin Islands. Also known as Peak Season.

History   Computer terminology signifying the record of reservation changes.

Hospitality Suite   A suite or room in a hotel used for entertaining during conventions or meetings. A hospitality suite may or may not have sleeping accommodations.

Hotel and Travel Index   A huge, one-volume hotel directory published quarterly and organized geographically and alphabetically by country, state, and city.

Hotel Chain   Hotels operating under the same name or designation. *Examples:* Marriott Hotels, Holiday Inns, Hyatt Hotels.

Hotel Package   Fixed-price, advertised hotel accommodations offer that includes room and other amenities such as meals, transportation, theater or attraction tickets, use of the hotel's recreational facilities, cocktails, and so on.

Hotel Representative (Rep)   Person or company retained by one or more hotels to serve as reservations and marketing outlets, usually with toll-free telephone service.

Hotelier   Hotel owner or manager.

Hovercraft   A high-speed boat that rides on a cushion of air over the waves.

Hub and Spoke System   The airline system of using a large city or area airport as connecting point for flights from smaller cities.

Hydrofoil   A high-speed boat whose entire hull is supported by fins or foils and is raised clear of the water when moving.

IATA   See International Air Transport Association.

IATAN   See International Airline Travel Agent Network.

ICTA   See Institute of Certified Travel Agents.

Illegal Connection   A passenger has an illegal connection when the time between the scheduled arrival of his or her first flight and the scheduled departure of his or her connecting (next) flight is less than the published, required minimum connecting time. Passengers on illegal connections are not entitled to airline compensation (meals, hotel, etc.) if they miss their connecting flights. However, no laws are broken. In this context, "legal" means "allowable" under airline/airport rules and regulations.

Immigration   The formalities associated with entering a country: passport control, customs, and so on.

IN or INF   See Infant.

Inbound   Arriving; coming into.

Incentive   Trip offered as a reward or prize to stimulate employee performance and company sales.

Incidentals   Personal items such as dry cleaning, telephone calls, and bar bills that are usually excluded from the price of a tour, package, or cruise.

Inclusive Tour (IT)   A tour offered at a fixed price that includes transportation, hotel accommodations, and so on. All charges (taxes, gratuities, meals, etc.) may not be included. Included items should be listed in the promotional literature.

Industry Agents Handbook   Also known as the *ARC Handbook.* A procedures manual for travel agents published by the Airlines Reporting Corporation. In addition to formats for tickets and other accountable documents, it contains the details of the contract between airlines and agents.

Infant (IN or INF)   A passenger under two years of age who does not occupy a seat (travels on the lap of a parent or adult).

In-Flight Service   Entertainment, meals, beverages, and miscellaneous items available during a flight.

In-Plant Agency   A travel agency located on the premises of a corporate client, doing business exclusively for that client.

Inside   On a ship/boat, a cabin with no windows or portholes.

Institute of Certified Travel Agents (ICTA)   The travel industry's primary educational organization. ICTA certifies agents who successfully complete a comprehensive course of study and pass a detailed examination. See CTC.

Interchange   Joint operation of one aircraft by two carriers. Primarily used with international flights.

Intercity Express   First-class train used throughout Western Europe to go quickly between large cities.

Interline   The use of a connecting service that includes two or more carriers.

Interline Agreement   An agreement between carriers that permits cross-services such as baggage handling and joint ticketing.

International Air Transport Association (IATA)   A voluntary membership organization of the airlines which, by setting rates and establishing conditions of service and safety standards, provides a unified system of worldwide air transportation.

International Airlines Travel Agents Network (IATAN)   A wholly owned subsidiary of IATA with voluntary membership among the airlines and other travel industry suppliers. It appoints travel agencies to sell tickets for international travel on IATA member carriers.

International Dateline   An imaginary line at 180 degrees longitude in the Pacific Ocean where the earth's day officially begins. When crossing the line eastbound, a day is gained. When crossing westbound, a day is lost.

International   Between separate countries.

Interstate   Between states.

Intrastate   Within the same state.

Involuntary Reroute (IRR)   A major schedule change imposed by the airlines requiring a passenger to leave much earlier or later than originally planned or to take a connecting flight instead of a direct one. By law, a ticketed passenger must be reaccommodated within a specified number of hours of the original flight on the original carrier or on another airline with no increase in fare.

IRR   See Involuntary Reroute.

Issue   The actual writing of a ticket or similar document to be used by the passenger. May be done by hand or by computer.

IT Fare   A special air fare available only to travelers who have purchased an advertised tour package. IT fares are not as common today as they once were and are offered only in international travel.

IT Number   Inclusive tour code number. The code assigned to an advertised package tour that is entered on the airline ticket to indicate authorized use of an IT number.

Itinerary   The complete schedule of a trip.

Jet Lag   Travelers on long flights cross several time zones. This causes a disruption of normal sleeping and eating patterns leading to a feeling of fatigue upon arrival known as jet lag. Also known as dysynchronosis.

Jet Stream   High-velocity wind that moves around the earth from west to east at high altitudes. The jet stream affects flight times; when a plane flies "with the wind" (west to east), flight times will be shorter than when a plane flies "against the wind" (east to west).

Jetway   The covered passageway that connects the airport (boarding/gate area) to the airplane.

Joint Fare   A fare using two or more carriers over specific routings and published as a single amount.

Junior Suite   A hotel room that is larger than a regular hotel room and may have separate sleeping and sitting areas.

Kilometer   A measure equal to 3,280 feet or 5/8 of a mile. The standard measure of distance in continental Europe is the kilometer.

King Room   A room with a king-sized bed.

Knots   Nautical miles per hour. A nautical mile is approximately 14 percent (1/7) longer than a land mile; 20 knots = 23 miles per hour.

Lanai   A room with a balcony or patio that is close to or overlooks water or a garden. The term originated in Hawaii, referring to a porch furnished as a living room.

Land Arrangements   Those elements of a trip provided to a client upon reaching his or her destination: transfers, hotels, meals, sightseeing.

Land Operator   Company that provides local travel services such as sightseeing. Also called a ground operator.

Last Seat Availability   The capability of an automated reservation system to provide users with up-to-the-minute information about an airline's available seats.

Layover   The amount of time a connecting passenger has between flights.

Leeward   Away from the wind. The Leeward Islands are a group in the Caribbean. The leeward side of an island is the less windy side.

Leg   A part of a trip. (Example: On a Miami–Atlanta–New Orleans trip, the Miami to Atlanta portion would be one "leg.")

Lido   A swimming pool and the area surrounding it.

Limited Availability   Means only a specified (or limited) number of reservations will be accepted at the advertised rate or on the special offer.

Linear Dimensions   Height + width + depth of each piece of baggage.

Local Fare   A fare for direct or through service on a single carrier and published in the local fares tariff.

Low Fare Search   Refers to any system (whether human or computerized) of monitoring reservations for the availability of lower fares for trips already booked, but not yet taken.

Low Season   Period when tourists travel to a given destination and rates for hotel and transportation are less than normal. Also known as the slow season or off-season.

Lower Berth   A berth on a ship or train that is under another berth.

Lowest Available Fare   The lowest fare that can actually be booked for a particular air itinerary. There may be a lower fare that can be quoted, but no seats are available.

Management Reports   Specialized reports an agency provides to its corporate clients so they can identify travel spending trends and control expenses.

Manifest   The official list of all passengers or cargo on a plane, train, ship, motorcoach, and so on.

MAP   See Modified American Plan.

Market   Current or potential customers. For airlines, the term "market" may also indicate the cities or areas to which they fly (i.e., the West Coast market, the Denver market).

Maximum Permitted Mileage (MPM)   The most mileage that can be traveled on a fare.

MCO   See Miscellaneous Charges Order.

Meet and Assist   An airline term meaning a client needs to be met by a customer service representative when his or her flight arrives and assisted with making a connecting flight. This request is most often made for elderly, disabled, young, or first-time flyers.

Meeting Fare   A specially discounted fare for a particular meeting or series of meetings that is arranged with one airline. The airline offering the fare is commonly referred to as the "official carrier."

Meeting Planners International (MPI)   A professional educational association for corporate and association meeting planners.

Metroliner   A high-speed, luxury train used by Amtrak for short and intermediate routes.

Mid-Ship   The location on a ship that is equal distance between bow and stern. Mid-ship cabins are considered preferable because there is less motion (pitch and roll).

Mileage Allowance   The miles a car renter may drive at no additional cost.

Mileage Charge   Charge made for each mile a rental car is driven beyond the established limit for the rental rate used.

Military Passenger   Traveler who is a full-time, active duty member of the U.S. Army, Navy, Air Force, Marines, or Coast Guard.

Minimum Connecting Time   The time required at individual airports to leave one scheduled flight and board another.

Minimum Land Package   The minimum in cost or components a passenger must purchase to qualify for either an individual or group inclusive tour fare.

Minimum Stay   The requirement of certain discounted or excursion air fares that the passenger "stay" at his or her outward destination for a defined period of time: one week, over a Saturday night, and so on.

Miscellaneous Charges Order (MCO)   A handwritten document issued by a travel agent or an airline as proof of payment for specified travel arrangements. An automated multipurpose document (MDP) is scheduled to replace the MCO in the future.

Misconnect   See Illegal Connection.

Modified American Plan (MAP)   A hotel room rate that includes lodging and two meals—breakfast and lunch or dinner.

Motorcoach   A bus with deluxe seating and sometimes bathroom facilities, wet bar, microwave, and TV monitors.

MPI   See Meeting Planners International.

MPM   See Maximum Permitted Mileage.

Murphy Bed   A bed that folds into the wall when not in use.

Narrow-Body   An aircraft with a single center aisle.

National Tourist Office (NTO)   A government-sponsored office that promotes tourism in a particular country. Tourist offices provide marketing assistance to travel agencies and destination information to the general public. Telephone numbers and addresses for tourist offices can be found in the *Travel Industry Personnel Directory*.

National Transportation Safety Board (NTSB)   An autonomous government agency that develops safety standards for all public transportation and investigates accidents. Whereas the FAA issues directives to prevent air crashes, NTSB investigates crashes after they occur.

Nautical Mile   The distance measurement used in air and sea travel. A nautical mile is equal to one minute of latitude or 6,076 feet.

Net Rate   (1) The air fare, tour price, hotel rate, or cruise price, less commission. (2) A price quoted to a sales agent without standard commission built in. Group hotel rates, chartered aircraft rates, chartered motorcoach rates, and group tour rates are often quoted net, noncommissionable by a supplier. The agency handling the trip must then add on its charges to cover handling and profit.

Neutral Unit of Construction (NUC) A synthetic currency used in the calculation of international air fares and designed to facilitate the equitable conversion of air fares from one currency into another.

Nonrefundable Payment, once made, will not be refunded to the client should he or she cancel his or her plans.

Nonrestricted Fares The airline imposes no penalties for changes or cancellations and does not restrict use according to date or time.

Nonstop Flight A flight that does not stop between point of departure and destination.

No Record (No-Rec) When a supplier can find no record of a reservation for a client even though the client may be holding a ticket or written confirmation. It is generally caused by a transmission failure in a computer system.

No-Show A passenger or guest who does not honor or cancel his or her previously confirmed reservation.

NTO See National Tourist Office.

NTSB See National Transportation Safety Board.

NUC See Neutral Unit of Construction.

Official Airline Guide (OAG) The published directory of flight schedules. There is a North American edition and a worldwide edition. There is a computerized format known as the electronic OAG and a printed pocket edition that is marketed to the frequent traveler.

Observation Car A railroad car specially designed for sightseeing.

Occupancy Tax The tax levied by many cities on a hotel stay. In addition to local taxes, there may be a set tax per room or per person added to the hotel bill.

Official Carrier The airline designated to provide transportation for a meeting or convention; also, occasionally used to designate a preferred airline for regularly scheduled travel: "Delta is the Official Carrier of Walt Disney World."

Official Hotel Guide (OHG). A multivolume collection of descriptions of hotels and resorts all over the world based on information supplied by the properties themselves.

Off-Line Connection When a passenger must change both planes and airlines to reach his or her destination.

One Way A trip from an origin point to a destination point with no return transportation arranged. A trip from Dallas to Phoenix only is "one-way."

On Request A reservation or service that has been asked for, but not confirmed.

Open Jaw (1) Air transportation from one departure point to a specified destination with a return to a point other than the original point of departure (i.e., Fly from Greensboro to Atlanta; return from Atlanta to Charlotte). (2) air transportation from a point of departure to a specified destination with the return from a point other than the specified destination to the original point of departure (i.e., Fly from Greensboro to Dallas; return to Greensboro from Houston). (3) A double open jaw is when origin, destination, departure, and return cities are all different (i.e., Fly from Greensboro to San Francisco; return from Los Angeles to Norfolk).

Open Ticket A ticket that allows the holder to secure a specific reservation at a later date. The ticket indicates air carrier, class of service, fare basis, and price only. The word "open" is printed across the sections of the ticket that normally indicate specific flight information.

Operates Frequency of service (i.e., Delta's flight #1011 operates daily between Atlanta and Dallas).

Option Date The date on which the deposit for a cruise, tour, or other service is due. If the deposit is not paid, the client will lose his or her reservation.

Optional An "extra" service, side trip, feature, or extension offered on a tour which participants may choose to take at an additional charge to the basic tour price.

Origin The point at which a trip begins.

Originating Carrier First carrier in the flight itinerary.

Outbound Departing; from home (originating) city to the furthest destination.

Outside Salesperson An employee working outside the office, generally on commission basis, to generate group or individual business. Some outside agents rarely appear in the office at all and many are not responsible for preparing their own tickets and documents.

Overbooking The intentional sale of more seats, rooms, or cruise cabins than actually exist in anticipation of a percentage of no-shows and cancellations.

Override Additional commission paid to agents by a supplier as a bonus for overall volume, increased sales, or as an incentive to book particular arrangements.

Package Travel arrangements put together and sold at a single, all-inclusive price.

Package Tour Any advertised tour that includes a combination of arrangements, such as transportation, accommodations, and sightseeing.

Parlor Car A railroad car or motorcoach with food and bar service.

Participating Carrier All operators involved in the transportation of a person or goods in a given itinerary.

Party (PTY) Refers to two or more people traveling together. *Example:* Mr. and Mrs. Jones and their two children are flying together; they are a "party of four."

Passenger Capacity The number of passengers a ship can accommodate. The ratio of the number of passengers to the number of crew (passenger/crew ratio) is usually an indication of the service that can be expected.

Passenger Facility Charge (PFC) Per passenger tax authorized by the U.S. Congress for airports to charge beginning in 1991. The tax can amount to no more than $3 by any one airport and no more than $12 for any individual trip. PFC revenues are specifically for upgrading and expanding local airport facilities.

Passenger Name Record (PRN) The computer term for a traveler's reservation information as booked and stored in the system.

Passenger Ship A ship that is used primarily as a means of transporting people from one point to another.

Passport A document issued by the traveler's native country that certifies his or her identity and citizenship and grants him or her permission to travel abroad and return to his or her home country.

Peak Season See High Season.

Penalty The amount charged for cancellation or change of a reservation.

Pension (French; pronounced *pawn-see-on*) Used widely in Europe, meaning guest or boarding house.

Per Diem The amount a traveler spends by day for his or her accommodations, meals, entertainment, and so on while on a trip.

Personal Accident Insurance (PAI) Optional coverage offered by car rental companies for renters to cover personal injury or death while using the rental car.

"Pick-Up Ticketing" Sometimes a client will make a reservation direct with the airline and then call an agency to have it issue the ticket. The agency will call the airline "to pick up ticketing" (i.e., get all reservation information and advise airline that the agency will be ticketing).

Pitch (1) The distance between rows of seats on an aircraft. (2) The rise and fall of a ship at sea.

POE Port of Embarkation.

Point-to-Point Fare Basic transportation rate from one city to another. These fares may be higher than round trip or excursion fares.

Port (1) The left side of a ship when you are facing the bow. (2) The cities or places where ships may dock.

Port Tax Fees levied by a port on each arriving or departing passenger.

Porterage Baggage-handling service. Tours including this service eliminate the need for the clients to carry their own luggage to their room or to pay (tip) for its carriage.

Ports of Call The stopping points on a cruise ship's itinerary.

Preferred Supplier/Vendor The suppliers an agency chooses to sell over others. The choice of preferred supplier is usually made based on commission rate paid, service, and quality. Some agencies have "preferred supplier lists" and sell those suppliers exclusively.

Prepaid Ticket Advise (PTA) An airline authorization that permits a ticket to be issued in one city and payment made in another. The agent accepts payment, but the airline issues the ticket.

Preregistration The completion of the check-in process before a guest's arrival. This service is useful for handling tours and meeting groups.

Pretrip Auditing An automated or employee review of trips booked but not yet taken to determine if savings opportunities exist or if travel policy is being followed. This auditing is usually done by agencies for their corporate accounts.

Printer The piece of computer hardware that prints the information stored in the computer onto the ticket, invoice, or voucher.

Priority Waitlist Special waitlist airlines offer travel agencies for their clients. Clients on priority lists receive preferential treatment in being given a confirmed reservation.

Profile Detailed computer file that contains information on a traveler or company and contains charge card numbers, frequent flyer numbers, addresses, phone numbers, travel preferences, and so on. Agencies use these profiles to insure speed and accuracy in making reservations for their regular clientele.

Promotional Fare   Lower than normal fare offered by a carrier to promote travel to new cities on its route, or to promote travel during off-season or slack periods.

Proof of Citizenship   A document that establishes nationality to the satisfaction of a foreign government. It may be an original or certified copy of a birth certificate, a voter's registration card, or a passport.

Proof of Identity   A document that establishes a passenger's identity to the satisfaction of a supplier or government. Proof of identity may be a driver's license, student i.d. card, birth certificate, voter's registration card, passport, and so on.

Property   A term often used when referring to a hotel or resort.

PTA   See Prepaid Ticket Advice.

Pullman   A sleeping car on a train.

Quad   A room/cabin that can accommodate four people.

Quality Assurance   Procedure for checking agency reservations for accuracy in faring, seat assignment, client information, and so on. Larger agencies may have employees or departments whose sole job is to check reservation records.

Quality Control   Same as Quality Assurance.

Queue   Term for a computerized filing/dating/messaging system. For example, when a schedule change occurs, the airline will send, via computer, all reservation records affected by the change to an agency. The schedule change messages will appear on a certain "queue," predetermined by the airline/agency. The agent then accesses the "queue" and all records that must be changed will automatically appear.

Rack Rate   The official posted rate for hotel rooms.

Rate Desk   The department of an airline in which complex air fares are calculated.

Rate Guarantee   (1) A guarantee made by a ship line that a passenger will receive his or her requested accommodations or better at the same rate quoted. (2) A supplier's guarantee that the price quoted for transportation or travel arrangements will not change.

Rate of Exchange (ROE)   The ROE is set by IATA, generally on a quarterly basis, for the purpose of converting NUCs into foreign currencies.

Rebate   The practice of giving a client credit for a percentage of the commission the agency earns on a sale.

Reconfirmation   A statement of intent by the passenger to the supplier to use a reservation. Passengers must reconfirm reserved space on international flights or risk losing their reservations.

Record Locator   The alphanumeric code assigned to a passenger name record (PNR) that identifies the PNR and gives the airline easy access to displaying the reservation data. Record locator numbers are randomly assigned in the reservation system and each existing PNR has its own record locator number.

Red-Eye   A long-haul flight during late night or early morning hours; usually from west to east. Refers to the "red eyes" of passengers who have flown all night.

Reduced Rate   Refers to the discounted price of an air ticket or other travel arrangement. Most commonly used in referring to lower rates for agents or travel industry personnel.

Refund/Exchange Notice (REN)   The combined ARC accounting form for issuing ticket refunds and exchanges.

Regional Carriers   Airlines serving specified areas or regions of the country. (i e., an airline that flies only in the west would be classified as a Regional Carrier.)

Registry   A statement indicating a ship's owner and the country under whose flag it sails. Registry is not necessarily related to the nationality of officers and crew.

Reissue   To write a new ticket because there have been changes to the itinerary or fare that cannot be handled through revalidation.

Release Space   To relinquish reservations or a commitment for space with a vendor. Most commonly used when working with group or block space.

REN   See Refund/Exchange Notice.

Rental Agreement   The contract between the car rental company and its customer that is executed/signed when a car is rented.

Rep   See Representative.

Representative (REP)   A person or company who acts on behalf of another, often in a reservations or sales capacity.

Request for Proposal (RFP)   A company's formal request to a supplier to bid for its business.

Reroute   The need to change a passenger's routing from what was originally confirmed, either on a voluntary or involuntary basis. See Involuntary Reroute.

Res   "Short" for reservation.

Reservation An agreement to hold a room, seat, or space for a specified day, flight, or time.

Reservationist A reservations sales agent.

Res Card The paper form on which an agent enters client reservation information if the records cannot be entered in the CRS.

Resort A hotel complex, usually in a popular vacation area (beach, lake, mountains) that offers many facilities: golf, tennis, swimming, dining, nightclubs, children's programs, and so on.

Responsibility Clause The section of a tour brochure or supplier sales contract that states the conditions under which a trip is sold. It should include the names of the companies financially responsible as well as bond coverage, if any.

Revalidation The authorized alteration of a ticket or other documentation.

Revalidation Sticker A change notice attached to a flight coupon showing that a change has been made on the original reservation. See Sticker.

Revenue Sharing See Rebate.

ROE See Rate of Exchange.

Roll The sway of a ship from side to side.

Room Block The number of hotel rooms reserved for a group.

Room Night One room occupied for one night at a hotel. A stay of two nights would therefore involve "two room nights."

Room Tax State or local tax charged on hotel stays.

Rooming List A list of the names of the members of a group, the type of rooms they are requesting, dates of stay, and so on that is submitted to a hotel prior to the group's arrival.

Round Trip A journey from origin point A to point B and back to point A, via the exact same routing, carrier, and class of service.

Routing The cities through which a passenger may travel for a particular fare. Fare rules specify which routings are allowed.

Run of the House (ROH) A hotel rate category that means that any room type available may be assigned to the guest. ROH is most commonly used with group bookings and means that no specific room type or location can be guaranteed for the price quoted.

Sales Report A detailed summary of air tickets sold during a seven-day period by a travel agency. This report is required by ARC.

Satellite Ticket Printer (STP) A ticket printer operated by an agency from a remote site. STPs are frequently used by agencies for issuing tickets for a corporate account at its location.

Schedule The published times of operation of a flight, tour, and so on.

Scheduled Carrier Refers to an airline offering regularly scheduled passenger service rather than to a charter airline, which operates only when requested and paid to do so.

Seasonal Rates A pricing structure that allows prices to vary depending on the time of year or consumer demand.

Seat Assignment The actual seat assigned to an airline passenger.

Seat Preference The seat assignment a client prefers on an airplane (smoking, nonsmoking, window, aisle, etc.).

Seat Rotation A system used on motorcoach tours to ensure passengers have an equal opportunity to sit up front. Passengers change seats frequently according to a preannounced pattern.

Security Charge In some countries (or areas), an extra charge is added to the air fare to cover the cost of airport/airline security procedures.

Segment A part of a trip; also called a leg.

Senior Citizen A passenger sixty-five years of age or older. Airlines, hotels, and other suppliers often grant discounts to senior citizens.

Service Charge (1) A fee added to a bill, usually in a hotel or restaurant, to cover the cost of certain services as a substitute for tipping. (2) A fee agencies may charge clients for specified, noncommissionable or nonrevenue-producing services.

Seventy-Five AD See AD-75.

Shell A brochure provided by a supplier complete with artwork and graphics, but with space for a travel agency or tour operator to imprint an itinerary, price, and booking information for its own tour.

Shore Excursion A tour of a port city or area usually by bus, which departs from shipside. Shore excursions are available for purchase in advance or on the ship.

Shoulder Season A travel season between high/peak and low/off peak.

Shuttle (1) Continuous ground transportation between airport terminals, rental car lots, or hotels. (2) A no-reservation, guaranteed air service operating on heavily traveled routes (i.e., there is hourly air shuttle transportation between Washington and New York).

Sightseeing Literally, "seeing the sights" or places of interest in an area. Sightseeing may be by a guided tour or independent.

Sine A set of initials or numbers that constitutes a reservation agent's identification symbol.

Single A room for one person.

Single Supplement The additional amount charged the single traveler to occupy a cruise cabin or hotel room on a package tour.

Skycap The person who checks baggage at airport curbside check-in.

Sleepers Train cars that consist of a private room with accommodations for one to four persons.

Sleeper Seats On long-haul flights with first-class compartments, there may be seats that recline to a more comfortable resting position.

Software Refers to computer programs. Each travel reservation system vendor has developed software programs to provide reservation, bookkeeping, reporting, and ticketing services to its users.

Sold Out No availability. All seats in a fare category or on a flight, rooms in a hotel, cabins on a cruise, and so on, are taken (i.e., "The morning flight is completely sold out, but there are seats on the afternoon flight.").

Spa Health-oriented resort.

Space Availability of seats on flights or accommodations for tours or lodging.

Space Available Generally applies to reduced rate or free passage and means "if the space is available." Travel or accommodations are subject to confirmation at the last moment after all full-fare passengers have been accommodated.

Special Interest Tour Tour designed for clients with an interest in a specific subject. It may be escorted by an expert in that particular field. *Examples:* Art tours, gourmet cooking tours, theatre tours, and so on.

Special Meals Most airlines offer special meals for passengers who have dietary restrictions. These meals must be requested in advance. *Examples:* Kosher, vegetarian, low salt, seafood.

Split Ticketing The practice of issuing two one-way tickets instead of a round-trip to obtain a lower fare as in international faring where exchange rates could favor such a transaction.

Stabilizer A device on a ship that reduces pitch/roll.

Standby A traveler, without reservations, who chooses to wait at the airport until departure time, for available space on a flight.

Starboard The right side of a ship when you are facing the bow.

STAR Service A collection of hotel and cruise ship evaluations prepared by travel industry representatives and characterized by frankness and attention to detail. These reports provide a counterbalance to the promotional literature provided by hotels, resorts, and cruise lines.

Stateroom Sleeping accommodations on a ship; also known as a cabin.

Status Confirmed, waitlisted, on request, cancelled, and so on (i.e., "What is the status of this reservation?").

Steamship Any large ocean-going passenger vessel including a cruise ship. The term is still currently used even though few ships are powered by steam.

Step-On Guide The guide who steps-on a motorcoach at a destination to give a local sightseeing tour. Also called a local or city guide.

Stern Rear of a ship.

Sticker To apply a revalidation sticker to a ticket.

Stopover A break in a trip that usually results in a higher fare. In the United States, a passenger has a stopover when he or she arrives at a connecting point and does not have a departure scheduled within four hours. In international travel, a passenger must depart within twenty-four hours or be charged an additional fee for a stopover.

STPN Satellite Ticket Printer Network.

Studio A hotel room with couches that convert into beds.

Substitute Service Authorization for one carrier to serve portions of a route assigned to another carrier. Usually refers to a commuter operating for a trunk or national carrier.

Suite Hotel accommodation that has a bedroom(s) and a separate living area. The rate is determined by the number of bedrooms. Typically, suites are one- or two-bedroom units.

Supplement An additional charge for special needs. The price of most tours is based on double occupancy, and single passengers pay a supplement.

Supplier An airline, tour operator, hotel, or car rental firm that provides or supplies the travel product.

Surcharge An additional payment imposed by a supplier, either at certain times of the year, or to meet exceptional circumstances (rising fuel prices or currency fluctuations).

Surface Segment   Referring to a segment of a trip itinerary that is traveled on land rather than by air. See ARUNK.

T & E   Travel and Entertainment is a classification for corporate travel expenses.

T & E Policy   The guidelines for business travel spending which a company determines for its employees.

Tariff   A published list of fares. Tariff also describes a supplier's comprehensive publication containing fares, rates, and the rules that govern their applicability.

Tee Time   When a golf game begins. Golf courses assign tee times to players (i.e., their reservations to play).

Teleconference   A meeting held via telephone/televideo.

Tender   A small boat used to transport passengers from a ship to shore and back when the ship cannot dock.

Terminal   (1) See CRT. (2) An airport, bus, or train station.

Terms and Conditions   That portion of a transportation or tour contract that states exactly what the purchaser is offered.

TGV   See Train a Grande Vitesse.

Theme Park   Manmade tourist attractions, such as Disneyland, Disney World, or Knott's Berry Farm.

Through Fare   Fare for travel from point of origin to destination.

Through Flight   See Direct Flight.

Ticket   When completed and validated correctly, the ticket is the contract of transportation between a carrier and a passenger.

Ticketing Deadline   The date by which a ticket must be issued and paid. If the ticketing deadline is not met, the client will lose his or her option to purchase the ticket at a specified fare.

Ticket Imprinter   When completed and validated with the imprinter, the handwritten ticket is the valid contract of transportation between a carrier and a passenger.

Ticket Lift   The actual number of tickets that were collected from passengers by an airline for its flight or flights.

Ticket Stock   Blank airline tickets used by airlines and travel agencies that become valid for transportation upon proper completion. Agencies are accountable to ARC for ticket stock and are required to follow its safekeeping procedures.

Time Share   A condominium concept whereby a person purchases the use of accommodations for a certain period each year. Others own the space during the rest of the year.

Tips   Gratuities for service personnel. Often determined as a percentage of a bill.

Tour   An organized, preplanned travel program that is promoted by a brochure and that qualifies for an IT number.

Tour Documents   See Documents.

Tour Escort   The individual who accompanies a tour throughout and is responsible for its smooth operation.

Tour Guide   (1) The individual with a special knowledge of a destination who joins the tour only while it visits that one area; also known as a local or step-on guide. (2) A tour escort who also serves as the guide throughout the tour.

Tour Leader   See Tour Escort.

Tour Manager   See Tour Escort.

Tour Operator   A company that packages or markets inclusive tours. Tour operators may sell their product through travel agents or sell directly to the public.

Tour Shell   See Shell.

Tourist Card   A document allowing entry into and departure from a foreign country, usually without a passport. Common in Mexico and Central and South America. Travelers must have them in possession before departure from their home city.

Tourist Class   Seating (as on airplane, train) or accommodation (as on a passenger ship) category. Also a classification for a hotel.

Train a Grande Vitesse (TGV)   High-speed train of French design that operates in Western Europe (primarily in France).

Transcanal   Passing through a canal. Usually refers to Panama Canal cruises.

Transfer   Local ground transportation, usually from airport to hotel. Transfers are frequently included in the price of tour packages.

Transient   Traveler passing through a destination for a short stay.

Travel Advisory   An official warning or caution issued by the U.S. State Department on travel to specified areas. *Example:* A travel advisory may be issued for a country experiencing political unrest.

Travel Agent   An individual working in the travel industry, serving as a counselor to the traveling public and as a salesperson of the travel product for industry suppliers.

Travel Industry Personnel Directory   A directory of industry suppliers, trade associations, national tourist associations, and related government agencies. An annual publication of *Travel Agent* magazine.

Travel Manager   The person in a corporation who books, plans, or controls business travel and business travel expenses. Very large companies often have travel managers; smaller companies leave the travel planning to the individual or the administrative/clerical staff.

Travel Planner   An OAG publication that contains extensive destination information on cities and countries throughout the world. A comprehensive and indispensable reference for travel agents.

Travel Volume   The amount of travel business a company books/purchases in a given period of time (usually yearly). Travel volume includes and may be broken down as air travel, hotel stays, car rentals, ground transportation, meals, and so on.

Triple   A room, cabin, or compartment for three people.

Trunk Carrier   An airline operating larger equipment and serving large areas of a country.

Tube   The British term for subway.

Turnaround Point   Location of outward destination of a trip from which the return trip begins.

Turndown Service   Service in a hotel involving "turning down" the spread and placing a mint or chocolate on the pillow.

Twin/Twin Double   A room with two beds for two persons. They may be single, but could be doubles or queens.

UATP   See Universal Air Travel Plan.

Unaccompanied Minor   A child (under twelve) traveling without an adult on an airline. There are age and fare restrictions for unaccompanied minors.

Unchecked Baggage   See Carry-On Luggage.

United States Tour Operators Association (USTOA)   Members must have been successfully operated by the same management ownership for three years, handle certain volume of bookings, and post bond and indemnity insurance of $1 million.

Universal Air Travel Plan (UATP)   An airline credit card that is recognized by most carriers. The UATP can be used only for air travel.

Universal Time Coordinated   Same as GMT.

Unlimited Mileage   A rental car contract that allows the renter to drive any number of miles without additional charges being made.

Upgrade   To move to a better class of airline service, cruise cabin, or hotel room.

Upper   A berth on a ship or train above another berth.

USTOA   See United States Tour Operators Association.

Valid Coupons   The negotiable coupons of an ARC document or carrier-issued ticket. Valid coupons are good for supplier services as indicated.

Validate   To imprint an airline document with the identifying mark of an airline or agency. This procedure is necessary to make a ticket a legally binding contract.

Validator   The imprinter used in the validation process of airline and rail tickets. Handwritten tickets must be imprinted in a validator. Automated (computer generated) tickets are validated when printed.

Validity Dates   Period during which a special fare or rate applies.

Value Added Tax (VAT)   A government-imposed tax on goods and some services common in European countries.

Value Season   Term used by some suppliers to indicate times of the year that are not "peak" or highest cost. Shoulder and low season are "value seasons."

VAT   See Value Added Tax.

Vendor   See Supplier.

Visa   An endorsement placed in a passport by a foreign government official that indicates that the passport has been examined and the holder may travel to that country. Not all countries require visas. Since the officials in the country in question have the final say, on rare occasions a visitor may be denied entry even though he or she has a valid visa.

Void   Not valid. Cannot be used (i.e., a voided ticket is one that cannot be used for transportation).

Volume   (1) See Travel Volume. (2) The amount of travel business an agency books/sells.

Voucher   A prepaid service order for transportation, accommodations, or other travel-related services. See Exchange Order.

Wagon Lits   Sleeping cars on European trains.

Waitlist   List of prospective travelers who are waiting for space that is sold out. Travel agents may ask airlines to put their clients on a priority waitlist to improve their chances of being confirmed as those who have confirmed space cancel their reservations.

Walk (Walked)   Term for when a traveler arrives at a hotel with a confirmed reservation, but the hotel has no rooms available. The hotel then "walks" the traveler to another hotel and (usually) pays for the accommodations.

Walk Policy   A given hotel's policy on overbooking and "walking" guests.

Walk-In   A guest without a reservation who literally walks in to a hotel to request a room.

WHO   See World Health Organization.

Wholesaler   A company that creates, plans, and markets inclusive tours and FITs for sale through travel agents. Distinguished from tour operators who often sell at retail as well as through travel agents.

Widebody   Oversized planes designed to carry large numbers of passengers on long-haul trips.

Windward   Facing the wind. The Windward Islands are a group in the Caribbean.

World Health Organization (WHO)   An agency of the United Nations that advises governments on vaccination requirements for travelers and tracks the spread of communicable diseases worldwide.

Yield   Revenue per unit. *Example:* An air carrier's yield is the average revenue per mile flown per paid passenger.

Yield Management   A system that a business uses to adjust its product prices up and down based on actual and anticipated demand. In sophisticated businesses such as airlines, yield management systems are automated.

INDEX

A

Adventure tour, 189
Agency, *see* Travel agency; Travel
    agent
AH & MA, *see* American Hotel &
    Motel Association
Air fares, 97–101
    base fare, 46
    class system, 97
    full coach, 99
    promotional, 100
    restricted, 99–100
Air/sea package, 126
Air Transport Association (ATA), 17
Air travel, 53
    domestic, definition of, 94
    history of, 70–72
    international, definition of, 94
Airline codes, 84
    decoding, 86
    encoding, 87
Airline Deregulatory Act, 73, 74. *see*
    also Deregulation
Airline industry, 12, 69–108
    automation, 15, 16
    "Big Three," 76
    commission payments, 46, 47
    commuter carriers, 75
    control of agencies, 53
    deregulation, 73, 79, 83, 99
    distribution (selling), 45
    employment opportunities,
        103–104
    regional lines, 73
    regulation, legislation, 7
    travel agency/agent relationship,
        44
    trunk lines, 73
Airline, *see* Airline industry
Airline route systems, 87–91
Airline system, *see* Automation
Airline ticket, 44, 46
    boarding pass, 28
    breakdown, 48
    commission, 46, 47, 48
Airlines Reporting Corporation (ARC),
    17, 44
    Industry Agent's Handbook, 61
    rail transportation, 177
Airport codes, 85
Airports, 91–95
    busiest, 93
    domestic, vs. international, 94–95

Frankfurt Main (Up Close), 95
    naming of, 92
    safety in, 94
Alamo Car Rental, 161
All-inclusive, 139. *see also* Resort
    Club Med (Up Close), 143–144
All-suite hotel, 138
Amadeus, 15
American Airlines, 16, 75, 76
American Express, 40, 54
    Up Close, 57–58
American Hotel and Motel Association
    (AH & MA), 17, 146
American Society of Travel Agents
    (ASTA), 17, 63
Amfleet, 174
Amtrak, 172–174
    equipment, 174
Apartment rental, 142
Apollo, 15
ARC, *see* Airlines Reporting
    Corporation
ARTA, *see* Association of Retail Travel
    Agents
Artificial hub, *see* Hub; Hub and spoke
    system
Association of Retail Travel Agents
    (ARTA), 17
Associations, 16
ASTA, *see* American Society of Travel
    Agents
ATA, *see* Air Transport Association
ATM, *see* Automated Ticket Machine
Auto Train, 174
Automated quality control, 66
Automated Ticket Machine (ATM),
    65
Automation, 14, 15
Avis Car Rental, 158, 161

B

"Baby boomers," 33
Barge cruises, 123–124
Base fare, 46
B&B, *see* Bed & Breakfast Inn
Bed & Breakfast Inn, 141–142
Best Western Hotels, 135
Boarding pass, 28
Brochures, 19
    cruise, 116, 125
    tour, 193
"Bucket Shop," 102

Budget hotel, 138
Budget Rent-A-Car, 156, 161
Bureau of Labor Statistics, 53
Business travel/traveler, 31, 54
    departments, 66
    influences on, 8
    international, 8
    Up Close, 33–34

C

CAB, *see* Civil Aeronautics Bureau
Cabin category, 117, 125
Canadian National Railways, 177
Canrailpass, 177
Capacity control, 100
Car class, 160–161
Car rental
    class, 160–161
    codes, 162
    foreign, 164
    insurance, 163–164
    international, 164
    off-site, 161–162
    on-site, 161–162
    pricing, 162–163
    reasons to use, 158–159
    requirements, 159–160
    see also Car rental industry
Car rental industry, 157–167
    commission payments, 47
    distribution, selling, 45
    employment opportunities,
        165–166
    insurance, 163–164
    international, 164–165
    see also Car rental
Carnival Air, 83
Carnival Cruise Lines, 112, 114–116
    Up Close, 114–116
Casa De Campo resort profile, 138
CDW, *see* Collision Damage Waiver
Centers for Disease Control, 41, 42
Certified Travel Counselor (CTC), 62
Chains, *see* Hotel chains
Channel Tunnel, *see* Chunnel
Charter
    air charter, 101–102
    definition of, 101
    Jax Fax, 102
    yacht, 124
Chunnel, 178
    Up Close, 180

City codes, 85
Civil Aeronautics Act, 73
Civil Aeronautics Bureau (CAB), 53, 65, 73, 74, 75, 79
Class of service
  in air travel, 97, 99
  in car rental, 160–161
  in cruise travel, 117–118
CLIA, *see* Cruise Lines International Association
Client/agent relationship, 50, 51
Club Med (Up Close), 143–144
Coach class, 26
"Cocooning," 2
Code sharing, 84–85
Codes, 14, 83, 86, 151, 162
Collision Damage Waiver (CDW), 163
Commercial agency, 55
Commercial hotel, 137–138
Commission, 46, 47
Commuter carrier/flight, 75, 76, 84
Competitive Marketing Decision, 65
Computer, *see* Automation; Computer Reservation System
Computer Reservation System (CRS), 16. *see also* Automation
  on-site, 55
Concierge (Up Close), 153–154
Condominium rental, 142
Connecting flight, 26
Consolidator, 102–103
Consulate, 36
Continental Airlines, 76
Continuing education, 61–62
Converters, electrical, voltage, 41
Cook, Thomas, 51–52, 184
Cook's Timetable, 176
"Cook's Tour," 52
Copper Canyon, 181
Corporate agency, 55
Corporate rate, 148–149
Corporate travel/traveler, *see* Business traveler
Couchette, 175
Covia Corporation, 15, 16
Crandall, Robert, 75
Cruise, cruising, 111–131. *see also* Cruise Line Industry
  booking, 162
  cabin category, 117
  deck plan, 116, 117
  dining, menus, 122–123
  passenger capacity, 114
  passenger/staff ratio, 121
  popularity of, 114
  pricing, 124–126
  scheduling, 124
  transatlantic, 111–112
Cruise Director (Up Close), 129–130

Cruise Line Industry. *see also* Cruise; cruising
  commission payments, 46, 47
  distribution, selling, 45
  employment opportunities, 128–129
  growth in, 128–129
  regulation, legislation, 7
  safety (SOLAS), 114, 126–127
  travel agency/agent relationship, 44
Cruise Lines International Association (CLIA), 17, 61, 127–128
  CLIA Cruise Manual, 116, 127–128
CRS, *see* Automation; Computer Reservation System
CTC, *see* Certified Travel Counselor
Cultural tour, 189
Currency, *see* Foreign currency
Custom tour, 188
Customs, 38–39

D

Datas II, 16
Deck plan, 116–117
Delta Airlines, 16, 75, 76
Demographic research, 32
Department of Commerce, 17
Department of State, 18
Department of Transportation (DOT), 18, 74
Deregulation, 73, 79, 83, 99
  international airline, 83
Destination Management Service (DMS), 190
Destination Specialist (DS), 62
Direct flight, 89, 91
Discretionary traveler, 30, 49. *see also* Vacation traveler
  use of travel agency, 49
Distribution, 65
  agency, 46
  supplier, 45
DMS, *see* Destination Management Service
Documents, 36
  cruise, 194
  tour, 194
Dollar Rent-A-Car, 158
Domestic carrier, 72–77
Domestic travel, 94
DOT, *see* Department of Transportation
Drop charge, 163
DS, *see* Destination Specialist; Institute for Certified Travel Agents
Dude ranch, 140
Duty (tax), 38
Duty-free, 38

E

Eastern Airlines, 76
Eco-tours, 189
Economy hotel, 138
Electrical current, foreign, 41
Embassy, 36
Employment opportunities, 2, 12, 21. *see also* specific industry
  qualities to cultivate, 22
Escorted tour, 187–188
Eurail, 175–178
  Eurail Guide, 176–177
  Eurailpass, 177–178

F

FAA, *see* Federal Aviation Administration
Familiarization (Fam) trip, 20
FAP, *see* Full American Plan
Fares, *see* Air fares
Federal Aviation Administration (FAA), 18, 73, 74
Ferry, 124
FIT, *see* Foreign Independent Tour
Flag carrier, 78, 82
Flight attendant, 49
  Up Close, 104–107
Fly/Sail package, *see* Air/Sea package
Flying Freedoms, *see* Freedoms of the Air
Ford's Freighter Travel Guide, 124
Foreign carrier, 72. *see also* International carrier
Foreign currency, 39–40
Foreign Independent Tour, 194–195
Foreign language, 40
Foreign travel, *see* International travel
Franchise (agency), 64–65
Frankfurt Main International Airport, 95
Freedoms of the Air, 80–82
Freighter, 124
Frequent flyer program, 26
Full American Plan, 149
Full-service agency, 55

G

Galileo, 16
Gambling (gaming) hotels, 140–141
Gateway, *see* International gateway
Gemini, 16
Gentil Organisateurs (GOs), 143
"Ghan" (train), 181
Golden Keys, 155
Golf and tennis resorts, 140
Gourmet tour, 188

Government
   agencies, 17
   airline regulation, deregulation, 73
   regulations, 7–8
   role in travel and tourism, 5
"Grand Tour," 184
Gray Line, 190
Ground transportation, *see* Car rental;
   Railways; Taxis; Transfers
Group travel/traveler, 30–31. *see also*
   Tour; Tour industry
Guide, 187
   services, 12
Guidebook, 19

H

"Heritage" (train), 174
Hertz Car Rental, 158, 161
Home rental, 142
Home television shopping, 66
Hospitality industry, *see* Hotel
   industry
Hosted tour, 186–187
Hotel, 137–138
   airport, 138
   all-suite, 138
   bed & breakfast, 141
   budget, economy, 138
   commercial, 137
   gambling, gaming, 140–141
   individually owned
   inns, 136–137
   rates, prices, 148–150
   ratings, 145–146
   reservations, 150–151
   resort, 138–140
Hotel chains, 135–136
Hotel concierge, *see* Concierge
Hotel industry, 133–156
   beginnings of, 134
   chains, 135–136
   codes, 151
   commission payments, 46, 47
   distribution, selling, 45
   employment opportunities,
   152–153
   individually owned properties,
   136–137
   ratings, 145–147
   references, 144–145
   regulation, legislation, 7
   size of, 134
   travel agency/agent relationship,
   44
Hotel management contracts, *see*
   Management contracts
Hotel rep/representative, 151
Hub, Hub and Spoke System, 89
Hyatt Hotels, 46, 135–136

I

IATA, *see* International Air Transport
   Association
IATAN, *see* International Airlines
   Travel Agent Network
ICTA, *see* Institute of Certified Travel
   Agents
In-house agency, 55
Incentive tour, 188
Independent contractor, 65
Independent tour, 185–186
"Indian Pacific" (train), 181
Individually owned properties
   (hotels), 136–137
Industry, definition of, 12. *see also*
   specific industry
Inns, *see* Hotel
Institute of Certified Travel Agents
   (ICTA), 17, 61–62
   Certified Travel Counselor (CTC),
   62
   Destination Specialist (DS), 62
Insurance, 195–196
   car rental,
International Air Transport
   Association (IATA), 78–79
   address of, 17
   "need clause," 79
   traffic conferences, 79
International airlines, *see* International
   carrier
International Airlines Travel Agent
   Network (IATAN), 17, 65,
   79
International carrier, 72, 77–82
   as source of travel information,
   36
International gateway, 38, 94
International travel, 35–42, 53
   complexities of, 8–10
   cultural differences, 8–10
   documents, 36
   health information, 41–42
"Iron Horse," 170
Itinerary, 185
   Fall Foliage (Up Close), 191

J

Japanese National Railways,
   179–180
Jargon, 13, 14
Jax Fax, 102
Jet transportation, 53

K

Kilometer, 164
"Know Before You Go," 39

L

LaGuardia, Fiorello, 92
Land arrangements, 185
Language, language barrier, 40–41
Laser imaging, 66
LDW, *see* Loss Damage Waiver
Legislation in travel and tourism, 7–8.
   see also Deregulation; Regulation
Leisure traveler, *see* Vacation traveler;
   Discretionary traveler
Les Clefs d'Or, 155
Limousines, 7
Linear routing, 87, 89
Loss Damage Waiver (LDW), 163

M

Maglev (Up Close,) 170–172
Major carriers, 75, 89
Major hub, *see* Hub, Hub and Spoke
   System
Management contracts (hotel), 136
MAP, *see* Modified American Plan
Marriot Hotels, 135–136
MCO, *see* Miscellaneous Charges
   Order
Meet and Assist, 27
Meeting Planners International (MPI),
   17
Meetings, 31. *see also* Group
   travel/traveler
Mega agency, 54–55, 56
"Metroliner" (train), 174
MGM Grand Air, 82
Michelin Guide, 146
Midwest Express, 83
Mileage allowance/mileage charge,
   162–163
Miscellaneous Charges Order (MCO),
   193
Mobil Guide, Mobil Travel Guide Rating
   Service, 145–146
Modified American Plan (MAP), 149
Motel, 137
Motor hotel, 137
Motor inn, 137
Motorcoach industry, 12, 190
MPI, *see* Meeting Planners
   International

N

National Association of Cruise Only
   Agencies, 56
National Business Travelers
   Association (NBTA), 17
National Car Rental, 158, 161
National carriers, 75
National Cruise Vacation Month
   (NCVM), 128

National Railroad Passenger
  Corporation, *see* Amtrak
National Tour Association (NTA), ??
National Tourist Office (NTO), 18
National Transportation Safety Board
  (NTSB), 18, 74
Natural hub, *see* Hub, Hub and spoke
  system
Nautical terms, 110–111
NCVM, *see* National Cruise Vacation
  Month
"Need clause," *see* International Air
  Transport Association
Net rate, 46
Nondiscretionary traveler, *see*
  Business/Corporate traveler
Nonstop flight, 26, 89, 91
North American Airlines, 82
Northwest Airlines, 16, 75
NTA, *see* National Tour Association
NTO, *see* National Tourist Office
NTSB, *see* National Transportation
  Safety Board

O

OAG, *see* Official Airline Guide
Observation car, 173
Occupancy tax, 149
Official Airline Guide, 84
Off-site car rental, 161–162
O'Hare, Edward "Butch," 92
On-site agency, 55
On-site car rental, 161–162
"Open skies", 73, 81, 83
Operator, *see* Tour operator
"Orient Express" (train), 181
Override commission, 47, 54

P

Pacific Rim, 82
Package 46, 184, 185. *see also* Tour;
  Hotel
Pan American World Airlines
  (Pan Am), 76
PARS, 16
Passport, 35–37
PC, *see* Personal computer
Persian Gulf War, 11
Personal computer, 65
Photography tour, 188
Piedmont Airlines, 76
Pitch, *see* Pitch and Roll; Seat Pitch
Pitch and Roll, 113, 125
Port taxes, 125
Porters, 52
Preferred supplier, preferred vendor,
  47. *see also* Supplier
Premier Cruise Lines, 123

Profile, 50
Proof of citizenship, 35–37
Proof of identify, 37
Proof of purchase, 39
Psychographic research, 33
Publications, list of travel trade, 19

Q

Quality assurance, quality control, 66

R

Rail industry, 169–182
  beginnings of, 170
  commission payments, 47
  distribution, selling, 45
  employment opportunities, 182
  foreign, 175–181
  future of, 174
  important dates in, 171
  regulation, legislation, 7
Rail travel, 174–182
  foreign, 175–181
  great train rides, romantic rides,
    181–182
  reservations, Europe, 179
  reservations, U.S., 174–175
Railroads, *see* Rail industry; rail travel
Railways, *see* Rail industry; rail travel
Receptive service, 190
Regionals
  airlines, carriers, 73, 74, 75, 89
  travel agencies, 55
References, 61
Religious tour, 189
Rental agreement, 163
Rental car, *see* Car rental industry
Resort, 138–140. *see also* Hotel Industry
  all-inclusive, 139
    Club Med (Up Close), 143–144
    golf and tennis, 140
    ski, 140
    spa, 140
Route, routing, *see* Airline route
  system
Royal Caribbean Line, *see* Sovereign of
  the Seas
"Royal Scotsman" (train), 181

S

Sabre, 16
Safety of Life at Sea (SOLAS), 114,
  126–127
Satellite printer, 55
Seat pitch (airline), 98, 99
Seikan Tunnel, 180
Service business 49, 59
  growth of, 4
  travel as, 2

Service charge, 150
Ship, *see* Cruise; Cruise Line Industry
Shore excursion, 123
Sightseeing, 12, 190. *see also* Tour;
  Tour industry
Single airline hub, *see* Hub, Hub and
  spoke system
Ski resort, 140
SODA, *see* SystemOne
SOLAS, *see* Safety of Life at Sea
Sovereign of the Seas, 116–121
Spa, 140
Sports tour, 188
Stateroom, 121
Steamship, *see* Cruise line industry
Steamship agent, 52
Step-on guide, 187
Superliner, 174
Supplemental carrier, 101
Supplier, 5, 13, 14, 44
  commission payments, 47
  distribution, selling, 45
  preferred supplier, 47
  travel agent/agency relationship,
    44–46
SystemOne, 16

T

Taxes
  air fare, 46, 48
  duty, 38
  hotel, 149
  port, 125
  Value Added (VAT), 164
Thomas Cook's Continental/European
  Timetable, 124, 176
Thomas Cook's Overseas Timetable,
  124
Thomas Cook Travel, 51–52, 54
Thrifty Car Rental, 161
Tour, 183–199. *see also* Tour industry
  booking, 192–193
  costing, 193
  custom, 188
  documents, 194
  escorted, 187
  Fall Foliage (Up Close), 191
  foreign independent (FIT),
    194–195
  hosted, 186–187
  incentive, 188
  independent, 185–186
  itinerary, 185, 191
  reasons to take, 189–190
  specialty, 188–189
Tour escort, 187. *see also* Tour manager
Tour industry
  beginnings of, 184
  commission payments, 47

distribution, selling, 45, 192
employment opportunities, 196
regulation, licensing, 8
Tour Manager (Up Close), 197–198.
    see also Tour escort
Tour operator, 185
Tour wholesaler, 185
Tourism. *see also* Travel & Tourism
    definition of, 4
    problems created by, 5–7
Tourist card, 35
Tourists, influences on, 10. *see also*
    Tourism; Traveler
Traffic conferences, *see* International
    Air Transport Association
Traffic rights, 81
Trains, *see* Rail industry; Rail travel
"Trans-Siberian Express" (train), 181
Trans World Airlines (TWA), 16, 76
Transfer, 184
Transit rights, 81
Transit visa, 37
Travel. *see also* Travel & Tourism
    definition of, 3–4
    developments, future, 3, 11
    pleasure, development of, 52
Travel advisories, 37
Travel agency, 13, 44–67
    as tour operator, 185
    beginnings of, 52
    commercial, corporate, 55
    cruise only, 56
    defined by concentration, 55–56
    defined by size, 54–55
    full service, 55
    future, 65–66
    in-house, on-site, 55
    in the travel industry, 12
    opening, owning, 62–65
    purchase of, 64
    reasons to use, 48–49
    regulation, licensing, 8
    today, 53–55
    vacation, leisure, 56
    yesterday, 53

Travel agent, 13, 44–67
    client/agent relationship, 50
    continuing education, 61
    entry-level, 59
    independent contractor, 65
    jobs of, 60
    "Morning in the Life", 57
    productivity, 59
    pros and cons of being, 62
    reasons to use, 48–49
    supplier/agent relationship, 44–46
Travel and tourism. *see also* Travel;
    Travel industry; Tourism
    development of, 5
    economic importance of, 4, 5
Travel career. *see also* Employment
    opportunities
    benefits of, 2
    growth in, 23
    requirements of, 2
Travel data bases, 66
Travel industry, 12. *see also* Travel;
    Tourism; Travel and Tourism; and
    specific industries
    associations, 16
    terms, 13, 14
Travel insurance, 194
Traveler. *see also* Tourist
    data sheet, 50, 51
    examples of, 26–28
    "gentle invaders," 29
    needs of, 5
Traveler data sheet, 50, 51
Treaty of Versailles, 70
Trip insurance, *see* Insurance; Travel
    insurance
Trunk lines, 73
"Turboliner" (train), 174

U

United Airlines, 15, 75, 76, 77
United States Tour operators
    Association (USTOA), 17
USAir, 15, 75, 76

U.S. airline deregulation, *see* Airline
    Deregulatory Act; Deregulation
U.S. Coast Guard, 126–127
U.S. Customs Service, 18. *see also*
    Customs
USTOA, *see* United States Tour
    Operators Association
U.S. Travel and Tourism
    Administration, 17

V

Vacation travel/traveler, 30, 31. *see also*
    Tourist; Traveler; Discretionary
    traveler
    development of, 53
Value Added Tax (VAT), 164
Vendor, *see* Supplier
VIA Rail Canada, 177
Videos, 20
Visa, 35, 37–38
Voltage, *see* Electrical current

W

Weather, 11
Western Air, 76
Wholesaler, *see* Tour wholesaler
WorldSpan, 16
World War I, 52, 70–72
World War II, 53, 78, 83

Y

Yacht charters, 124
Yield management, 100–101